First edition by Dr John Sugden published 2000

Cover Design by Nikki Moore, Pigsty Studio, Feltons Farm, Elmers Green, Skelmersdale, Lancashire.

British Library Cataloguing in Publication Data
A catalogue record for this book is available from the British Library

ISBN 1 899016 25 2

Printed by Regal Litho, 352 Selbourne Road, Luton, Bedfordshire, LU4 8NU. Tel: (01582) 493332.

ACKNOWLEDGEMENTS

The British Horse Society is indebted to Dr John Sugden for giving freely of his expertise and time in the writing of this book. Dr Sugden's association with the BHS goes back many years, to at least the early 1980s if not before and his professional experience has given him an invaluable insight into rights of way law and practice, in particular regarding exquestrian matters. Dr Sugden is one of a band of voluntary workers who do a tremendous amount of work on behalf of the British Horse Society and to whom to all equestrian users have reason to be lastingly grateful.

supported by

The Countryside Agency

The British Horse Society would like to thank the Countryside Agency for the generous financial support they have given to the production of the book, however, as part of their grant aid conditions we must stipulate that they have played no part in approving the text.

PREFACE

This book was written to help ordinary horseriders and drivers of horse drawn vehicles who want to play their part in securing more and better bridleways and byways. The number of people who ride for pleasure continues to increase rapidly. So, unfortunately, does the level of traffic on motor roads. There has never been so great a need for bridleways and byways as now and the need can only increase. Whilst there are more than 20,000 miles of bridleways recognised in England and Wales, a substantial proportion cannot be ridden because of obstruction or neglect. It is believed that there are many miles of old bridleways that are still legally in existence but not officially recorded. This book, then, is dedicated to those people who are prepared to work to bring all the ancient bridleways and byways into a usable condition and to establish new links to create a network for riding and driving in the 21st century.

Throughout this book the word *bridleway* is used as a shorthand for *bridleways and byways* and *riders* for *riders and drivers* simply to save space; where there is a difference in the law between bridleways and byways then this will be made explicit.

Public rights of way are highways in law and highways are dealt with by several hundreds of assorted laws.
The legislation referred to or implied in this book is that which is in force at 1st October 2000. Parliament is currently dealing with the Countryside and Rights of Way Bill, which if enacted, will give a statutory right of access on foot to certain types of country – mountain, moor, heath, downland and registered common land. The CROW Bill also contains provisions that will alter some of the existing law regarding public rights of way and will introduce greater protection for wildlife. At the time this book is published, the law remains valid and the ensuing advice is sound. It is recommended that readers obtain a copy of the new Act when it is published and use this in conjunction with this book. The Act will be available from the Government website free of charge and also from HMSO and their agent at cost. Guidance and advice regarding the new legislation will be published by, and available from the Countryside Agency.

CONTENTS

		Page
1: Introduction		
1.1	Our debt to walkers	15
1.2	British Horse Society training courses	16
1.3	Rights of way work and the law	17
2: Some simple concepts of highway law		
2.1	Introduction	19
2.2	Rights of way	19
2.3	Trespass and the civil law	20
2.4	Types of highway at common law	21
2.5	Statutory types of highway	22
2.6	Green lanes and byways	23
2.7	Once a highway, always a highway	24
2.8	Ownership of the highway	25
2.9	Creation of highways by dedication	26
2.10	Dedication subject to conditions and limitations	27
2.11	Creation of highways by statute	29
2.12	Maintenance of highways	29
2.13	Privately maintained highways	31
3: Official records of public paths and byways		
3.1	Introduction	34
3.2	Importance of the definitive map	34
3.3	The definitive map	35
3.4	Meanings of the routes shown	36
3.5	Meanings of the types of route – a summary	38
3.6	The definitive statement	38
3.7	How the map was prepared	40
3.8	Review of the map	42
3.9	Removal of rights from the definitive map	45
3.10	Rupps and byways	45
3.11	Records of council maintained roads	47

4: Ordnance Survey maps

4.1	Introduction	50
4.2	The National Grid	50
4.3	The 100km square system	51
4.4	Map scales	53
4.5	The 1:10,000 maps	53
4.6	The 1:25,000 maps	56
4.7	The 1:50,000 series	57
4.8	Giving a grid reference	58
4.9	Historic maps	61
4.10	The six inch maps	61
4.11	The 1:25,000 first series	62
4.12	The one inch series	62

5: Surveying public paths and byways

5.1	Introduction	64
5.2	Getting around	64
5.3	What you will need	65
5.4	Understanding the 1:25,000 map	65
5.5	Planning a survey	67
5.6	Following the path	68
5.7	Compass bearings	69
5.8	Recording information	70
5.9	Handling aggressive people	72

6: The government machine

6.1	Introduction	74
6.2	Central and local government	74
6.3	Central government	75
6.4	Other national public bodies	76
6.5	Local government	77
6.6	County councils	78
6.7	District councils	79
6.8	Local councils	80
6.9	The structure of local government	81

6.10	The members	82
6.11	The political dimension	84
6.12	Access to council information	84
6.13	The role of officers	85
6.14	The officer structure	86
6.15	How to make friends and influence people	87

7: Collection of user evidence
7.1	General points	90
7.2	Types of evidence	91
7.3	Creation of highways at common law	92
7.4	Presumed dedication under statute	93
7.5	Dedication by statutory bodies	95
7.6	Selecting the witnesses	96
7.7	Permissive use	98
7.8	Collection of user evidence – a summary	100

8: Adding paths to the definitive map
8.1	Introduction	103
8.2	Preparation of a report of evidence	103
8.3	The duty of the surveying authority	105
8.4	Formal application for an order	105
8.5	Making the order	107
8.6	Changes to the order	109
8.7	Enforcing the duty to make the order	109

9: Deletion of paths from the definitive map
9.1	Introduction	112
9.2	Background	112
9.3	History of the deletion process	113
9.4	Circumstances in which deletions are allowed	114
9.5	Rights that cease to exist	115
9.6	Alleged errors on the definitive map	116
9.7	The ground rules	117
9.8	Evidence of lack of use	120

9.9   Evidence of obstruction   122
9.10   Information from OS maps   123
9.11   Obstructions recorded on the definitive map   124
9.12   Drafting errors on the map   125
9.13   Claims based on documentary evidence   127
9.14   Use subsequent to the definitive map   129

10: Closure and diversion of highways
10.1   Introduction   131
10.2   Highways act – magistrates court orders   131
10.3   Magistrates court procedure   132
10.4   Highways act – public path orders   134
10.5   Modifications to the network – diversions   135
10.6   Modifications to the network – creations   137
10.7   Modifications to the network – closures   137
10.8   Level crossing orders   138
10.9   Town and county planning powers   140
10.10   Assessing proposals to change paths   141

11: Traffic regulation orders
11.1   Introduction   145
11.2   General points   145
11.3   Routes subject to traffic regulation   146
11.4   Classes of traffic subject to regulation   146
11.5   Types of restrictions   147
11.6   Reasons for traffic regulation orders   148
11.7   Duration of orders   149
11.8   Making a traffic regulation order   150
11.9   Enforcement of traffic regulation orders   151
11.10   Traffic regulation through planning powers   152
11.11   Traffic regulation without orders   152

12: Paths affected by new roads
12.1   Introduction   155
12.2   Background to road proposals   155

12.3	Types of new road	156
12.4	The planning process	157
12.5	Public consultation stages	159
12.6	The legal framework	161
12.7	Forming alliances	163
12.8	Preparing the ground	164
12.9	Grade crossings of main roads	165
12.10	Grade-separated crosssings	167
12.11	Planning rights of way crossings	169
12.12	Design standards	170

13: Legal orders and public inquiries

13.1	Introduction	173
13.2	Orders affecting public paths	173
13.3	The making of the order	174
13.4	Should an objection be made?	175
13.5	Negotiations	176
13.6	Public inquiries – what are they?	178
13.7	Applications for costs	180
13.8	Procedure at public inquiries	181
13.9	Preparing the ground	184
13.10	Presenting the arguments	186
13.11	The site inspection	188
13.12	Written representations	188
13.13	The results	189

14: Documentary evidence of public paths and byways

14.1	Introduction	191
14.2	The importance of documentary evidence	191
14.3	The nature of documentary evidence	192
14.4	Is the document a forgery?	193
14.5	Was the writer telling the truth?	193
14.6	How did he know that anyway?	194
14.7	Official documents	195
14.8	Interpretation of records	196

14.9   A systematic approach   197
14.10   The dossier of evidence   199
14.11   The time capsule   200

15: The historical development of roads
15.1   Introduction   204
15.2   Prehistoric and Roman roads   204
15.3   The Dark Ages   206
15.4   The Norman Conquest   210
15.5   The Middle Ages   211
15.6   From Tudor to Georgian times   213
15.7   Common and private ways   214
15.8   The enclosure period   217
15.9   The turnpike roads   218
15.10   Macadam and the gravel road   219
15.11   The building of the country roads   220
15.12   The end of the private ways   222
15.13   Urban streets   223
15.14   The coming of the motor vehicle   224
15.15   County roads and trunk roads   225
15.16   The post-war years   226
15.17   Local government changes   228

16: Private Acts of Parliament
16.1   Introduction   230
16.2   What acts are available?   230
16.3   Why were private acts required?   231
16.4   Finding private acts   232
16.5   Plans, sections and books of reference   234
16.6   Interpreting the records   235
16.7   Value of the records as evidence   237
16.8   Private act evidence for deletion of rights of way   238

17: Tithe surveys
17.1   Introduction   242
17.2   Background to tithes   242

17.3	Parishes	243
17.4	Tithe commutation	245
17.5	Tithe records as evidence	246
17.6	Roads belonging to the parish	247
17.7	Roads not belonging to the parish	249
17.8	Summary	250

18: Historic maps

18.1	Introduction	252
18.2	Development of cartography	252
18.3	Estate maps	253
18.4	County maps	255
18.5	The ordnance survey	258
18.6	The county series of maps	258
18.7	The county grid	260
18.8	Information shown on county series maps	261
18.9	Interpretation of ordnance survey maps	264

19: Enclosure awards

19.1	The objectives of Enclosure	268
19.2	The process of Enclosure	268
19.3	Enclosure awards	269
19.4	Types of road set out	272
19.5	What did the commissioners mean?	274
19.6	What happened to the private ways?	276
19.7	Powers of the commissioners	279
19.8	Construction of public roads	281
19.9	Boundary problems	284
19.10	Ownership of enclosure roads	286

20: Court records

20.1	Introduction	289
20.2	Why the courts are involved	289
20.3	Highways duties of the magistrates	290
20.4	Quarter sessions records before 1889	292

20.5   Records relating to closures and diversions   293
20.6   Interpreting closure and diversion orders   295

21: Highway authority records

21.1   Introduction   297
21.2   The structure of local government   298
21.3   Urban districts   299
21.4   Lists of streets   301
21.5   Rural areas and the county road   302
21.6   Handover maps   303
21.7   Interpretation of county roads maps   304
21.8   Consolidation of the records   306

22:1910 Finance Act records

22.1   Introduction   308
22.2   Background to the records   308
22.3   Why the records are useful   309
22.4   How the valuation was carried out   310
22.5   Location of the records   311
22.6   Interpreting the records – public roads   312
22.7   Interpreting the records – public paths   314
22.8   The way ahead   315

23: Negotiating skills

23.1   Introduction   317
23.2   Why negotiation is helpful   317
23.3   Negotiating from strength   319
23.4   The other angle   319
23.5   Establishing diplomatic relations   321
23.6   Our allies   321
23.7   Neutral parties   323
23.8   The other side   323
23.9   The professional approach   324

24: Management of volunteers

24.1   Introduction   327
24.2   Why management is important   327
24.3   Changes in management techniques   328
24.4   Centralised management   329
24.5   Devolution and empowerment   330
24.6   Devolution and empowerment in the voluntary sector   332
24.7   How volunteers can achieve their objectives   333
24.8   Organisation within a local rights of way group   335

25: Working with the media

25.1   Introduction   337
25.2   Who are the media?   337
25.3   Why we need the media   338
25.4   Why the media need us   340
25.5   How the media works   340
25.6   Making friends with the media   342
25.7   Telephone approaches   343
25.8   News releases – the story and its timing   343
25.9   Writing a news release   345
25.10 Radio interviews   346
25.11 Television   347

1
INTRODUCTION

1.1. Our debt to walkers

It is only in the last twenty years or so that riders have really taken an active part in the protection of bridleways. This reflects the increase of recreational riding over the same period; before that, those who rode were so few and scattered that little concerted action was possible.

Riders should recognise the great debt owed to the various walkers' organisations who fought for so many years to protect public rights of way which, of course, include bridleways. In the early fifties when the network was for the first time legally defined it was walkers who, literally, did the legwork that established the protection that rights of way now enjoy. Where they believed that bridleway rights existed these were usually recorded. We believe that a great many were missed off simply because they were not known about, but this should not reduce our gratitude for the many that were recorded and without which riding on bridleways and byways would now be virtually impossible.

In their championship of rights of way over more than a century, the walkers have built up an impressive degree of expertise. Whilst this certainly extends to literature on the protection of rights of way, it has become clear that the needs of bridleway workers are slightly different. In particular, our work has a degree of emphasis on correcting past errors of omission which is largely absent from footpath work, essentially because of the thoroughness with which rights of way on foot were recorded in the fifties. The intention of this book, then, is not to supplant existing books dealing with the protection of footpaths but rather to complement them by the development of additional themes with which many footpath workers may not be so familiar (1).

In this sense it is hoped that this book will be of value even to those whose primary purpose is to protect rights of way on foot. If so, it may in some way help to repay the debt which riders owe to those early pioneers as well as to those of today.

The growth in recreational riding has been followed by renewed interest in carriage driving and by an explosion of mountain biking. Only now are participants coming to realise the importance to them of the preservation of the networks of byways and bridleways. We welcome the new activists as our allies and in this book try to give them the opportunity to take advantage of the experience that we have acquired over the past twenty years.

1.2. British Horse Society training courses

The starting point of this work was the need to provide adequate training for the voluntary workers of the British Horse Society. It was recognised that extremely valuable work was being done, but by a small core of skilled and dedicated volunteers who were only able to scratch the surface of the problem. If real progress was to be made it was essential for very many more people to assist, but it would also be necessary to provide the new volunteers with training to bring them up to the standards already set. To achieve this it was decided to devise a series of training days with a structured programme starting with a new volunteer with no previous experience and leading through to more advanced work with the possibility of different people specialising in different areas of work. This book is effectively the textbook for the course.

The book follows the same progressive structure. Chapters 2 to 7 provide the technical background for the first training day which is intended for volunteers with no previous experience of rights of way work. It aims to give them the skills to start taking an active part in rights of way work as private individuals rather than a representatives of any organisation. The reader is introduced to the basic framework of highways law, how to find and record local paths, how to collect evidence of usage, find the way through the corridors of power and hence how to lobby for improvements.

The next stage of development is when the volunteer assumes responsibility to some voluntary organisation for paths in an area. The necessary topics are dealt with in Chapters 8 to 13 which represent a second day of training. The work described here is mainly associated with legal orders, both those made by authorities that potentially threaten the network but also the promotion of orders adding paths to the definitive map. The reader is also introduced to public inquiries and to the methods that should be followed to give a reasonable chance of success.

However, this is by no means the whole story. The skills learned on the second day of training represent the absolute minimum that are needed to be an effective representative. Many workers go on to achieve other skills. Often these skills are so specialist that it is not feasible for all workers to have them; it is often more efficient for a number of people within a group to specialise in particular areas. To accommodate this a different approach is used for the more advanced courses. These consist of a series of modules dealing with different aspects of the work each of which assume a knowledge of the first two days. This means that it is not necessary to study all the modules, nor does any module depend on any other.

The more advanced modules require skills that are learned more through experience than from books and so not all are dealt with. However, one of the more important skills does require to be dealt with at some length. This is the researching from documentary sources of evidence that will allow the addition of paths to the definitive map and is described in detail in Chapters 14 to 22.

To end the book, a brief introduction is given to three topics which relate to inter-personal skills that are mainly attained through practice but for which a few hints might be useful. Chapter 23 deals with negotiating skills and attempts to show how diplomacy can be used to achieve our objectives. In Chapter 24 the reader is introduced to some management skills, bearing in mind that progress can only be made through team effort and that somebody has to lead the team. Finally, it is often forgotten that publicity is vital in our work and so Chapter 25 gives an insight into the techniques needed to handle the news media.

1.3. Rights of way work and the law

To be an effective rights of way worker requires a wide variety of skills and knowledge. However, most beginners quickly begin to feel inadequate in their knowledge of highway law. It is important not to become too concerned about this; the various processes have been designed to accommodate the amateur. This book is intended to show how objectives can be achieved without the need to beat the lawyers on their own ground. However, to do this it is useful to have a working knowledge of the relevant law.

Whilst the subject is dealt with at length in many learned and expensive books for lawyers, these are hardly adequate for the layperson who knows little or nothing of the background of many legal concepts. In any case, lawyers' textbooks tend to concentrate on particularly obscure points that lawyers need guidance on but which the normal person is unlikely to come across. On the other hand, problems that are very common are glossed over because, of course, the lawyer knows the answer anyhow.

This book aims to avoid these problems by dealing with the sorts of problems that are frequently found in a way that the ordinary person can understand. Inevitably, in a book of this sort it is not possible to deal with all the obscure problems that might arise. The intention is to indicate at least where the pitfalls are and, most importantly, when is the time that professional advice should be sought.

On the assumption that readers will neither have access to nor the time to follow up obscure case law, the text aims to explain what the law means rather than citing cases. Inevitably, a book of this length has to deal rather superficially with what is potentially a lifetime's study. However, for any reader who wishes to make a more detailed study of the legal aspects, there are numbered references to legal notes at the end of each chapter.

It should be noted that highway law differs significantly between the countries of the United Kingdom and this book deals only with the law applying in England and Wales; the law in Northern Ireland is somewhat different and that in Scotland much more so. Yet another system applies in the Isle of Man.

Notes to Chapter 1

1. All rights of way workers find essential reading what has become known as the *blue book*. This is *Rights of way - a guide to law and practice* written by John Riddall and John Trevelyan and published jointly by the Commons, Open Spaces and Footpaths Preservation Society and the Ramblers Association. (Second edition 1992.) Of particular value are the appendices which include all the more important laws relating to rights of way together with the text of orders and Government circulars. Reference to these is often necessary and they are not readily available to the amateur.

2
SOME SIMPLE CONCEPTS OF HIGHWAY LAW

2.1. Introduction

The purpose of this chapter is to set out the broad framework of law that affects all highways. Footpaths, bridleways and byways are highways in exactly the same way as are the busiest trunk roads and the same body of law applies, although obviously there are differences in detail.

Roads have always been indispensable to civilisation. In this country Roman roads built almost 2000 years ago still form the basis for some main roads. It seems clear that many Roman roads themselves followed even earlier trackways. With such a long history it is inevitable that the law relating to highways should also have a very long history. Some of it appears to be based on Roman law and many of the basic principles form part of the common law. Common law is the basis of many of our laws and, indeed, our freedoms. It is based on the immemorial customs of the nation as they existed before the Norman invasion and before a formal legal system was created. The principles of the common law have never been laid down by either the monarch or Parliament, but over the years they have been codified through successive decisions of the various courts.

On the foundation of common law there has been built a complex structure of statute law, that is law laid down by the monarch or Parliament. In view of the antiquity and importance of the highway system, it is not surprising that there are records of statutes concerning highways going back at least 800 years. Since then there have been very many different laws about highways. This creates particular difficulties for rights of way work where it is often necessary to consider old documents whose importance can only be judged by a knowledge of not only what the law is now but also of how it stood at the date of the document. It is more a study of history than of the law, and it should not be assumed that present-day lawyers will necessarily have great expertise on what the law was in times past.

2.2. Rights of way

Central to highway law is the concept of a right of way. This is where one or more people have a legal right to pass and repass over the land of another person. There are private and public rights of way, the difference being as to who has the right to

3)   A carriageway or cartway is a right of way for all traffic including vehicular traffic as well as rights on foot, on horseback and for driving. Originally, of course, vehicular rights applied only to horse-drawn vehicles but on the development of motor vehicles it was accepted that these were carriages as well. Motor cycles and pedal cycles are also regarded as carriages although the latter have now been granted additional rights as are described in the next section.

Footpaths and bridleways are together described in modern law as public paths. They are often also loosely described as public rights of way, although this is confusing in that all highways right up to motorways are also public rights of way.

2.5. Statutory types of highway

In addition to the traditional common law types of highway described in the last section, there are other types that have come into existence through statute, that is to say through laws that have been passed by Parliament. Whilst any person who wishes may create a common law type of highway over his land, the statutory types can only be created where procedures laid down by Parliament have been carried out by central or local government. The main types of statutory highway likely to be met with are cycle tracks, motorways and canal towpaths.

The invention of the bicycle seems to have caused the problem of how to fit it within the traditional types of users. Was it a modern form of horse or a narrow type of carriage? Originally it was decided that it was a carriage and thus restricted to carriageways. But with the growth in motor traffic this century a more sympathetic attitude has prevailed. Since 1968 bicycles have been granted a statutory right to use bridleways with the proviso that they give way to horse riders and walkers. This facility has been little-used until the recent development of mountain bikes (2). But in addition provision has been made for the creation of cycle tracks which are a right of way on pedal cycles and normally on foot. This effectively creates an additional statutory type of highway lying between a footpath and a bridleway in the traditional tier (3).

A motorway is a statutory form of highway on which non-motorised traffic consisting of pedestrians, pedal cycles, horses and horse-drawn vehicles is prohibited. In most cases motorways are of completely new construction and the right of way is created by the making of an order. It is possible to convert an existing road to a motorway by means of an order, but this is relatively unusual because of the difficulty of making provision for the traffic excluded and for access to premises served by the road. Our main interest in the creation of motorways lies in the effect on existing routes for non-motorised users which need to be taken over or under the motorway, closed or diverted. These proposals need to be watched carefully to ensure that adequate provision is made and this will be dealt with in detail in Chapter 10.

A canal is a statutory highway for boats. The rights of navigation need not concern us but the rights of way on the towpath are of interest. The statutory rights along towpaths are restricted to the needs of navigation; for example, horses are only allowed if being used to pull barges. However, it is possible for a towpath to become a normal footpath or bridleway and some towpaths, particularly along disused canals, now have this status. In recent years the recreational potential of towpaths has been more generally recognised, particularly in that towpaths usually form a continuous network with bridges under many roads separating recreational users from motor traffic. On most towpaths, walkers and cyclists are allowed on a permissive basis. Unfortunately, this has not been extended to horse-riders even though towpaths are probably the only properly constructed routes specifically designed for use by horses.

2.6. Green lanes and byways

It is important to appreciate that the legal status of a highway in terms of what rights of way exist over it is quite separate from the physical condition of the highway. This works both ways. The owner of land over which a highway lies may construct a road so long as he does not obstruct the rights of the public. Many farm access roads lie along footpaths or bridleways, and it is not particularly unusual today for these private roads to have a tarred surface. On the other hand, by no means all public carriageways are surfaced. Roads were not generally surfaced at all before the nineteenth century when stone surfaces were introduced. Tarred surfaces were not generally introduced until the development of motor traffic from about 1920. Although most of the ancient carriageways were improved to become the basis for the surfaced road network of today this did not happen in all cases. There remain significant numbers both of pre-nineteenth century roads that were never surfaced and of the improved stone roads that were never tarred.

Many of the roads that were never surfaced are now grass-grown and are thus referred to as *green lanes*, although the term has no legal meaning. The nineteenth surface of the highway. Although there was a public duty to maintain the highway there was no power to improve it. If the highway authority tried to improve the highway the owner could take action against it for trespass (8). If this had continued modern roads would have been impossible and so the law was changed to make the highway authority the owner of the surface and to allow it to carry out improvement works. The law was changed at various times for different types of highway as described in Chapter 21. The modern position is that the surface of all highways that are maintainable at public expense now belongs to the highway authority which is also allowed to improve it.

2.9. Creation of highways by dedication

At common law a highway can only exist either because it existed in the year 1189 or has subsequently been dedicated by the owner and accepted by the public. The year 1189, incidentally, marks the death of Henry I during whose reign the English legal system was started. Customs of any sort which existed prior to that date are assumed to have existed from time immemorial and to be legally binding and this extends to highways. This is the legal basis of our very ancient highways such as those based on Roman roads.

Normally, however, highways come into existence by dedication and acceptance. This means that the owner voluntarily dedicates the route to public use and the public indicate that they are prepared to accept it as a highway. For a highway to come into existence both elements have to be present; it is no use to have dedication without acceptance or acceptance without dedication.

This process may be a formal one with the owner entering into a legal agreement to dedicate the highway and the highway authority formally accepting it on behalf of the public. But for many older routes there is no record that any formal process was ever gone through. In such cases, however, the law can presume dedication. If a route has been used by the public for a good many years as if it were a highway with the public believing it to be a highway and the owner has known this and has done nothing to show that he disagrees, then the law will presume that it must have been dedicated and accepted at some period now lost in the mists of time and has been a highway ever since.

It is important to note that public use alone does not create a highway; it creates a presumption that the owner dedicated it which can be overturned by other factors. For example, if the owner put up a sign to the effect that he did not intend to dedicate

26

then irrespective of the level of use he could not be presumed to have dedicated it. Where an owner allows the public to use a route but does not wish it to become a highway it is sometimes the practice to close the route one day a year to demonstrate that no dedication is intended. By a similar argument, a dedication cannot be presumed where use by the public is so secret that the owner could not have become aware of it.

Under the common law there is no fixed period of use which must elapse before a dedication can be presumed. Each case is considered on its merits. Where use by the public is considerable or where the owner has acted in a way consistent with dedicating the way, then the period can be quite short. On the other hand, if public use is slight then a very long period would be required for dedication to be presumed. To simplify the process, a more precise set of rules has been laid down by Parliament although the common law rules continue to apply as well. Under the statutory procedure, if public use can be proved over a twenty year period then dedication will be presumed unless the owner can show not only that he had no intention to dedicate but also that he made this clear to the public (9).

The main value of the legal principles concerning presumption of dedication is in deciding arguments concerning alleged highways. If an owner disputes that a particular route is a highway it is not necessary to establish when or how the route first came to be used by the public. It is only necessary to consider use over the previous twenty years. This is obviously of importance in protecting the many highways that have existed for centuries and where there are no records as to how the route came into existence.

It will be more difficult where a route has been little used for many years; although a highway cannot cease to exist through disuse it will become increasingly more difficult to prove that it is a highway if the fact is disputed by the owner. This is clearly more of a problem for footpaths and bridleways than for motor roads and formerly led to many disputes. To reduce the scope for argument the system of definitive maps was introduced as described in Chapter 3.

2.10. Dedication subject to conditions and limitations

Because highways are assumed to have come into existence through the voluntary dedication of the owner, it is only reasonable that the owner is allowed to make some conditions. There are limits on this; a highway must be available to all the public all the time so that it is not possible to dedicate a highway only to residents of a particular area or to make it open on certain days only. The owner may, however, retain the right to do things on his land or to maintain structures that would otherwise be an illegal obstruction.

It is possible for a highway to be dedicated subject to a condition allowing the owner to maintain features that would otherwise be regarded as an obstruction. The most common example is a condition that the owner may have gates and stiles. If there is a stile or gate on a highway at the time that it is accepted then the owner has a right to keep there. Where a stile or gate is known to have existed on a path for as long as anyone can remember then it will normally be presumed that it must have been there at the time the path came into existence. This only applies in the absence of evidence to the contrary; if it can be shown that the path once existed without stiles or gates then the path cannot have been dedicated subject to them as a condition.

Under common law there was no other way in which the right to have a gate or stile could come into existence, although it is now possible for the highway authority to authorise additional gates or stiles on bridleways or footpaths (10). It is important to note that it is impossible to dedicate a highway subject to conditions that prevent it being used; for example, it is not possible for a bridleway to be conditional on the right of an owner to maintain a stile on it that prevents use on horses.

Another frequently met condition is the common law right to plough. If at the time a highway is accepted it is regularly ploughed then the dedication is assumed to be subject to a condition that the owner may continue to plough it.

There was no other right to plough until the 1939-45 war when temporary powers were introduced, being incorporated into the law in 1949 (11). In view of the greatly increased use of public paths since that time, and the fact that the food shortages of the 1940s have been replaced by food mountains, it is perhaps time for Parliament to reconsider whether this temporary concession to the farming industry should still continue.

Similar to the right to plough is the right to hold a market in a public street. It is interesting to note that the courts have held that where a market was not held for more than twenty years the right to obstruct the highway ceased because there was a later dedication not subject to the condition (12). It would appear from this judgement that where a path is not ploughed for a period exceeding twenty years then the common law right to plough will similarly disappear. Also if a gate or stile which is a condition on a dedication is removed and not replaced over a period of twenty years then that condition also ceases.

A key principle is that the public must take the highway as they find it. This means that if a highway was difficult to use at the time that the public accepted it then they later have no basis for complaint against the owner if it remains in the same condition. Features which legitimately make the highway more difficult to use are described as limitations on the dedication. For example, if a path runs over rough and stony ground then the owner is under no obligation to make the way smooth. There are even some highways that run over sands covered by the sea at high tide; obviously the owner is not required to do anything to prevent this!

2.11. Creation of highways by statute

Although the normal method of creating highways is by dedication and acceptance, it is also possible for highways to be created by statute. In some cases acts of Parliament specifically create a highway; more frequently the law authorises a procedure to be carried out which will create a highway. The highway will not come into existence until all the procedures specified in the law have been carried out, but once this has been done there is no need for the highway to be accepted by the public. This means that, in theory at least, a statutory highway may exist that has never been used by the public. Highways created by statute are of particular interest to rights of way workers because there are normally records available of the process by which the highway was created and these may be conclusive evidence of the existence of the highway today, even if long obstructed or disused.

It should be noted that as there is no dedication of a highway created by statute, there can be no conditions or limitations on the dedication other than those specified in the process by which the highway was created. For example, a highway created by an enclosure award cannot be subject to a common law right to plough or to any conditions of gates and stiles other than those set out in the enclosure award.

2.12. Maintenance of highways

For as long as there have been highways it seems to have been accepted that the public had a duty to maintain them. Traditionally this duty fell on the inhabitants of each parish who had the job of maintaining the highways in the parish for the benefit of all the public. Originally this was done directly by the inhabitants' own labour. In most areas this gradually evolved into a system where a payment was made instead of providing labour, the money being used to pay for maintenance to be carried out. The old system was not fully done away with until 1835 at which time the *statute labour* system was replaced by the modern system of rates. Since then various reorganisations have taken place and now the responsibility for maintenance rests with county councils, unitary councils or metropolitan district councils except for trunk roads which are the responsibility of central government through the Highways Agency.

Until the nineteenth century it was the rule that all highways were the responsibility of someone. In most cases the inhabitants of the parish were responsible but there were some cases (discussed in the next section) where private individuals or corporate bodies were responsible instead. As a general rule, however, once a highway came into existence it had to be maintained by the public. It was found that this could give rise to abuse because someone could dedicate a highway that was essentially a private access road and then the public would be obliged to maintain it. With properly constructed road surfaces increasingly coming into use in the nineteenth century this could have caused a serious financial burden on the public. To avoid this the concept of adoption was introduced. This means that a new public highway is not automatically maintainable by the public until it has been formally adopted. Highway authorities have the option not to adopt roads that are not properly constructed or of little value to the public. The adoption process was first introduced in 1801 for new carriageways created as part of enclosure awards (13) and was extended to all carriageways in 1835 (14). It was not extended to new footpaths and bridleways until 1949 (15).

As it was not essential for all highways to be adopted, it follows that nobody may be responsible for the maintenance of a highway. In the early years the test of public utility was applied fairly rigidly and roads that were essentially local access roads were not adopted. Later, however, it was found that this gave rise to public health problems and local authorities were given powers to force urban streets to be properly constructed and then adopted. This applied even if they were of little use to the public, for example in cul de sacs and courtyards. The effect of the different approach in the early years has been a legacy of private streets; that is streets which are not maintained by the public although they may well be public highways.

It should be noted that many local authority staff confuse adopted highways with highways maintainable at public expense. Because roads will not now be adopted unless they are properly made up it tends to be assumed that unless a road is made up then it cannot be maintainable at public expense. But this is a fallacy as highways maintainable at public expense include roads which existed prior to 1835, roads formally adopted in the nineteenth century which have never been made up to modern standards and most public paths. This issue will be discussed in more detail in Chapter 21.

The requirement to maintain a highway essentially means to keep it in the same condition as when it was dedicated. The common law responsibility to maintain did not allow even an optional power to improve the highway and a highway authority attempting to improve could be sued for trespass by the owner. But in modern times the highway authority has been given wide powers to improve any highway which is maintainable at public expense. In addition, the highway authority now owns the surface of a highway which is maintainable at public expense. This was introduced originally to allow the authority to have control of adopted streets but as it has been extended to all highways maintainable at public expense it now includes the surface of rights of way even where there is no made up surface.

2.13. Privately maintained highways

The public have a duty to maintain most highways. There are some highways which came into use from the nineteenth century for which the public have no responsibility. Although private individuals may maintain these, they cannot be compelled to do so. However, there are a small number of ancient highways which private individuals have a legal duty to maintain. It is frequently impossible to establish the exact process by which highways became privately maintainable. The only basis for believing a privately maintained highway to exist is the discovery of records showing that a particular highway has always been regarded as having that status.

The fact that a highway is required to be maintained by a private individual does not affect the rights that the public have over it. The highway authority still has a duty to make sure that it is not obstructed and can take legal action to enforce maintenance. The duty to maintain only extends to keeping the highway in the same condition as it has always been, which, bearing in mind the ancient origin of such roads, normally means only to green lane standards.

Notes to chapter 2

1. Harrison v Duke of Rutland (1893) 1 QB 145. See also Hickman v Maisey (1900) 1 QB 752. These cases set out the law as it now stands. However, it is not clear that this was always the same, as the law seems to have evolved during the nineteenth century. In earlier times the ability of the owner to take any action

against users of a right of way may not have been recognised, even where the users were exceeding their legal rights.

2. Countryside Act 1968, Section 30. Most legislation dealing with cycling refers to pedal cycles which term includes cycles with more than two wheels. The reference in this Act to bicycles seems to restrict use of bridleways to cycles with two wheels only, presumably bearing in mind that bridleways need only be wide enough for a horse.

3. The Highways Act 1980 allows the construction of cycle tracks within an existing vehicular highway. A highway authority has powers to purchase land and construct a new highway which can be designated as a cycle track. In addition, the Cycle Tracks Act 1984 allows orders to be made to convert a footpath into a cycle track. In this case the land remains in the original ownership and the public have a right over it on foot or cycle (including tricycles etc).

4. Byways (or Byways Open to All Traffic to give them their full title, sometimes abbreviated to BOATs) were first introduced by the Countryside Act 1968. However, they were given a wider definition under the Wildlife and Countryside Act 1981 and may now be regarded as a statutory type of highway. Any highway that meets the definition is a byway whether or not it is recorded as such on the definitive map. See Chapter 3 for more information on this.

5. In Regina v Wiltshire County Council ex parte Nettlecombe it was held that a highway with vehicular rights which could not be used because it was obstructed was not a byway because it was not used on foot and horseback.

6. As this is such a fundamental principle it is of interest to note the earliest recorded case in this book: R v Inhabitants of St James, Taunton (1315) Selwyn's Nisi Prius Reports.

7. The leading case is Attorney General v Stokesley RDC (1928) 26 LGR 440. Here a road was known to have been a public highway in the 1840s but a shorter way had been substituted and the old way went out of use. There was no evidence that it had been legally stopped up and the courts held that in the absence of such evidence it must be assumed that it retained its original status.

8. Radcliffe v Marsden UDC (1908) 7 LGR 1186. In this case the Urban District Council erected stone posts alongside a moorland bridleway to enable users to find

their way in mist. It was held that they had no authority to do this and their action was thus a trespass against the owner. It is important to note that bridleways (other than streets) which lay in urban districts did not become vested in the highway authority until the Highways Act 1959 although similar bridleways in rural districts had vested in county councils since the Local Government Act 1929 (see Chapter 21 for more details). At the time of the Marsden case the UDC had only a power to maintain the highway which did not include erecting stone posts. Such work would be perfectly legal today as bridleways vest in the highway authority which does have a wide power of improvement.

9. A statutory process for assuming dedication was first introduced by the Rights of Way Act 1932 and is now to be found in the Highways Act 1980, Section 31. This is an important issue and is dealt with at length in Chapter 7.

10. Highways Act 1980, Section 147. This allows stiles or gates to be authorised on a footpath or bridleway where necessary for agriculture and on the application of the owner or agricultural tenant. Presumably, this does not authorise the blocking of a bridleway by the provision of a stile without a gate, although this is not specifically stated in the legislation.

11. Until the 1939-45 war there was only a power to plough a public path where the path had originally been dedicated subject to a condition allowing it to be ploughed. During the war emergency special powers allowed paths to be ploughed. With continuing food shortages, the National Parks & Access to the Countryside Act 1949 allowed paths to be ploughed during agricultural operations, if they were then restored again. The powers were amended by the Rights of Way Act 1990 and are now contained in Section 134 of the Highways Act 1980.

12. Gloucestershire CC v Farrow (1985) 1 WLR 741.

13. Inclosure (Consolidation) Act 1801. See Chapter 19 for more detail on roads created under enclosure acts and awards.

14. Highways Act 1835.

15. National Parks & Access to the Countryside Act 1949.

3
OFFICIAL RECORDS OF PUBLIC PATHS AND BYWAYS

3.1. Introduction

This chapter considers the official records of public paths and byways. There are other routes that exist and are not officially recorded, but it is obviously best to start with those that are recorded. There are two main sets of records. The key record is known as the definitive map and is supposed to show all public paths together with minor carriageways that are mainly used on foot or horseback, that is to say byways. Unfortunately, for reasons that are not entirely clear, many definitive maps miss off many of the byways.

However, there are normally completely separate records of the roads and streets that are maintained by the highway authority. Most of these, of course, are normal tarred roads but the record usually also shows all the byways that are maintained by the authority. Sometimes byways recorded in this way are also shown as byways on the definitive map, but often they are omitted or shown only as public paths. It follows that to obtain the full picture of the available routes it is necessary to look at both the definitive map and the other records and so both will be considered here.

3.2. Importance of the definitive map

The importance of the definitive map in the protection of public rights of way cannot be exaggerated. For most highways there are no surviving records as to how the route first came into use. Any challenge to the status of the route can normally only be tested in the light of use over the previous twenty or so years. In theory, the owner of the land under the busiest main road could dispute its status as a highway but clearly the challenge would fail because public use would indicate that the route had been a highway all along. Although the same principle is true for rights of way, it would be very much more difficult to prove it because of the much more limited use and the way in which illegal obstructions are often overlooked for years on end. If the normal rules were used to make the decision, a very large part of the rights of way network would be subject to continuous dispute.

Fortunately, this problem was recognised and in 1949 Parliament introduced the definitive maps (1). These were intended to record all rights of way although the possibility was recognised that there might be others left off. The definitive map is conclusive of all the rights of way shown on it and can thus be used to resolve any disputes as to whether they exist or not.

It is important to note that although the current definitive map is conclusive, there are provisions for the map to be changed to keep it up to date or to correct errors. Because it is recognised that there might be rights of way not recorded, there are provisions for adding new public paths and byways as well as changing the status of routes to show additional rights, for example by changing a footpath to a bridleway. This latter point tends to be important in bridleways work as many bridleways appear to have been wrongly classified as footpaths at a time when there was little riding in many areas. There is also the possibility of paths being removed from the map, or reduced to a lower status, if it is found that an error was made when the path was first recorded. This can potentially be a threat to the security provided by the definitive map and needs to be treated very seriously. This point is considered further in 3.9 and dealt with at length in Chapter 9.

3.3. The definitive map

The definitive map is the official record of public rights of way. It is prepared and kept up to date by the county council except in places where there are unitary or metropolitan districts who will then be responsible. The map has a relevant date and it is conclusive evidence of the existence of all rights of way recorded but only on that date. This means that unless the right of way has been properly closed or diverted, the map must also be evidence of the right at any later date as highways cannot cease except by the proper legal process.

It should be noted that there are some small areas still not covered by definitive maps. Under the original scheme the former county borough councils were not compelled to prepare maps but could if they wished. Many opted out and thus some of the largest towns and cities did not have a definitive map. County boroughs were abolished in 1974 and in most cases boundary changes mean that new districts do not correspond. This means that modern districts corresponding to the old county boroughs sometimes have a "hole" in the middle where there is no definitive map. Often, however, these are built up areas with few public paths in the rural sense. Since 1981 the idea has been that the whole country should be covered and definitive maps should eventually be available for all areas.

The intention was that all rights of way should be recorded on the definitive map. In practice this was never achieved and there are many rights of way that were

CRF is a particularly baffling hybrid; the normal use was said to be as a footpath, the conclusive rights are as for a bridleway but it was believed by the surveying authority to be a carriageway!

Because of the confusion, in 1968 it was decided to introduce the concept of a byway and to phase out RUPPs (4). The RUPPs already on the map were supposed to be reclassified as footpaths, bridleways or byways. This was supposed to be done at one stage in a special review so that there should not be RUPPs and byways on the same definitive map. In practice the re-classification brought about a great many other problems which will be considered further in 3.10.

3.5. Meanings of the types of route - a summary

The implications of the different types of route shown on the definitive map can be summarised as follows in terms of what were thought to be the rights of way available as against what rights conclusively exist through the path being shown:

(a) A footpath was believed to be a footpath. It conclusively has rights on foot and **may** have rights on horseback or for vehicles.

(b) A bridleway was believed to be a bridleway. It conclusively has rights on foot and horseback and **may** have rights for vehicles.

(c) A RUPP was believed to be a carriageway. It conclusively has rights on foot and horseback and **may** have rights for vehicles.

(d) A byway was believed to be a carriageway. It conclusively has rights on foot, on horseback and for vehicles.

3.6. The definitive statement

Associated with every definitive map is a statement. In some cases this is a few lines giving only the relevant date, but more usually it is a complex document including a schedule listing all the paths shown on the map. The schedule may include information under three headings - the position and width of the path, limitations and conditions, and other information.

Definitive maps exist in several scales with many authorities choosing the smallest permitted scale of 1:25,000. At this scale it is impossible to tell precisely where a path is to a few metres; after all a line 1mm wide on the map scales at 25m wide on the ground! Consequently, it is sometimes helpful to have a schedule which describes exactly where the path goes in terms of features on the ground, for example on which side of a hedge it runs. Also, the map cannot indicate how wide a path is but this can be recorded on a schedule to the statement.

Where the position or width of a path is described in this way then it becomes conclusive evidence of the position or width at the relevant date. This is helpful if the statement gives additional information to fill in lack of clarity on the map, but what happens if the route described in the statement clearly differs from that on the map? It is generally believed that in such circumstances the route described in the statement will be conclusive but this has never been fully decided by the courts (5).

The statement may also include information as to legal limitations and conditions. The most common are paths subject to a right to have stiles and gates and subject to a common law right to plough. If a condition or limitation is set out in the statement then this is conclusive evidence that it existed at the relevant date but this is without prejudice to other conditions or limitations that might also exist. It should be noted that subsequently the limitations or conditions might be different because of the power to authorise new gates or stiles and the fact that conditions may lapse due to lack of use.

The statements were required to contain the relevant date and whatever details of the position and width of paths and of limitations and conditions that the surveying authority felt expedient to include. This gave a wide discretion to the authority as to what was included. Some limited the statement to a few lines stating the date whilst others included a great deal more information than would strictly have been required to meet the legal requirements. This was encouraged by the instructions given to authorities as to how to carry out surveys for the maps.

Authorities were told to record obstructions along the path and whether the path had been ploughed throughout living memory or only in recent years. This was particularly important when the surveys commenced around 1950 as many paths had been authorised to be temporarily obstructed during the 1939-45 war. The authorities were advised that the information collected as part of the survey would form the basis for the definitive statements and so it is hardly surprising that in many cases the information as to obstructions and ploughing also appears in the statement. It was never a requirement for this to be included in the statement and thus the information has no real legal status. Nevertheless, it should be regarded as strong evidence of the state of affairs which existed at the time of the survey.

The different types of information in the statement should not be confused. It appears that the statement is only conclusive of a condition or limitation if it is

The results of the survey were then passed on to the county council or county borough council as surveying authority. The council had then to prepare a draft map showing paths which it believed to exist, or were reasonably alleged to exist. The draft map was then advertised and the public could object either that paths that existed had been missed off or that paths shown did not exist. There then followed a complex process of public hearings with further opportunities to object to any proposals to add or remove paths from the draft. Eventually, the council arrived at what they believed to be a correct map and this was then published as the provisional map. Further objection was then only allowed from people aggrieved by the showing of a path who could challenge the decision in the courts with the council defending their decision to show the path. Once all such cases had been decided, then the provisional map as amended by any court decisions to remove paths became the definitive map.

It is worth noting that the extent to which the evidence for the showing of a path was tested depended on whether objections were raised. If a path was recorded on a parish survey, perhaps on the basis of user evidence, then unless the surveying authority had any contrary information, it would be *reasonably alleged* and would be recorded on the draft map. If the owner objected then the evidence of use would have to be presented and a decision taken as to whether it was sufficient to justify a presumption of dedication. If no objection was raised then the path would simply go forward to the provisional and definitive maps. The extent to which the evidence supported the inclusion of the path would probably be known only to the people who carried out the survey; even the surveying authority would not know the strength of the evidence.

3.8. Review of the map

The definitive map is only conclusive evidence on the relevant date. Although this will prove the existence of any path shown that has not been legally extinguished, it nevertheless becomes less useful with the passage of time as the network changes. There is a need for a review procedure to change the map from time to time.

The map needs to be modified to take account of legal events after the relevant date such as the creation, diversion or extinguishment of paths. There is also a need for paths to be added where sufficient use has occurred to give a presumption that a path has been dedicated and accepted. In addition to the need to modify the map in respect of changes that have actually occurred, there is also provision for errors in the map to be corrected. Originally this only applied to adding paths that had been left off, including recording extra rights such as changing a footpath to a bridleway. There was originally no provision for removing or downgrading paths but this was added by the Countryside Act 1968.

Under the original law, reviews were supposed to be carried out every five years. However, most authorities did not keep up this programme and indeed some had not even carried out the first 1954 review by the time the system was changed in 1981. On a review the council had to produce a completely new map for the whole area including any changes that it felt necessary to make. There was provision for objection and public inquiries which could mean the whole process taking a very long time. Eventually, the new map became definitive and completely replaced the previous map which then had no status at all.

A problem was that if the authority made an error in re-drawing the map and nobody noticed then it would be difficult to correct. For example, if a path shown on the old map was missed off the new map, when it was noticed it could only be replaced if the evidence of its existence could be found. The fact that it had been on the old map would not be relevant because the map would no longer have any definitive status. Thus in practice the review process could lead to the map becoming less accurate rather than the reverse.

For a variety of practical reasons, the review process was changed by the Wildlife and Countryside Act 1981. The new system is one of continuous review and operates by the making of definitive map amendment orders. An order has its own relevant date and adds or deletes a path from the map. Thus there should always be an up-to-date definitive map. Different paths may well have different relevant dates but this is no real problem. If this becomes too complex there is provision for a consolidation process where a new map is drawn up with a new relevant date to include all paths with earlier relevant dates that have not been extinguished. The continuous review can then start again from the new base.

Definitive map amendment orders can be of two types which may be regarded as being the full process or the short cut.

The surveying authority has a duty to make an order by the full process on the discovery of evidence that the map is incorrect. This could be because a route is missing, either because it was there all along but was missed off the original map or because it has since come into existence. Or a route shown on the map may be found not to exist, either because it never did exist and was shown on the map in error or because it later ceased to exist. Similar arguments apply, of course, where the evidence indicates that a path has the wrong status; for example a footpath shown on the map may be really a bridleway or vice versa. The authority making the order has to publish the proposals and serve notice on all landowners affected. The public and the owners have a right to object to the order and if so then a public inquiry is held.

If members of the public find information that indicates that the map is wrong, then they can inform the surveying authority which should then investigate the matter and, if it agrees that the map is wrong, should then make an order. If the council takes no action then a formal notice may be served; if the council still takes no action, or having investigated the matter feels that there is no basis for an order, then there is right of appeal to the Secretary of State. Unfortunately, a convenient folk-lore has developed within many local authorities that an order can only be made when a member of the public actually serves the formal notice. This means that where evidence is found that a route should be added to the map it is frequently found necessary to go through the full process of serving notice on the council; this will be discussed in greater detail in Chapter 8.

The short cut method is only available for recording changes due to legal events. The main use of this procedure is to record the effects of public path orders creating, extinguishing or diverting paths. When an order of this sort has been confirmed, then an amendment order is made with its own relevant date to bring the map up to date. It should be noted that a diversion comprises concurrent extinguishment and creation orders and can be dealt with by deleting the old route and adding the new route. Other legal events which can be dealt with under this process include a variety of powers under which highways can be closed together with the creation of highways by formal methods which cannot be disputed. Examples are the creation of a highway under statute or by the owner formally dedicating the way and it being adopted by the highway authority. It should be noted that the process is not restricted to recent events; an order can be made in respect of legal events which happened many years ago, even before the first definitive map was prepared.

Orders under the short cut procedure can only be initiated by the surveying authority. However, if a member of the public or a landowner alleges that a legal event has taken place then there should be evidence of the fact and thus an application can be made under the full procedure dealing with the discovery of evidence.

A potential problem arises from the fact that orders under the legal events procedure are not advertised and there is no provision for objection. What happens if an order is made and confirmed and it is subsequently discovered that the alleged legal event never took place? Although the situation is not entirely clear, it seems that the validity of an amendment order made under the legal events method depends on the validity of the legal event itself; if it is later proved that the original order was not valid then neither is the amendment order.

3.9. Removal of rights from the definitive map

Originally, under the 1949 Act, paths could only be removed from the definitive map where they ceased to exist after the relevant date and were thus not in existence at the next review. There was no provision for paths to be removed even if it was established that before the first definitive map there had been no right of way (7). This was felt to be wrong, and under the 1968 Act provision was made for paths to be deleted or downgraded where it was found that a mistake had been made. This remains the position.

It is important to be clear that a path can only be removed or downgraded where new evidence is discovered which clearly shows that the original decision must have been wrong. There is not a provision for the owner to simply challenge the map and require evidence for the inclusion of the path to be produced. The opportunity to do this ceased when the map became final. The map must be assumed to be right unless it can be shown otherwise. It is also important to note that the new evidence must refer to matters arising before the original map was prepared. This is normally more than forty years ago and as time passes the evidence needed must refer to an increasingly distant past. In general, it seems likely that there will only be a few unusual cases where sufficient evidence will be available to justify the deletion or downgrading of a right of way.

Unfortunately, some owners appear to regard the power to delete paths as an opportunity to have paths removed wholesale and thus seriously undermine the whole concept of the definitive map. Any such attempt needs to be strongly opposed. In view of the importance of this, the issue will be considered in more detail in Chapter 9.

3.10. Rupps and byways

On the original definitive maps there were no byways and the term was not defined in law. On the map there were Roads Used as Public Paths (RUPPs) which were believed to be vehicular routes but were conclusively rights on foot and horseback.

In some areas the RUPPs were further classified as CRF or CRB depending on whether they were mainly used on foot only or by pedestrians and horses.

This gave rise to some confusion and so in 1968 it was decided that in each area there should be a special review dealing only with RUPPs and reclassifying them all. They could be reclassified as footpaths, bridleways or byways. Byways were to be a new concept and were defined as rights of way for all traffic, that is carriageways. Byways were still only a classification of a route on the definitive map and could only arise through the reclassification of a RUPP. This gave the curious anomaly that once the special review had been carried out there was no provision for adding carriageways to the definitive map if any more were found.

In deciding how to classify RUPPs, authorities had first to determine whether vehicular rights existed. If they did then authorities had to consider whether the routes were suitable for vehicular traffic and whether hardship would arise if vehicular rights were to be extinguished. These are, of course, tests to establish whether to reclassify as a bridleway or byway and gave no guidance as to the circumstances in which a path could be reclassified as a footpath. This inevitably gave rise to conflict in that many authorities believed that they had a freedom to reclassify as they thought fit and many CRFs were changed to footpaths. This led to the British Horse Society bringing a test case (8). The courts held that the power to reclassify a RUPP as a footpath was restricted to the situation where new evidence was discovered that the wrong status had been shown in the first place. Apart from this, as RUPPs had rights on horseback then they could only be reclassified either as a bridleway or a byway.

The position was changed yet again by the Wildlife and Countryside Act 1981. The tests of suitability and hardship were dropped and any remaining RUPPs were to be reclassified as byways if vehicular rights were found to exist. An important change was to allow additional routes to be added to the map as byways where they met the appropriate definition. A byway also became a sort of highway as well as a line on the definitive map. Now all public carriageways used mainly on foot and horseback are byways irrespective of whether they are shown on the definitive map or not.

For many years there was some doubt as to the status of RUPPs which had been reclassified. It has now been held by the courts that the normal definitive map principles apply and that changes to the map can neither create nor extinguish rights. Thus if vehicular rights existed, they were not extinguished if a RUPP was reclassified as a bridleway or footpath (9). Similarly, riding rights were not extinguished where a RUPP became a footpath. However, the existence of the rights needs to be proved; it is not possible to argue any conclusive case based on the former definitive map. However, records of the special review can be very valuable; if the authority established that vehicular rights existed but then reclassified as a bridleway or footpath on the basis of suitability then this does provide good evidence that vehicular rights still exist and that the route should now be shown as a byway.

3.11. Records of council maintained roads

In theory, all byways ought to be recorded on the definitive map, either as byways or as RUPPs where the special review has not yet been carried out. However, experience shows that there are many byways not recorded. This is not always because the council does not regard them as public highways; on the contrary, many of them are officially recorded as roads maintainable at public expense. It follows that an examination of these records is essential in establishing the full set of routes that are officially recognised.

The records are sometimes a little difficult to follow because they derive from former local authorities as they existed before the re-organisation of 1974. Before that time there were urban and rural district councils. The urban council was the highway authority for all highways other than classified A and B roads, for which the county council was responsible. Urban authorities were required by law to keep lists of all "streets" that were maintainable at public expense (10). These records (which are usually a map as well as a schedule or list) are often described as the adopted street record although this is a little misleading as it should include streets adopted since 1835 but should also include all streets already in existence at that time and thus maintainable at public expense.

In rural districts the highway authority for all highways was the county council, which was not obliged to keep any records of which were maintainable at public expense. In reality, however, it seems to have been the invariable practice to have a map which was usually described as the *county roads map*. The term *county road* strictly meant any highway maintained by the county and thus includes public paths, but in practice the maps produced seem to have only shown carriageways or what would normally be described as roads.

The Local Government Act 1972 extended the requirement to keep a list of streets to all highway authorities. Thus the county roads maps and the adopted streets maps should now have been consolidated into a record of all the streets maintained at public expense. Inspection of these records frequently shows a significant number of roads that have never been tarred and which are arguably byways, but are not shown on the definitive map.

For some reason, county staff are often rather secretive about the existence of the records, or even try to charge people for looking at them. If necessary, it should be pointed out that the requirement to have a list of streets maintained at public expense has now been extended to cover all areas and that such records are, by law, open to public inspection (11).

It should be noted that these records are not conclusive in the way that the definitive map is. However, they are the official record available for public inspection and the public are entitled to assume them to be correct unless the contrary is proved. Thus for the purposes of recording and surveying the rights of way network, the byways recorded only on the county roads records should be regarded as every much a part of the network as those actually shown on the definitive map.

Notes to chapter 3

1. National Parks & Access to the Countryside Act 1949. The equivalent legislation is now contained in the Wildlife & Countryside Act 1981.

2. R v Secretary of State for Environment ex parte Riley (1989) JPEL 921. See note 9 below.

3. Ministry of Town & Country Planning. Circular no 81, February 1950. This approves the methodology set out in the pamphlet: Surveys and Maps of Public Rights of Way for the Purposes of Part IV of the National Parks and Access to the Countryside Act 1949. Commons, Open Spaces & Footpaths Preservation Society in collaboration with the Ramblers Association. January 1950.

4. Countryside Act 1968.

5. "Definitive Map and Statement". Paul Coughlan, RWLR 8.1. 1992.

6. DoE Circular 1/83 argued in paragraph 20 that where an obstruction is recorded in the definitive map and statement then the use of the path is subject to that obstruction. The same error was carried forward to DoE Circular 2/93 (Welsh Office 5/93) where it appeared in paragraph 31. However, this error was corrected by a revision dated 22nd July 1997.

7. Morgan v Hertfordshire County Council (1965) 63 LGR 456. In this case it was established that through an error a right of way had been included on the map where no right of way had ever existed. Nevertheless, the map was conclusive. It appears to have been this judgment that led to the change in the Countryside Act 1968 allowing previous errors to be corrected.

8. R v Secretary of State for Environment ex parte Hood (1975) QB 891. This case established that under the 1968 Act a RUPP could only be re-classified as a footpath if there was evidence that the original classification was wrong. This rule was incorporated in the Wildlife & Countryside Act 1981. However, the judgments are important in describing the rules for removing or downgrading paths and are discussed in more detail in Chapter 9.

9. R v Secretary of State for Environment ex parte Riley (1989) JPEL 921. This case dealt with a RUPP which was known to have vehicular rights but had been reclassified as a footpath on the basis of suitability under the Countryside Act 1968. The principle that deletions or downgradings in error do not actually extinguish any rights is of wider importance.

10. Public Health Act 1925. There is some doubt as to what a street actually means which is discussed in more detail in Chapter 21. At this stage it is sufficient to note that the lists of streets and county road maps may point to the existence of additional routes. Whether they show all of them is a different matter.

11. Highways Act 1980. Section 36 requires highway authorities to maintain lists of streets that are highways maintainable at public expense and these may be inspected by any member of the public, free of charge.

4
ORDNANCE SURVEY MAPS

4.1. Introduction

Those who seek to protect public paths and byways frequently require skill in the use of maps. This chapter describes the various maps published by the Ordnance Survey, how they are keyed to the National Grid and how to determine the grid reference of any point. It also looks at some of the maps produced by the Ordnance Survey in the past, as some knowledge of these is often useful in researching paths missed off the definitive map.

4.2. The National Grid

It is necessary to have some appreciation of the National Grid. This is the system in which there is a set of north-south and east-west lines forming a grid over the whole country. The numbering of these lines is used to identify map areas as well as to give grid references of any point.

The grid system is known as a national one because there is only a single one covering the whole country. It is based on metric measurements. The system was introduced to replace the earlier system in which there was a separate grid (in imperial measure) for each county. As the individual county grids were based on arbitrary origins (for example the Yorkshire grid had an origin at York Minster) the grid lines in adjoining counties did not join up. On the National Grid this problem does not arise.

The National Grid has its origin at a point in the sea off the Isles of Scilly such that all points in Britain are both to the north and east of it. It may be of interest to know that it was arranged such that the grid line 400km to the east and running roughly down the centre of England corresponds to line of longitude 2 degrees west. This grid line is thus due north and south; all other lines are very slightly out of true north because of the need to make a spherical surface fit on a flat map.

Every 1km both north and east of the origin there is a grid line which appears on the OS maps. The lines every 10kms are shown slightly bolder. Although they are not shown any differently the lines every 100km are of special importance.

Any point can be uniquely defined as a distance east and north of the origin. It is vital to remember that the eastings are **always** given before the northings. The principle may be remembered from school mathematics as the cartesian system of coordinates; x the distance across is always given before y the distance up. Or it may be remembered by the more picturesque system taught to RAF navigators; go along the passage and then up the stairs!

4.3. The 100km square system

Although it is possible to define points simply as the distances from the origin, this gives rise to long numbers and an alternative system is generally used. This consists of having a two-letter code for each of the 100km squares. The 1km grid lines are then numbered within the square so that they have numbers from 00 to 99 instead of including the number of hundreds. This is the system used on the maps where only the two-figure number is shown beside each 1km line. If it is clear which square is being used then this is adequate on its own, but to give a unique reference it is necessary to quote the 100km square letters as well.

The method of lettering the squares is best seen on a diagram (see Figure 1). This shows the first 500km east and north of the origin which includes the greater part of England and all of Wales. It will be seen that there are 25 of the 100km squares. They are lettered simply enough with 25 letters of the alphabet (excluding I which could be confused with 1). The top row is lettered A to E, the second F to K and so on). All are then prefixed with an S so that the top row is SA, SB, SC, SD and SE.

There are two other 500km squares to the east and north of the one shown. There is not one to the north-east as that would be all in the North Sea. The eastern square uses the same set of 25 letters but instead of an S the letter is prefixed with a T. Thus the top line is TA, TB, TC, TD and TE. The same system is used for the northern square but here the prefix is N so the top line is NA, NB, NC, ND and NE.

see figure 1 on next page

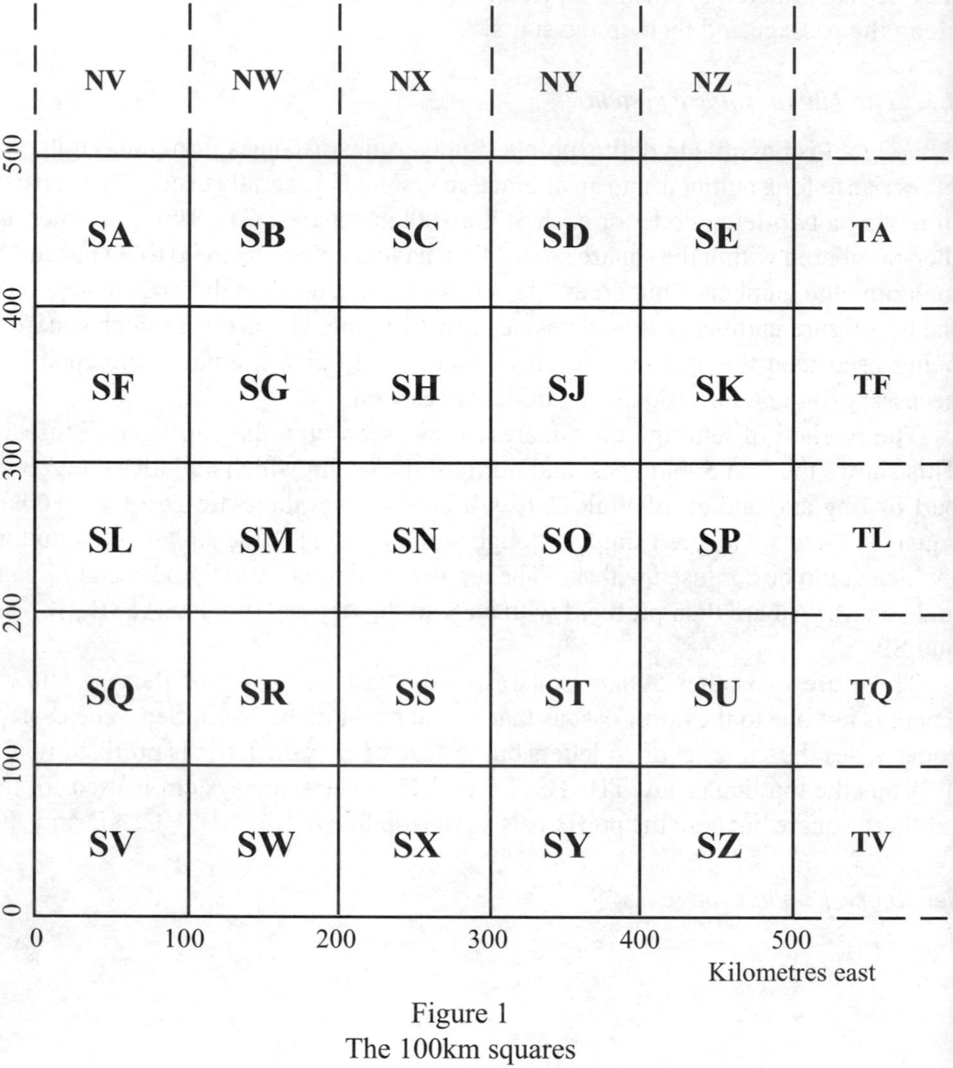

Figure 1
The 100km squares

4.4. Map scales

The Ordnance Survey produces maps to a variety of scales. They are normally specified as a ratio, for example 1:10,000. This means that a measurement of 1mm on the map will correspond to a distance of 10,000mm on the ground or 10m.

The very largest maps are at scales of 1:1,250 and 1:2,500. These show the greatest amount of detail but are far too large to be of much use in bridleways work. At the other extreme the OS produces maps on scales as small as 1:1,000,000 but these small scale maps are also of little use because they show hardly any detail. The key scales to be used in bridleways work are those at 1:10,000, 1:25,000 and 1:50,000 and these will be discussed in more detail.

4.5. The 1:10,000 maps

These maps are a relatively recent product of the OS and replace the traditional maps at a scale of 6" to one mile (ie 1:10,560) which will be noted later under historic maps.

These maps are intended for sale to professionals rather than the general public and are very expensive. They are printed in black and white with brown contours. They show a tremendous amount of detail but restrict themselves to physical features. So, although every hedge, fence or wall in the countryside is shown together with physical tracks, rights of way as legal entities are not shown.

The importance of 1:10,000 maps is that they are the most common base map on which the official definitive map is drawn. So rights of way workers rarely work with the base maps only but may well be concerned with 1:10,000 maps on which the rights of way have been superimposed.

Each sheet of the 1:10,000 series covers an area 5km square. The sheets stick rigidly to the National Grid system with the sheet boundaries being every 5km grid line east and north from the origin. There are thus four sheets within each 10km square. The sheets are identified by the 10km square in which they are, followed by NW, NE, SW or SE for each corner. The 10km square is specified by the two letter code of the 100km square, followed by two numbers which represent the bottom left hand corner of the 10km square. For example, the square whose corner is line 30 east and 60 north will have the numbers 36 (remember eastings are always given first!). To make the matter clearer Figure 2 shows the numbers for all 100 10km squares within a 100km square.

An example may help. Suppose we want the 5km sheet that contains the centre of York which is on 100km square SE and 60km east by 51km north. Thus the 10km square will be SE65. The easting is between 60 and 65 and thus in the western half; similarly the northing is between 50 and 55 and thus in the southern half. So the corner we want is the SW one. The full description of the sheet is thus SE65SW.

It should be noted that these 5km squares have been used as a sampling basis for carrying out national surveys of the condition of rights of way. The method used was to select at random a relatively small sample of squares from the vast number that cover the whole of England and Wales. Then the rights of way within those squares were accurately surveyed and the results expanded to provide an estimate of the condition of rights of way as a whole. It is likely that more surveys of this type will be carried out in order to plot progress towards the government target of bringing all rights of way into a usable condition.

see figure 2 on next page

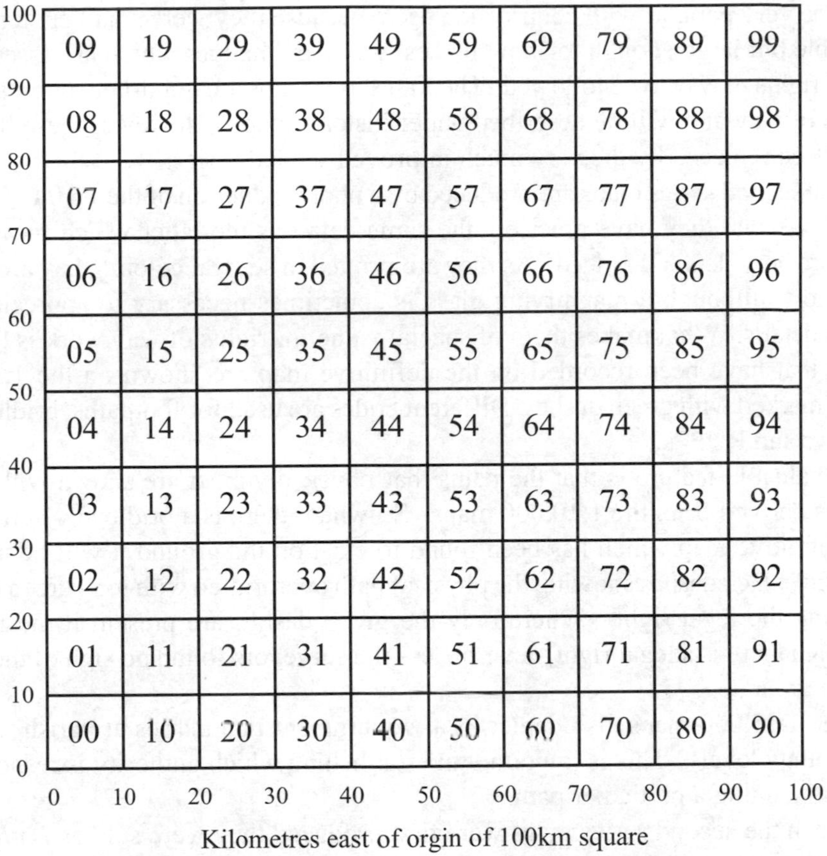

100										
	09	19	29	39	49	59	69	79	89	99
90	08	18	28	38	48	58	68	78	88	98
80	07	17	27	37	47	57	67	77	87	97
70	06	16	26	36	46	56	66	76	86	96
60	05	15	25	35	45	55	65	75	85	95
50	04	14	24	34	44	54	64	74	84	94
40	03	13	23	33	43	53	63	73	83	93
30	02	12	22	32	42	52	62	72	82	92
20	01	11	21	31	41	51	61	71	81	91
10	00	10	20	30	40	50	60	70	80	90
0	0	10	20	30	40	50	60	70	80	90	100

Kilometres east of orgin of 100km square

Figure 2
The 10km squares

4.6. The 1:25,000 maps

There were no maps of anywhere near this scale until the late 1940s. At that time the 1:25,000 series was introduced. They are often described as "two and a half inch maps" because the scale is approximately 2.5 inches to the mile. These maps became very popular with countryside users because they were small enough to be portable but large enough to show fences, walls and hedges which are essential to allow rights of way to be followed. The first series maps are important in researching rights of way and will be described under historic maps. However, these have all now been replaced by the very much improved second series.

The second series maps are produced by a photo reduction of the 1:10,000 maps. It follows that they have precisely the same detail as the latter which means that they are very detailed indeed. As they are printed in several colours they are easier to follow, although a magnifying glass is sometimes necessary to appreciate the finest details. What makes them of special value for rights of way work is that the paths that have been recorded on the definitive map are shown on the 1:25,000 maps marked with green dashes. Different codes are used for footpaths, bridleways, byways and RUPPs.

A valuable feature is that the paths that physically exist are shown with black dashes derived from the 1:10,000 maps. So where there is a bridleway defined on the definitive map which has been found to exist on the ground it will be marked with fine black dashes showing the physical path overprinted with long green dashes showing the legal right. Where only the green dashes are present it means that although there is a legal right, nevertheless the surveyors found no sign of the route on the ground.

The 1:25,000 maps also depict local government boundaries at parish, district and county levels. This is important in establishing which authority is responsible for maintaining a particular path.

When the second series maps were first produced they were sold as *Pathfinder* maps to emphasise their importance for users of rights of way. They have green covers and normally show an area of 20km by 10km. In most cases they correspond to two 10km squares side by side and are identified by the square numbers, for example NZ60/70. This rule is not invariably followed, however, and there are some odd sheets around the coast. It should be noted that the Pathfinder sheets each have a name describing the area depicted. Confusingly, they also have a second number but this is of little value as the sheets are consecutively numbered and thus the number gives no information as to which area is covered.

Later the Ordnance Survey started to publish *Outdoor Leisure* maps with yellow covers for tourist areas like national parks. These have a similar specification to the Pathfinder maps but with more colours and overprinted with tourist information. Where Outdoor Leisure maps were published, then the equivalent Pathfinder maps were withdrawn from sale. More recently the Ordnance Survey has started to publish a further series of 1:25,000 maps known as *Explorer* maps with orange covers. These have a very similar specification to the Outdoor Leisure maps and will eventually replace all the Pathfinder maps. Unlike the Pathfinder maps, their replacements do not have any consistent pattern nor numbering system.

4.7. The 1:50,000 series

These are by far the best-sellers of the Ordnance Survey range. Now marketed as *Landranger* maps with pink covers, they were introduced in the 1970s to replace the very popular one inch to the mile series.

Although very popular as touring maps for motorists, they are not anything like as useful as the 1:25,000 series for rights of way work as they are too small a scale to show field boundaries. This makes it difficult to follow paths unless they are well marked. But the maps are very helpful as a key map in that they are the smallest scale to show all the paths from the definitive map. As on the 1:25,000 series the paths are shown by dashed lines, this time in a magenta colour. Bridleways are shown by long dashes but unfortunately the printing is such that care is needed to tell bridleways apart from footpaths. The maps show county and district boundaries but not parish boundaries. They are useful in giving a broad picture of the availability of bridleways in an area, for identifying which authority is responsible and for use as a key to the numbers of the larger scale maps.

A recent innovation is to show information based on local authority records of highways maintained at public expense, which will generally be unsurfaced public roads. However, the Ordnance Survey refuses to show routes which are not physically evident on the ground. It is difficult to see the logic of this when they find no difficulty in showing invisible paths based on the definitive map. It also needs to be remembered that the council records are not definitive and the routes recorded may be open to challenge by the owners, either on the basis that the council is wrong in alleging that there is a highway at all, or if there is a highway, that it is only a footpath or bridleway and not a byway.

Each 1:50,000 map covers an area 40km by 40km. Unlike the larger scales there is no uniform pattern and the areas covered sometimes just meet each other and sometimes overlap. Each map has a name and also a number; the full set comprises 204 maps.

4.8. Giving a grid reference

The National Grid system allows any point in Britain to be given a unique reference. This is very useful in rights of way work as it allows, say, an obstruction to be recorded so that anybody else can find the same point.

The normal method of giving references is to start with the two letters of the 100km square. All points in the square are then referenced from the left-hand bottom corner. The reference is the distance the point is to the east, followed by the distance it is to the north.

It is possible to give a reference to the nearest metre. A reference would then consist of the distance in metres that the point was east of the origin followed by a similar northing. As points could be up to 99,999m from the origin it would be necessary to use up to 10 numbers to give the reference; such a reference is called a ten-figure reference. However, for many purposes this level of accuracy is unnecessary. For rights of way work it is normally quite adequate to give the reference correct to the nearest 100m; this means that the actual point is within 50m either side of the exact reference which is usually quite good enough. In quoting the reference the final noughts are left off and only the hundreds are written down. This is known as a six-figure reference. So that people know that it is a six-figure reference it is necessary to quote the leading zeros. For example, a point 500m east and north of the origin has to be described as 005005.

Let us consider in more detail how to give a six-figure reference for a point shown on the map. The first thing is to identify the two-letter code for the 100km square. These will be found shown in blue on 1:50,000 maps. The larger scale maps are even easier because the number of the map starts with the code; for example a 1:25,000 map NZ60/70 is obviously in 100km square NZ.

Next, the eastings have to be determined to three figures. The first two figures are the number of the kilometre square, that is the number shown beside the grid line to the left. The final figure is the distance from the grid line in tenths of a kilometre. The easiest way of measuring this is to make a little scale out of a piece of card with tenths of a kilometre marked along the edge. The distance between the marks depends on the scale; it will be 10mm for a 1:10,000 map, 4mm for a 1:25,000 map and 2mm for a 1:50,000. With the aid of this simple tool the distance from the grid line is measured and this becomes the third figure.

Finally, the northings are measured. This is done in precisely the same way except working up instead of across. The first two figures are the number of the grid line below; the final figure is measured up from this line using the card.

This is shown on Figure 3 which represents a part of the 100km square TA showing 1km grid lines and a point whose reference is required. The nearest grid line to the left is number 61. The point is measured as 400m to the east; thus the easting is 614. The grid line below is 23. The point is measured as 200m north of the line; so the northing is 232. The full six-figure reference is then TA614232.

see figure 3 on next page

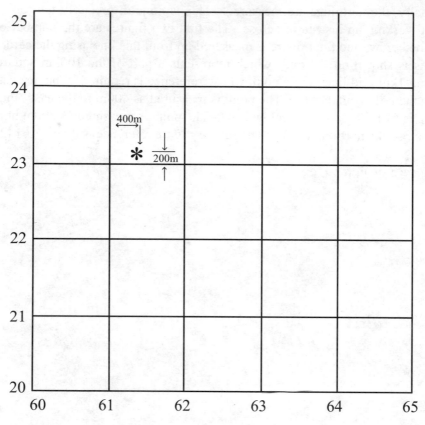

Figure 3
Taking a grid reference

Point* is TA 614 232

4.9. Historic maps

A knowledge of the modern maps described above will be found essential in following the public paths and byways that have been officially recorded. In addition, a knowledge of the types of map used in the past will often be valuable when disputes arise as to the accuracy of the current records. The scales that are found to be of most use are the six inch to the mile maps, the first series 1:25,000 maps and the one inch maps

4.10. The six inch maps

In the early days of the Ordnance Survey, maps were produced for different areas at a variety of scales. However, in the 1840s the whole of Ireland was surveyed at a scale of six inches to the mile and the success of this was such that it was decided to extend the coverage to all of Great Britain. The survey was carried out very quickly such that by the end of the 1850s all of England and Wales had been covered.

These maps were produced on a separate grid for each county and are known as the county series. Indeed, the very earliest maps only show up to the county boundary and leave the area beyond blank. The grid was an imperial one of half-mile squares but it is not shown on the maps except as the sheet boundaries. Each sheet is a rectangle six squares wide by three squares deep. The maps are identified by consecutive numbers like the Landranger maps of today.

In those days the Ordnance Survey was an offshoot of the Army and each sheet has the name of the officer responsible for the survey. Their obvious pride in their work is justified for these maps are surely the most beautiful works of cartography ever produced in Britain They were engraved on copper plates and printed by a process which allowed extremely fine lines and hence a great deal of detail. For example, individual hedgerow trees are identified. The importance of these maps in researching the history of rights of way cannot be exaggerated.

The county series maps were revised and re-issued at various times. The process of converting them to the National Grid and then to 1:10,000 scale was only completed in the last few years. But of particular note are the maps produced between about 1890 and 1940 because these make a distinction between footpaths (shown FP) and bridleways (shown BR). There was, of course, no definitive map at that time and these classifications do not necessarily correspond with the legal status but nevertheless the evidence is important; this point will be discussed in more detail in Chapter 18.

Copies of the various editions of the county series maps can be obtained from the British Library, but unfortunately they are quite expensive.

4.11. The 1:25,000 first series

As explained above, these maps were first produced in the late 1940s and have always been at a ratio scale and keyed to the National Grid. The first series maps each cover only a 10km square, or half the area of a modern Pathfinder map. The maps are described simply by the reference of the 10km square, for example NZ50.

These maps were originally produced before the definitive map and were not generally updated to show rights of way information. The exception is that there were some early Outdoor Leisure Maps which were based on first series mapping and these were overprinted with rights of way information in green. The main interest of first series maps is that they were current at the time of the surveys for the definitive map and in many cases they seem to have been the basis for the rights of way recorded.

Of particular interest are the very earliest editions which are now very difficult to come by. These are different from the later maps in that they show bridleways and footpaths by different line types, whilst the normal first series maps lump them all together. This appears to be based on the similar depictions on the old six inch maps but is shown rather more clearly and conveniently on the first series maps. They are always worth looking for in junk shops or old attics. They can be distinguished by the name of the map which instead of using the two letter code for the 100km square uses two numbers: the eastings and northings of the 100km square in 100s of kilometres. Thus map SE78 is instead described as map 44/78. This rather cumbersome system was used by the OS at one time before the more convenient two letter codes were introduced.

4.12. The one inch series

One inch maps are among the oldest products of the Ordnance Survey, with some being made as early as the eighteenth century when they were the largest scale mapping then carried out. With the completion of the six inch mapping for the whole country, the OS produced a full set of one inch maps. Re-prints of these are available both from the OS and commercial publishers.

Coloured versions were later introduced, the most common being the appropriately named *Popular Edition* produced from the 1920s and widely used by walkers, cyclists and motorists in the leisure boom of that time. They were replaced from the late 1940s onwards by the Seventh Series maps which were a considerable improvement in clarity and showed the National Grid. They originally showed physical paths in black but later included information from the definitive map in red. Popular and Seventh Series maps are frequently found in junk shops, flea markets and so on.

They are of some interest in researching rights of way, but like their modern equivalents they are most useful as a key to the larger scale maps. If a disputed path is shown on a one inch map, it is worth trying to find the six inch map of the same date which will provide much more useful information.

5
SURVEYING PUBLIC PATHS AND BYWAYS

5.1. Introduction

Once the theoretical existence of public paths and byways has been determined from the definitive map or the county roads map, the next stage is to go and find them on the ground. This is not always as easy as it sounds. Some routes that have not been used for many years may be quite invisible and the very fact that there is a right of way may be disputed by the owner. Even more confusing may be a route in use that over the years has diverged slightly from the official line. In all cases it is necessary to check out the line of the path and to make a record of what has been found.

This chapter deals with how to follow on the ground a path that is marked on the map. It includes some hints on reading the map and navigating, including how to use a compass. It also covers the efficient recording of what has been found and how to deal with any awkward people found along the route.

5.2. Getting around

The best way of getting around will depend on the sort of network being surveyed. If the intention is to survey all public paths and byways in an area, then it will be necessary to travel on foot as this is the only method allowed on the footpath parts of the network.

Where the survey is intended to cover only bridleways and byways, perhaps to develop riding or cycling routes, then it might be possible to carry out the survey from horseback. However, this is not as simple as it might seem as it is often found that a significant proportion of bridleways are blocked in ways that make it impossible to get through on horseback. In any case, in many areas of the country the bridleways are relatively infrequent with significant distances between; although a horse can cover the length of the bridleway quickly, it may take a long time to get to the next one. Finally, not every horse is patient enough to stand quietly whilst its rider studies maps or makes notes.

The cyclist fares rather better in that a mountain bike can be lifted over most obstacles, can be ridden along roads between bridleways or byways and carried by car for the longer sections. Even so, it has to be recognised that not all routes can be easily cycled along because of mud, undergrowth or deep ruts so walking may still be the best option.

5.3. *What you will need*

It is useful to have a checklist of what will be needed before setting out; nothing is more infuriating than getting to the path then being unable to complete the task because of lack of equipment.

The most vital piece of equipment is an Ordnance Survey 1:25,000 map showing the path to be surveyed. In the case of county roads it will be necessary to have previously recorded their routes on the map. Remember that any extra information added to a map should be in a waterproof medium as it might rain. In practice pencil is as good as anything for this.

A magnetic compass can sometimes also be of assistance. The orienteering type is best. You will not need a very expensive model as great accuracy is not needed in rights of way survey work. The method of using a compass will be described later in 5.7.

You will also need to be able to record the condition of the path. Some sort of notebook will be needed. It is as well to have a robust one or it will not survive the rigours of outdoor work. Probably the best is a spiral bound artist's sketchbook with good-quality cartridge paper; the A5 size fits conveniently in a pocket or bag.

To write in the book it is hard to beat an ordinary pencil (HB for preference). It is reliable even on damp paper, waterproof if rained on and can be easily rubbed out if a mistake is made. So remember to take a soft rubber for corrections. Finally, remember to take spare pencils or a means of sharpening them. If you do not, sod's law dictates that you will drop your pencil and break the lead miles from anywhere!

You will, of course, need ordinary outdoor gear, including waterproofs, boots and any necessary food and drink. As most surveys do not involve walking immense distances but over paths that are very muddy, wellington boots are often more useful than ordinary walking boots, particularly in the winter.

5.4. *Understanding the 1:25,000 map*

To survey a path it is necessary to follow precisely the route depicted on the 1:25,000 map. It is not possible to do this without knowing how to understand the symbols marked on the map. Whilst it is impossible to give here a complete guide to reading a map, it is hoped to include the features that are most commonly met with in following public paths and byways.

(a) Streams are marked by a blue line. These vary from very thin lines for minor ditches, through thicker lines for streams to larger rivers marked with a blue line on each bank with pale blue between. Where there is a bridge or culvert, the blue line is broken. If there is an actual bridge, the bridge symbol is shown. If the stream simply disappears through a culvert the blue line is merely broken.

(b) Buildings are marked by a grey block. Individual buildings are shown unless the gap between two buildings is small in which case they will be shown as continuous.

(c) Boundaries between enclosures are shown by a thin black line. This can mean a fence, a hedge or a wall; the various types of boundaries are not distinguished. Gates are not shown; a boundary line crossing a track may mean that it is fenced over or that there is a gate or stile. In some cases a boundary is shown by a dashed black line; this means that there is a marked boundary but that it is not continuous. This usually means either an old hedge that has been allowed to grow into a gappy row of bushes (common in grazing areas), or a dry stone wall that has been allowed to fall down.

(d) Roads, tracks and paths are also shown by black lines. Where there is a fence, wall or hedge on each side of the route then there will be double continuous lines. If there is a tarred surface the space in between will be coloured; otherwise it means a green lane or stone track. If there are no fences but the route used is visible then a dashed line indicates the edge of the track. A double dashed line means that the route is wide enough for vehicles; where there is only a footpath or bridleway width visible then a single dashed line is used. Where a route has a fence on one side but not the other a continuous line is used on one side and a dashed line on the other. Note that in this case there is an ambiguity as to how wide the route is because a lane with a fence on one side is shown the same as a footpath following a wall. The dashes are slightly longer than those for a ruined wall or hedge, but it is often difficult to distinguish these and it may not be clear whether a single dashed line is a path or a non-continuous boundary.

(e) Boundaries of counties, districts and parishes are also shown as lines of dashes. It is important not to confuse these local government boundaries (which are, of course, invisible on the ground) with the physical boundaries. The former can be distinguished by being in black but thicker than the latter. Parish boundaries are dotted. District boundaries (which are also parish boundaries) are dashed. County boundaries (which are also district and parish boundaries) are shown as alternate dots and dashes. It should be noted that the local government boundaries often follow physical field boundaries such as ancient hedges.

(f) Useful features of 1:25,000 maps are the faint symbols which show the type of vegetation. The key indicates special symbols for heath, rough grassland, bracken and various types of woodland. Where there are no symbols the land is ordinary arable or pasture land. Knowledge of these symbols can be useful in following a path.

(g) Finally, the most important symbol: the path itself. Where the path is recorded on the definitive map then the path will be marked in green on the 1:25,000 map. Different symbols are used for footpaths, bridleways, RUPPs and byways. These lines are like local government boundaries in that they are legal lines but there is not necessarily anything to see on the ground. If the legal line corresponds with a physical track of any sort then the physical feature will be shown by thin black lines as above with the green line overprinted. If there is a green line only it means that there is a right of way but it is not actually visible on the ground.

5.5. *Planning a survey*

Opinions differ as to the extent to which it is sensible to plan a path survey. One approach is simply to go to the end of the first path and start walking. A possible problem is that the 1:25,000 map will be correct at the date printed on it, but paths may subsequently have been diverted or even closed completely. So some people first visit council offices to study the definitive map and see if they need to make any alterations to the paths shown. This can conveniently be done at the same time as adding county roads.

Which is the best way depends on how inconvenient it is to go and check the definitive map. If the records are only held at a distant central office, open only on weekdays, then checking may be quite difficult. If a reasonably up-to-date Ordnance Survey map is being used then there are unlikely to be very many paths that have been diverted. Even if they have, it is accepted good practice that a new path is signposted at each end of the new route and clearly waymarked. So it is still possible to survey the new path even though its route was not known before visiting it. Situations where the path has been diverted but the new route not marked should be very rare and arguably it may not be worth the trouble of checking the definitive map first to avoid such rare problems.

It will, however, be worth a little trouble to plan the route used so as to minimise the amount of walking. In the case of a single path with no other connections, it will be necessary to walk it both ways, first to survey it and then to get back to the starting point. Where there is a more complex system of paths there will be a number of different ways of making the tour, preferably working outwards on one path and back on another. It is worth taking care that the tour is planned so that odd bits and pieces of path are not left over for another day if they can only be reached by having to walk long sections of paths already covered.

5.6. *Following the path*

The matter of surveying a path is simple enough in theory; you walk along the path and record its condition in your notebook. However, there is the important practical problem that you have to be able to follow accurately the line shown on the map. In practice, it is found that beginners often have problems with this. It is not possible within this book to give a full course of map-reading but it is hoped that the following hints will be useful.

Know where you are on the map. The vital rule is to keep looking at the map and to always know precisely where you are on it. Once you veer away from the route you are following and cannot tell your position on the map, then it is often difficult to retrieve the situation.

Start from the right place. It follows from the above that unless you start from precisely the right place you will rapidly become disorientated. If the path starts from a road then there ought to be a sign. But be careful; it is not unknown for the point signposted to be different from that marked on the map.

The Ordnance Survey is always right. The OS maps are prepared with meticulous care and errors are virtually unknown. Of course, they are only right at the date of survey and may not correspond with features later if things have changed. But before jumping to the conclusion that the map is incorrect due to changes, consider whether the change is really plausible. For example, suppose the map corresponds to features on the ground with one exception; there is an additional building not shown on the map. If that building is a modern barn then it is likely that it will have been built after the map was drawn. But what if the building is a Tudor farmhouse? It can hardly have been built recently, nor is it plausible that the map was drawn in error. The correct conclusion is that you are not where you think you are.

This brings us to a key point. After allowing for any plausible changes, the features on the ground should correspond precisely with the map. Far too often mistakes occur because people say "well its nearly the same". The rule must be that if it is not the same then you are not there. Sometimes when it is difficult to work out where you are, a compass bearing will help. For example, if you become disorientated in an area of small fields with limited visibility it may be useful to be able to see what direction a particular hedge is running in so that you can compare it with a possible hedge on the map. The method of taking compass bearings will be described in the next section.

5.7. *Compass bearings*

The use of a compass is often felt by rights of way workers to be an excessively complex matter, but it is hoped to show here that this is not the case and that a compass is from time to time a very useful piece of equipment.

The purpose of a compass is to determine a direction, or bearing relative to the reference direction which is due north. Bearings are the angle from north, measured clockwise in degrees. There are 360 degrees in a full circle so a bearing of 90 is due east, 180 due south, 270 due west and so on.

The easiest compass to use is the sort used by orienteers. In rights of way work it is not necessary to have high accuracy and the cheapest model will be quite adequate. Orienteering compasses are made with a rectangular base which is laid on the map. There is a line with an arrow which is used to indicate the direction for which a bearing is required. The compass proper is circular and fits onto the rectangular base. It can be rotated and has a scale of degrees marked round it. The arrow marked on the base is arranged such that the bearing of the line can be read off the circular scale on the compass. Within the compass there is the magnetic needle, one end of which will point north and is usually painted red.

The compass can be used in two ways. It can be used to find the bearing of a particular point seen on the ground and to transfer it to the map. It can also be used for the reverse process of pointing to some feature which has been found on the map. These processes will be described separately.

Suppose you can see a feature in the distance and want to identify it on the map. First point the arrow on the base of the compass towards the feature. Then rotate the circular part of the compass until the red end of the magnetic needle corresponds to the 355 degree mark on the compass. The bearing to the feature can now be read off where the line of the arrow meets the circular scale.

Why 355 degrees and not 360? There is a slight complication here in that the magnetic north pole is not quite at the normal pole but is actually in northern Canada. This means that the needle points a little to the west of true north. The exact variation differs between areas and is gradually reducing; in 2000 the variation was roughly 5 degrees. For the sort of accuracy with which we are concerned, the use of 355 degrees as the assumed bearing of magnetic north is good enough and has the advantage that it is likely to be clearly marked on the compass.

To transfer this bearing to the map it is necessary to place the base of the compass on the map such that the arrow line goes through the point on the map where you are. Then rotate the whole base until the compass is orientated with its north point in line with the north to south grid lines. The arrow line on the base now has the same bearing as that measured on the ground and should pass through the feature on the map corresponding to that seen on the ground.

Now consider the same thing the other way round. A feature is seen on the map and it is necessary to find its direction on the ground. For example, a path may go in a certain direction but if it is invisible on the ground and goes to a destination which cannot be seen over a hill, then a compass bearing is the answer.

First place the compass base on the map with the arrow pointing along the marked feature, for example the path. Then rotate the circular part of the compass until the north point is in line with the north south grid lines. The required bearing can be read off where the arrow line intersects the circular scale.

To find the direction to be followed, stand and rotate the whole base until the red needle in the compass points to 355 degrees. The arrow line is now pointing in the direction which you need to go in.

To try and make this clearer, Figure 1 shows the compass set on the map showing a line with a bearing of 60 degrees.

5.8. Recording information

As a route is followed on the ground, relevant information needs to be recorded in a notebook. There are many different ways of doing this but they should all achieve the following:

(a) All information that is likely to be needed in the future should be recorded. It is infuriating to have to re-survey a path because on the first try some important information was forgotten.

(b) It is particularly important that the location of any problems should be recorded in such a form that when a complaint is made to the appropriate body, sufficient information is available for the problem to be easily found.

(c) It should not be assumed that certain features are easily remembered and need not be recorded. After surveying many paths over a long period, the details tend to blur together. The notebooks should provide a record which looked at many years later, or by another person, provides clear information about the path.

A method of recording the information that has been found to be particularly useful is based on the methods used by land surveyors. The idea is to draw a little sketch map of the path as you walk along it. This can include the detail of the side of the path using symbols for walls, fences, hedges, marked but unfenced and unmarked. Any gates are marked by a line across the path, together with fences, walls or hedges running away from the path and any streams, railways and so on that are crossed. Buildings adjoining the path are also marked. Figure 2 shows a typical page from a field book giving details of a bridleway. This enables a good picture of the path to be gained even years later. It also allows any problems to be marked (in this case with a *). The detail allows the path to be compared with the OS map and the location of any features found on the survey to be located using a grid reference. There are a number of forms in use for recording information on paths, such as that used for the Countryside Commission 5km square sample surveys. Although excellent for recording certain information for analysis by computer, they have the disadvantage of not giving the full picture in the way that a sketch map does. It is suggested, therefore, that the best way is to collect the information in the field using sketch maps in a field book and then, if necessary, to transfer appropriate information to survey forms for analysis.

There may also be advantages in taking photographs of any obstructions or misleading signs in case at some stage in the future there should be any dispute as to whether they existed or not. Modern light-weight automatic cameras make this easy to do, but it is essential to make a note at the time the picture is taken as to what it records. Otherwise, by the time the film is developed you may well have forgotten! The location of any photographs should be marked in the field book for future reference.

6
THE GOVERNMENT MACHINE

6.1. Introduction

It is inevitable that anyone who sets out to protect public paths and byways must have an understanding of the role of government, both central and local. Central government is responsible for making the laws, and local government has much of the responsibility for implementing them. Local authorities have a great many powers and duties that concern public rights of way, and the way in which these powers are exercised cannot properly be understood without a knowledge of the way in which local government operates.

Although highway authorities have duties laid on them by Parliament that theoretically they are obliged to carry out, the reality is that they only do as much as they want to. Where there is no public pressure to do something, local authorities generally find ways of avoiding doing it, whatever the law may say. It follows that a key part of our work consists of ensuring that public support for rights of way is mobilised and that key decision-makers are made aware of it.

To lobby and influence decision-makers requires a knowledge of where power lies and the ways in which decisions are made. This chapter, therefore, gives an introduction to the government machine with particular emphasis on the role of local government; this tends to be where the key decisions are taken that affect the local public paths and byways.

6.2. Central and local government

In understanding the workings of the public sector it is important to appreciate the difference between central and local government. To many outsiders there is only one government machine and local government is simply its local branch. Although this concept is carefully fostered by central government, it is not correct. There are two quite separate branches of government; central government and local government. They are both rooted in great antiquity and have their different approaches and cultures. The most important point to understand is that both are democratic and controlled by separate elected bodies. Although the framework within which local government works is set by central government, nevertheless local government is entirely independent and ultimately reports back to the public and not to central government.

74

Central government originated from what were originally the totally despotic powers of the monarch. In our more democratic age this power is controlled through the election of Members of Parliament. The implementation of action decided upon by Parliament is in the hands of paid employees known as civil servants.

Local government, on the other hand, is derived from the self-governing communities of the Anglo-Saxon world and can thus claim an even greater antiquity than central government. The public control it through the election of councillors. Implementation of action decided by councillors is in the hands of paid employees known as local government officers. It is worth pointing out that there is considerable jealousy between the two types of government and that a state of cold war generally exists between civil servants and local government officers. It is thus important not to confuse the two. Local government officers do not like being described as civil servants, and will be even more upset by any suggestion that the local Member of Parliament has any influence over them.

6.3. *Central government*

The origin of central government goes back many centuries to the time of the Norman kings who had completely despotic powers. The King made the laws, but in doing so took the advice of his friends who constituted the court. To implement his decisions he needed particularly trusty friends who were appointed his ministers and who governed the country. Over the years the theoretical framework has remained the same but has gradually evolved to meet the needs of a more democratic age.

The King's friends have been replaced by the elected House of Commons and the unelected House of Lords, today most of the power rests with the former being the Members of Parliament elected by the public of each constituency. In theory, the Queen still makes the laws which are ratified by Parliament but in practice it is the other way round. The Queen acts as the guardian of the unwritten constitution; it would, for example, be her duty to refuse to approve laws that abolished elections or free speech.

Separate from Parliament is the Government which advises the Queen and decides policy. The Queen appoints a Prime Minister who is asked to form a government. In theory, the Queen can ask anybody to be Prime Minister but there is the practical restraint that policy proposed by the Government can only be implemented through laws that are approved by Parliament. So, in practice, the Queen appoints as Prime

Minister the leader of the political group that has the most Members of Parliament or otherwise there would be stalemate.

The policies of the Government are actually implemented through civil servants who are permanent and non-elected public employees. The Civil Service is arranged in departments and ministries each of which is headed by a member of the Government. In rights of way work the main body involved is the Department of Environment, Transport and the Regions (DETR) which was formed in 1997 out of the previous Department of the Environment (DoE) and the Department of Transport (DoT).

The DETR is responsible for town and country planning matters including rights of way. In particular, the Secretary of State effectively acts as arbiter where a local authority has made a public path order which has been objected to by a member of the public. Some orders can only be made by the Secretary of State rather than a local authority. Thus the DETR is responsible for public inquiries and for the Planning Inspectorate which makes the decisions on them.

The combined department also has responsibility for road and rail transport. It is the highway authority for the trunk road network which includes most of the motorway network. The Secretary of State has the power to make orders that alter existing highways, including public paths and byways, to allow new trunk roads to be built. In addition, the DETR controls in a variety of ways the actions of local authorities in the provision of highways. This includes acting as arbiter in disputed orders and in some cases making orders on the request of the local authority.

6.4. Other national public bodies

As well as the Civil Service which is directly controlled by the government, there are a variety of public bodies that operate nationally but are not directly under government control.

Until recent years, public corporations were of importance. These were effectively companies whose shares were all owned by the public and which controlled the various nationalised industries such as gas, electricity, the railways and so on. However, most of these have now been privatised and are no longer under public control. The new companies that replace the former public corporations may still have an important influence on public paths and byways. In particular, Railtrack now owns all the former British Rail tracks, but does not operate any trains. As very many rights of way cross railway lines by bridges or level crossings, Railtrack can exercise a considerable influence, especially as there is increasing concern over level crossings in the light of faster modern trains.

Of increasing importance are what are known as quangos (standing for Quasi Autonomous Non-Government Organisation). These organisations are set up by the government which funds them and appoints their controlling bodies. This means that unlike elected bodies which might include inconvenient people critical of the government, quangos can be controlled by carefully selected supporters. Even if they incline to doubts they tend to be reluctant to voice them as they will simply not be selected again. In addition the fact that funding is arbitrary means that quangos tend to toe the government line. Effectively, they are little different from bodies directly controlled by the government, but with the advantage that being notionally independent the government can quickly distance itself from any unpopular decisions! There are said to be several thousand quangos, but those most likely to be met with are the Sports Council and the Countryside Agency. The latter applies to England only; the Welsh equivalent is the Countryside Council for Wales.

6.5. Local government

Local government consists of elected councils which have powers given them by Parliament to make decisions on specified topics within defined areas. The constitutional position is that local government can only exist at the behest of Parliament. Nevertheless, local government pre-dates central government by many centuries; indeed there was local government based on manors before there was even a nation.

Over the centuries there have been many changes in the way that local government operates. Our present system is largely a Victorian creation. Local government was substantially reformed such that by the 1890s there were three levels of elected councils at county, district and parish levels. This pattern has remained broadly the same to this day, although there were substantial changes in 1974 when many boundaries were altered together with the respective powers of the councils. From that date the whole of the country was covered by district councils and county councils. The boundaries were arranged such that each county was a group of districts and each of the two tiers had their own duties and powers. Most, but not all, of the country was further sub-divided into parishes which have their own powers but no duties; this allows parishes to be optional.

In 1986 there was a further change when certain county councils were abolished and the district authorities became unitary, that is to say they are effectively both a county and a district at once. They are known as metropolitan districts. Further county councils were abolished in the 1990s with the district councils being given the powers of a county council; these districts are known as unitary districts in England and county boroughs in Wales. Their powers are virtually identical to the previous metropolitan districts. In addition, some individual districts were taken out of a county area and designated as unitary authorities but with the two-tier approach retained in the rest of the county.

The remainder of this chapter is written in terms of separate county and district authorities. Where unitary authorities exist it should be remembered that they are simply a county and a district rolled into one.

6.6. County councils

Counties or shires appear to have had some significance in the government of the country even before the Norman conquest. But they became more important during the Middle Ages with the setting up of a national system of courts. The King's judges travelled around the country holding assize courts in the county towns. At a more local level the various justices of the peace, as well as administering justice in the various parishes, also met four times a year at the quarter sessions.

Few people now realise that the quarter sessions were not merely criminal courts. The justices of the county in quarter sessions also had an administrative role. Among other matters, they were responsible for overseeing the maintenance of roads which was then carried out at a parish level. They were also directly responsible for the maintenance of major bridges. They had the power to levy a county rate, and could also force the parishes to levy rates to carry out their duties.

Justices of the peace were, and are, appointed by the monarch and not elected by the public. This was hardly a democratic approach and so from 1888 county councils were set up. These councils were elected and took over the administrative role of quarter sessions.

Over the years, counties have acquired more and more duties concerned with highways. Since 1974 they have been responsible for all highways except trunk roads. It should be noted, though, that in some areas the actual maintenance work is carried out by district councils under what are known as agency agreements. County councils also have responsibility for recording rights of way on the definitive map.

County councils also have important responsibilities in strategic planning. They have to prepare what is known as a structure plan which is the blueprint for the development of the whole county over the next fifteen years. This can have important implications for the future development of rights of way.

6.7. District councils

District councils are the newest tier of local government. For many centuries the parishes were the main form of local government carrying out such functions as the provision of highways and social services. But in Victorian times it became accepted that the parishes were rather too small to carry out these duties effectively and a variety of special boards were set up so that groups of parishes could act jointly. However, these were found not to work too well and by the 1890s they were replaced by a system of urban and rural districts covering the whole country. Some districts had the status of boroughs, of which some were described as county boroughs meaning that they also had the powers of counties and did not come under the county councils for the area in which they were.

All these districts originally had responsibility for highways, apart from some main roads that were the responsibility of the counties. However, the responsibility for minor roads was transferred from the rural districts to the counties in 1930 and the remaining roads from urban districts in 1974.

Although district councils are no longer responsible for highway maintenance, in many areas they have agency powers. This means that they do the maintenance work for the county who foot the bill. In some areas the counties have also delegated to the districts the highway responsibility for public paths.

It should be noted that despite not being the highway authority, district councils still have the right to make a variety of orders altering public highways. This is in parallel with the similar power of the county council and does not require the consent of the county.

District councils also have an important role in planning in that they are the local planning authority. Not only do they prepare local plans for their districts within the framework of the structure plan, but they are also responsible for deciding on most applications for planning permission. Associated with this are a number of powers to vary public highways in connection with proposed developments that have been granted planning permission. Such orders may well affect public paths and byways.

Whatever the relationship, there is a fundamental difference in culture which inevitably seems to surface. To an officer, consistency is a virtue. The ideal council would be one that had clear and consistent policies which the officers could easily understand and implement. But to politicians expediency is a virtue and consistency of little importance. Members tend to prefer not to have overall policies so that they have the ability to take individual decisions as expediency dictates. This approach clearly makes it difficult for officers to take operational decisions and often leads to a degree of friction between the two groups.

6.10. The members

Let us now look in a little more detail at the members and the constitutional framework in which they work. It is necessary to appreciate this theoretical framework first, although it will be shown in the next section that this has been somewhat modified in practice by the introduction of political systems.

Members are elected by the public to act as their representatives. The area served by the council is usually divided into wards and one or more members are elected by the voters who live in that ward. The ward members then have a special responsibility for representing the people of that ward (whether or not they actually voted for them) but they do have to balance this against the needs of the public of the area as a whole.

The method of election varies. In some authorities there are elections every year with an equal number of members retiring each year. In other areas the whole council is elected at once. But either way it is important to note that the council as a body is continuous; only the members change. This means that at any time the council is legally responsible for any decisions it has made in the past even if there are no longer any of the same members on the council. It should also be noted that this applies even where local government is re-organised. For each function a new authority is made responsible and is in precisely the same position as the old authority had it continued. For example, county councils as highway authorities are now responsible for the decisions made by urban districts before 1974 where they were acting as the highway authority. There is no equivalent in local government of the Parliamentary system whereby after a general election a completely new Parliament and government is formed with no connections with the previous ones.

At a very simple level, the council meets and takes decisions. It elects a chairman (sometimes dignified by the title of a mayor) who is there to control the meeting.

Whilst this is often still adequate for some parishes, in counties and districts it is no longer practical to conduct all business at council meetings and there is a system of committees where most of the decisions are actually taken.

This works by the council appointing a number of members to form a committee to deal with certain specified matters. There may well be a second tier of sub-committees to deal with even more detailed matters. For example, a county council might have a committee to deal with highways matters with that committee having a sub-committee to deal with public paths. Although committees actually make most of the decisions in local government, strictly speaking their decisions are recommendations to the main council who ratify the recommendations as decisions of the council. This ratification process allows members who are not on a particular committee to query decisions of that committee. If they can persuade members of the council as a whole that a wrong decision is being made then the council can refer the matter back to the committee for further consideration.

There are, however, some matters on which a fast decision needs to be made. In such cases the council can give a committee what are known as plenary powers. This means that on decisions of a particular type, the committee have delegated to them the powers of the full council. For example, most district councils have committees to deal with planning applications and these generally have plenary powers to make immediate decisions as otherwise applicants would be unreasonably delayed.

Each committee has to elect a chairman. In principle, chairmen are simply there to control the meetings and ensure that decisions actually do get taken. However, in practice their role tends to be wider than this. Committees often delegate to an officer the taking of urgent decisions between meetings, subject to consultation with the chairman. Although the officer is not bound to take the advice of the chairman, in practice it would be most unwise not to! This means that in practical terms the chairman may well have a very significant executive role and is thus a person of considerable power in the local government system.

In recent years the Government has encouraged a streamlining of local government through reducing committees to the bare minimum necessary to decide strategic policy with the routine decisions to implement these policies being delegated to officers. The officer will normally be required to consult with a specified lead member having responsibility for a particular policy area. Given the large range of issues delegated in this way, the lead members will have an even greater executive role than the chairmen under the previous system.

6.11. The political dimension

It will be seen from the above that there is an important difference between central and local government in that in the latter there is no direct equivalent of the split between Parliament and government. The council, which includes members of all political colours, is responsible for taking all decisions and for running the area. In theory, the system does not acknowledge the existence of political groups.

In practice, of course, politics play a considerable part in local government. Today there are few independent members; most are associated with a political party. The members of a council of a particular political colour are described as a group. Obviously, the most important group is that which has the most members and is known as the controlling group.

The controlling group is so described because, given that all its members vote the same way, they can effectively control all decisions of the council. In advance of the formal meetings of council or committees, the groups hold private and unofficial meetings where they discuss the matters on the agenda and decide on the group policy. Once this has been agreed, all group members vote the same way irrespective of what their initial views were. This extends to the appointment of members and chairmen of committees. At present the law requires that the various parties have their members on the various committees in the same proportion as on the council. This ensures that each committee can elect as chairman a member of the controlling group. Given the power that the chairmen have, it follows that they form an inner "government" within the controlling group. This is headed by the leader who is selected by the controlling group and is the real power within the council. The chairman of the council (or mayor), although the titular head of the council, actually has very little power in practice.

Following an election, control frequently passes from one political group to another as a result of changes in the numbers of councillors of each political party. The new group may well revise the policies of the council. On obviously political issues the group will normally follow the party line; on less political issues like rights of way the approach may simply reflect the personal priorities of the leader.

6.12. Access to council information

It is appropriate in passing to note another difference between central and local government, which stems from the wider responsibilities of councils. This is in the degree of openness in which decisions are taken. Central government is somewhat obsessive about secrecy. Although meetings of Parliament are of public record, all the real decisions are taken by the government whose meetings are anything but open. Government papers are kept from public gaze for at least thirty years and often sixty. What is often not realised is that this applies equally to succeeding governments who thus have no information on how similar problems were solved in the past. With such a bizarre system it is perhaps not surprising that central government seems prone to repeatedly making the same errors! The central government approach to secrecy is summed up by the Official Secrets Act which effectively says that everything is secret unless a specific decision is made to release information. Whilst this is clearly justifiable in matters of national security, there seems little doubt that this is used by governments as a convenient way of hiding information to which the public is entitled but which would be politically embarrassing.

The local government approach is the absolute opposite. Decisions are taken by the council or by committees that are open to the press and public (except in special cases where there are good reasons for confidentiality, such as confidential information about a child in the care of a social services department.) The meeting at which decisions are taken is therefore open to the public who may also inspect in advance any reports that are to be made by officers (1). Further, all files and papers that were taken into account in the writing of the reports are also available for inspection. This can be very valuable although it is worth remembering that it works the other way. For example, if an individual writes to claim that a path has been missed off the definitive map then the owner is entitled to inspect the files and find out who has made the claim.

Where decisions are delegated to an officer then a record is required to be kept of the decision made and the reason for it and again the files and papers taken into account have to be available for inspection. The Government has indicated clearly that it expects the streamlining of local government to make it more transparent than before although it remains to be seen whether some councils or individual officers will use the new system to mirror the secrecy found in central government.

6.13. The role of officers

Let us now look at the other side of the local government system and consider the officers. In theory, the officers advise the members and implement their decisions. It should be obvious, though, that in practice this gives officers a great deal of control over day-to-day matters. This is for two reasons. Firstly, in most cases where officers advise members this advice is accepted without question. It follows that the key decision is in deciding what advice should be given and this is made by officers rather than members. In addition, once a policy decision has been made by members, officers are given authority to implement it and this means taking many decisions. Thus in practical terms, key policy decisions tend to be taken by members whilst less important decisions are taken by officers. Given that rights of way work tends to have a low priority in most authorities, it follows that the main players in rights of way work tend to be the officers rather than the members.

An example may make this clearer. A county council will need to take a decision as to how much money it intends to spend in the coming year and how this will be divided between the various committees. Such a decision is essentially a political one and taken by members. But suppose that an allocation for highways has been made; the next question is how this is to be divided between the various aspects of highways work. Although this is also a member decision, the only basis for making this decision is on the basis of officer advice as to the best value for money. The members are very unlikely to ignore technical advice on such a matter so this is effectively an officer decision. Suppose this decision provides an allocation of finance for maintenance of rights of way. It would be very unusual for members to want to know precisely how the money was being spent and the normal practice would be for operational decisions of this type to be delegated to officers.

6.14. The officer structure

Parallel to the members structure that has been described there is a quite separate officer structure. Like most large organisations this is hierarchal with all staff reporting ultimately to the most senior officer who is usually described as the chief executive. Next in line are the chief officers who are each in charge of a department. In general, the departmental structure is arranged to correspond with the committee structure so that a particular department exists to carry out the functions of an associated committee. For example, there may be a planning department headed by a chief planning officer which is to advise and implement the policies of a planning committee.

An implication of this is that the role of the chief executive is less important than would appear at first sight. The chief officer tends to act as the link between a department and the members who control it so that the chief executive has little input in the decision-making process except for strategic issues that affect the whole council. It is the chief officer who has the greatest influence on the way in which services such as rights of way are actually supplied to the public.

Because different councils operate in different ways, there are different departments in which rights of way matters may be handled. The most common seems to be to regard rights of way as minor highways and deal with them in an engineering or highways department. In county councils such a department is often described as a county surveyor's department, taking the historical title of the chief officer from the time these functions were in the hands of quarter sessions. Another common approach is to include rights of way matters with other countryside matters in a planning department. Increasingly, though, engineering and planning departments are being merged as technical services or environment departments.

Whatever the name of the department, it will be further sub-divided into divisions, sections, groups, teams and so on. Somewhere within this will be the staff who actually deal with rights of way. Unfortunately, in most authorities the rights of way work is regarded as of little importance and the staff engaged in it of little influence in the officer structure. Almost invariably, though, they will be found to be extremely enthusiastic supporters of rights of way. Shortcomings in the way in which the work is carried out are usually due to the inadequate resources made available rather than the failure of the staff employed.

6.15. *How to make friends and influence people*

An important advantage of local government over central government is that the former is much more responsive to the needs of the public, or at least the opinions expressed by the more articulate! There are a number of reasons for this. The simple fact is that general elections are decided on national issues. Although, for example, the route of a new trunk road is technically a government decision, it is hardly the sort of decision that brings down a government. Indeed, it is very rare indeed that such matters are even debated in Parliament. Ministers are on fairly safe ground in assuming that they can take any decision they want without risking their own position.

By contrast, local government exists to take local decisions. Matters that are regarded as minor distractions by ministers will be the subject of intense debate in the council chamber, not to mention the local newspapers and bars! The public want to know what the attitude of their ward member is and are liable to take it into consideration when casting their vote at the next election. It should be remembered that the number of electors in a ward is very small compared with the constituents of an MP. Moreover, turnout at local elections is low and the results largely depend not so much on floating voters but what proportion of each side's supporters can be motivated even to go the polling station. Consequently, councillors tend to take no risks and lean over backwards to gain the support of electors in their ward.

There is an important implication of this. Local authorities have legal duties to do certain things. But the reality is that authorities can almost always wriggle out of their duties; they are much more likely to respond to demands of the electors. It follows that the best way of influencing a local authority is by approaches from people who actually live there. For example, suppose a bridleway is obstructed. An official approach from, say, the British Horse Society will probably go in the waste paper basket. A complaint from a resident will almost certainly have more effect. Even better will be lots of complaints! Many rights of way workers tend to try and act as a channel of communication between users and the council. This tends to be counter-productive; it will be much more effective to try and persuade the people to make their own complaints. Indeed, there may well be an argument for reversing the process with rights of way workers arranging for problems coming to their notice to be farmed out to as many different people as possible to make the actual approach.

However, to make the most effective use of public opinion it is essential to ensure that it is applied in the right place. It is important to know precisely which local authority is responsible for each type of problem, and who is the officer within that authority who actually makes the relevant decisions. It is necessary to know which members are most likely to take up the cudgels if officers fail to act, and which of their electors is prepared to urge them on.

In short, to influence the local government system to maximum effect it is essential to have a detailed knowledge of precisely how the machinery works in each particular area.

Notes to Chapter 6

1. Local Government (Access to Information) Act 1985. This amended the Local Government Act 1972 and the requirements are in Sections 100A to 100H of the 1972 Act. Where decisions on rights of way matters are taken by committee then the meeting should be in public and the public should be able to obtain copies of the officers' reports three clear days in advance. Any other documents taken into account in the writing of the report should be listed, and be available for inspection at the same time.

7
COLLECTION OF USER EVIDENCE

7.1. General points

This chapter deals with the collection of user evidence to show that extra paths should be added to the definitive map or that paths should be upgraded, for example by changing a footpath to a bridleway. If evidence can be found then a formal application can be made as will be described in Chapter 8.

It is important to be clear that the definitive map is intended to be a record of the rights that actually exist; not of paths that would be desirable. Paths can only be added to the definitive map where there is evidence to show that the right already exists. There are quite different procedures available for creating new paths where they can be shown to be required.

The other side of the coin is that if evidence shows that a right of way exists, then it is required to be added to the map irrespective of how inconvenient it is to the owner. Objections to the addition or upgrading of paths on the map can only be on the basis that the alleged rights do not exist; arguments as to whether there should be a path are not relevant.

However, it will be clear that the addition of a right of way to the map may well financially affect the owner. Although it may have existed all the time, the recording of it on the map will clearly indicate its presence to any future purchaser of the land who may not be prepared to pay so much in consequence. Nobody should be surprised if owners go to a great deal of trouble and expense to dispute the existence of rights of way alleged to lie over their land. To most rights of way workers, the finding of additional rights of way is an entertaining piece of detective work; the owner whose pocket is hit is likely to see it in a much more serious light!

The law, quite reasonably, takes the line that paths can only be added following a rigorous testing of the evidence. It should be noted that the standard of evidence now required to add a path to the map is different from that used when the map was first produced. Then a path could be put on the draft map simply on the basis of a reasonable allegation that it existed. If the owner objected then the evidence was properly tested, but if no objection was raised then the path went forward to the final definitive map. To add a path later, the surveying authority is required to check out the evidence and make sure that it is adequate before even making the relevant order (1).

There is an important conclusion to be drawn from this; the rights of way worker should play to win. The objective is to get extra paths on the map, not to make some ineffective gesture in favour of rights of way. One application that is properly researched and succeeds is far better than ten that fail. If resources are inadequate to fully check all paths for which some evidence exists then the best plan is to research fully the most promising but also to record all the information on the others. This last is an important point; large amounts of valuable evidence have been lost simply because people committed it to memory and then died, moved or lost interest before recording it properly.

7.2. *Types of evidence*

The evidence needed to show that a highway exists normally falls into one of two categories. Firstly, there is evidence of usage where the intention is to show that a dedication can be presumed. As a general rule, evidence of this sort refers to fairly recent times. Secondly, there is evidence of reputation where it can be shown that the route in question was or is believed to be a highway. Perhaps the oldest inhabitant says that when she was a girl everybody regarded a particular route as public. Or documentary evidence may be used to show the same thing.

A highway can be proved on the basis of either of these forms of evidence alone. However, in many cases both types of evidence are available and this is always a more satisfactory state of affairs. Where a right of way is proved by usage then the use by the public raises an inference that it was either already a highway at the start of the period of use or the owner dedicated it at that time. It is clearly better if this can be supported by evidence from some earlier time that the route was believed to be a highway, even where this would be inadequate on its own. Similarly, although a highway can be claimed through evidence that it was reputed to have been a highway at some period in the past, without it having being used in living memory, under such circumstances the evidence would have to be very strong. It is always better to have both types of evidence which serve to strengthen each other.

The researching of documentary evidence to establish evidence of reputation is a complex matter which will be dealt with at length in Chapters 14 to 22 of this book.

7.3. Creation of highways at common law

Under common law, there are only two ways in which a highway can have come into existence. The highway may already have been in existence in 1189 in which case it is described as an immemorial highway and there is no need to speculate on how it originally came to be. If the highway came into use any later then it could only have been through dedication of the owner to the public and acceptance by the public. Until relatively recently all new highways were automatically maintainable by the public and thus the public had, in theory at least, the power not to accept that responsibility by not using the route offered (2).

If there is a dispute over whether a particular route is a highway or not it is not necessary to prove how or when it first came into existence. If it can be shown that the public and the owner treated the route over a long period of time as if it were a highway, then an inference can be drawn either that it was already a highway at the start of the period or, if not, that the owner dedicated it at that time. The legal principle involved is similar to the concept of a *lost grant*.

Since people are always losing written records, the law has developed a series of assumptions that come into play when the evidence cannot be found. Basically, where a set of conditions which could have had a legal origin have been found to exist for very many years it will be assumed that there was originally a proper legal document creating the position which has since been lost, hence a *lost grant*. The position on a public highway is similar except that no lost document has to be imagined as a highway can be dedicated by simply throwing it open to the public. Where the public have used a route for many years, believing it to be a public highway, and the owner has known about this and made no moves to dispute it, then this is consistent with the route being a highway all along and this will be assumed in the absence of any conflicting evidence.

Under common law there is no fixed time period laid down as to what use will allow a dedication to be assumed. Each case has to be considered on its merits. Where there is very strong evidence, the period can be quite short; there is a recorded case where use over only eighteen months was sufficient for a highway to be presumed (3). More usually, of course, an inference can be drawn only after use for many years.

The common law approach poses a number of problems. A difficulty is that there are circumstances where nobody has the power to dedicate a highway, for example if the owner is a minor. If nobody has the power to dedicate then dedication cannot be presumed. In general it is only possible to prove public use for a finite number of years into the past and it has to be assumed that the use commenced at that date and the dedication took place then. Where there was nobody with a power to dedicate at that stage then the courts have refused to assume any dedication. Thus there might be situations where a route has been clearly used by the public for a great number of years and yet it is impossible to prove at common law that the route is a highway.

To simplify the matter, a statutory process was introduced in 1932 and today most attempts to prove the status of a route through public use are based on the statutory rather than the common law approach (4). However, it should be remembered that the common law approach still exists and might yet be appropriate where there is strong evidence of dedication and acceptance by the public, but over a period of less than twenty years. For example, where an owner tries to divert the public away from a section of path that is inconvenient to him by putting up signs that another route is a public path, then he would probably be regarded as having positively dedicated the route. Then usage by the public over a relatively short period of time would probably satisfy the common law test and the new diversion would become a highway without, of course, the old route being extinguished.

7.4. Presumed dedication under statute

Where a route has been used by the public as of right and without any challenge from the owner for a period of at least twenty years then the way is presumed to have been dedicated as a highway. This presumption can be overturned by the owner proving that he had no intention to dedicate, but the burden of proving it falls on him and he must be able to show that he made it generally known that he had no intention to dedicate.

The public means everybody. It is not, of course, necessary to show that every one of the Queen's subjects has used the alleged highway but the implication has to be that any of them could have used it. The actual users have to be a sample of the public and not special individuals. They must use the route believing themselves to have a public right to use it and not because they have the special permission of the owner or because they have a private right of way over it. As the acceptance of the owner has to be inferred from his failure to intervene, then the public use has to be sufficiently open such that it can reasonably be assumed that the owner knew about it.

It should be noted that the objective is to show that the public used the route for a period of at least twenty years. There has to be evidence of members of the public using the route over the whole period, but it is not necessary to show that any one person used it over the whole time. Evidence of a large number of people using the route for quite short periods would suffice, so long as the periods overlapped enough to indicate that there was continuous use by the public during the whole twenty years.

There is no precise answer as to how many users are required. As it has to be inferred that the owner knew about the use but did not challenge it, it must follow that evidence from those who used the route frequently will be much more valuable than those who used it rarely. A normal rule of thumb is that there ought to be at lease ten users. In theory, it might be possible to infer public use with less witnesses if they had used the path very frequently, for example to go to work every day, but in such cases it would be necessary to be able to show clearly that there was no explicit or implied permission from the owner.

It is important to note that a claim cannot succeed where the owner has challenged the right during the twenty year period. This might be through erecting barriers which prevent the use of the path, by putting up signs prohibiting use or informing the public that there is no intention to dedicate. It is also possible for the owner to serve notice on the highway authority that there is no intention to dedicate a highway, but this is rarely done in practice (4).

It is a requirement that the twenty years use has to be calculated backwards from the date that the right to use the path became disputed. In theory, a claim can be made for a path which the public were prevented from using many years ago, but the twenty years have to run backwards from that date. In practice, of course, it becomes increasingly difficult to find evidence for early years and most successful claims will be where use is up to a recent date. It should be noted, however, that it is not possible to make a claim for a path where public use ceased without the owner challenging the right. Occasionally there will be examples where there is good evidence of use up to some time in the past which was never challenged by the owner, but the use ceased because of some other change. For example, people might have used it to reach a railway station which was later closed. In such cases it will not be possible to use the statutory approach, but it might still be possible to use the common law approach.

In other cases, there may be routes not on the definitive map that continue to be in regular use and where the owner has never challenged the public right. As there has been no challenge, the statutory presumption of dedication cannot be invoked. If there is good user evidence going back at least twenty years from the present date, then the surveying authority would appear to have an adequate basis for adding the route to the definitive map on the basis of repute. If the owner continues to accept this by not objecting, then the evidence of repute is substantiated and the matter can go forward. If he does object, then there is a challenge and the statutory approach to presumption of dedication comes into play.

7.5. *Dedication by statutory bodies*

It should also be noted that a highway cannot be assumed to have been dedicated where the land belongs to some body whose purpose is incompatible with the dedication. For example, if a water company owns land for the construction of a future reservoir then a dedication cannot be presumed for a route which would prevent the reservoir being built. This will apply where use can only be proved back to a date after the land was purchased; if the period of use runs back before the land was purchased then a dedication can still be presumed by the then owner at the commencement of use.

The courts also take into account whether the alleged dedication would be likely to have had an adverse effect on the body even where the alleged path would not have actually prevented the use for which the land was obtained. For example, it was held for many years that a railway company could not be presumed to have dedicated a highway over an occupation bridge, that is, one provided to give a private right of way to someone affected by the railway. The logic was that if the need for the private right ceased then the railway could demolish the bridge and save the maintenance cost. They would not be able to do this if they had dedicated a public right and this was thus inconsistent with their purpose of running the railway as cheaply as possible.

This has practical implications because it appears that when the original definitive maps were produced in the 1950s, the then British Transport Commission objected to very many routes which crossed bridges and even level crossings where these were originally provided only as occupation routes. However, in 1955 it was held by the courts that the traditional logic was too tenuous and that it was possible for paths to be presumed to have been dedicated over occupation crossings or bridges (5). However, many of the definitive maps had already been produced by that time and this resulted in many missing links over railway lines which are still missed off

95

the map today despite the fact that they continue to be regularly used. There is a clear need for the definitive maps to be tidied up in this respect, especially as many of the rural railways involved have long since been closed and the tracks removed.

7.6. Selecting the witnesses

As user evidence leading to an alleged presumption of dedication is the most common method of trying to add paths to the definitive map, it is worth looking a little more closely at the practical problems. It is very much more difficult than it looks at first sight and many attempts have failed simply through not enough care being taken over the collection and vetting of evidence.

The first problem is to establish the exact location of the right of way being claimed. To prove a path through presumption of dedication requires that the precise route of the path can be specified and that all the users have gone that way. Unfortunately, it often proves to be the case that different people have travelled broadly between the same points but using slightly different routes. This cannot be used to prove the path; there must be adequate use over precisely the route claimed. Of course, if there is considerable use over a number of separate but clearly defined routes then there might be sufficient evidence to establish a separate right of way over each route but this will be rare. In general, it will be very difficult to establish any right at all where the users have not restricted themselves to a single route.

The next thing to check is whether there is any need to collect user evidence anyway. If, for example, a path has been used for many years on horseback and continues to be so used then this may well be because the owner already regards it as a bridleway. This is the first thing that should be checked because the owner may well have no objection to the existing situation being regularised by showing the path on the definitive map. If this is the case there is no need to collect any further evidence.

If the owner does dispute the right then the next stage is normally the collection of statements from witnesses using evidence forms. Most surveying authorities have their own standard forms which they like people to use. There are some problems here which need to be considered arising from the forms being intended for general rights of way use. In particular, the forms often ask whether the witness regards the path as a right of way without asking whether as a footpath, bridleway or byway. Similarly, forms often ask about use without specifying use on foot, horseback or by vehicle. Clearly these points are of importance in proving a bridleway or byway and it may be necessary to endorse the forms to make clear what status of highway is being claimed and what type of usage the evidence refers to.

Many rights of way workers adopt the wrong approach in collecting evidence. It should be remembered that the intention is not to produce a petition of people who want the path; it is to produce evidence that will stand up in a court of law. Quality not quantity must be the key principle. It is perfectly possible to prove a path on as few as ten good evidence forms although clearly more are preferable. Forms that are irrelevant will simply be discounted and are of no value. Worse still, if people can be shown to have given untrue information this will weaken the case far more than if they were never involved as it throws doubt on the accuracy of all the others. The surveying authority has a duty to check the evidence submitted and it is the normal practice to interview the key witnesses. If they are unable to substantiate what they put on the form then the authority will be unable to process the order. It is essential that those who collect evidence are aware of all the pitfalls and take every precaution to ensure that the evidence collected will stand up to examination.

It is worth being clear from the outset that evidence forms that have been submitted to the surveying authority will become public documents if it is decided to make an order. This arises from the access to information requirements that were described in Chapter 6. The forms have to be listed as documents used in the preparation of the report to the appropriate committee and as such are open to inspection by the landowner.

This is only fair in that if the owner believes that the information is incorrect he has the opportunity to challenge the evidence or produce his own evidence to refute the claim. Unfortunately, it also allows the unscrupulous owner to put pressure on the witnesses to withdraw their claims and intimidation of witnesses is not unknown. It is particularly a problem in bridleway claims because most riding is very local and hence the owner is likely to know the witnesses. Whilst all this is most improper, it would be naive to ignore the possibility. It means that witnesses must not only be sure of their facts but they must also have the strength of character to refuse to be browbeaten. Obviously, this makes the collection of evidence more difficult but it important to be clear of the problems before starting. It should be made clear to prospective witnesses that the owner will have access to the statements; if they are then frightened to give evidence that is unfortunate but there is not a lot that can be done.

Whilst forms of evidence are useful, it is far better if witnesses are prepared to give evidence in person at any future public inquiry. This is because it is relatively easy to lie on paper but more difficult in public and under cross-examination. Thus it is useful to prepare for this by checking whether witnesses will be prepared to give evidence. Again, it is necessary to check that their story is consistent and, of course, true. If a witness at a public inquiry is proved to be lying then doubt is thrown on the whole case.

Often the most useful witnesses are very old people who can give information from very many years ago. As disputes over paths can drag on for years there is a real risk that they may die before a public inquiry can be held or that they will not be well enough to attend. Here a statutory declaration will be of assistance. A statutory declaration is the modern equivalent of the traditional statement under oath. In general it is immoral but not illegal to tell lies, even at a public inquiry. But in a court of law witnesses undertake to tell the truth and if they lie they then commit the criminal offence of perjury for which they can be jailed. A statutory declaration operates under the same rules and anyone who makes one which is untrue is guilty of perjury. A statutory declaration has to be made before a solicitor, who will charge a fee. The declaration can be presented as evidence and is of much greater value than a simple evidence form because of the possible results to the witness if he is shown to be lying.

It is necessary to be able to prove twenty years of use working backwards from the current time if the path is still in use. If the path is blocked or disputed then the twenty years has to be backwards from the time that it became disputed. During the whole of the twenty years the owner must not have done anything to indicate that he did not accept the right of way. If in any way he has disputed the right, even without preventing the public from using the path, then a claim that it is a right of way must fail. It is important to check this with witnesses because there is a kind of folklore that use alone will create a right of way. People will confidently claim that a path must be a right of way because everybody has used it for years and then admit that the owner tried to prevent it. If this is the case then it is no use going any further unless it is possible to prove twenty years use prior to the last time that it was disputed, or unless there is alternative evidence of repute.

7.7. Permissive use

An owner is perfectly entitled to allow the public to use a route by permission, on the basis that this can be withdrawn. If it can be shown that this occurred, for example by the owner putting up a sign inviting people to enjoy the route but stating that it is not dedicated as a right of way, then no dedication can be presumed. In a similar way, owners often allow specific people permission to pass over their land. This can be an important point in that the owner may allege that individuals giving evidence of use did so by separate permission and not as of right.

If possible, this problem should be avoided by finding witnesses who have no connection with the owner. They should not be relatives or friends and preferably not even be known to the owner. Also to be avoided are people who have a business dealing with the owner, for example his tenants. If there are any links with the owner then it can be alleged that they used the path not as sample members of the public but under some special arrangement. This is an important point which again runs contrary to folklore. People often allege that a particular path must be public because the owner gave them permission to use it; in fact such permission is taken as tending to refute the proposition that the path is public.

This is frequently a serious practical problem to the claiming of bridleways through presumption of dedication. Most people ride locally and thus even when a path is well-used it is frequently the case that the use is by a relatively small number of local people who use it regularly and are likely to be known to the landowner. It is thus perfectly plausible for the owner to claim that the users are not a sample of the general public but merely local people to whom he has given special permission. To make matters worse, it is often true! If an owner tells users of a path that he is giving them special permission to use that path they are unlikely to dispute the matter even if they believe the path to be public. It is then not possible to present such people as sample members of the general public. In any case, if the owner has said the same thing to all the regular users then this will be evidence that the owner had no intention to dedicate. Remember that public use will produce a presumption that the owner intended to dedicate but that presumption can be overturned by clear evidence that the owner had no such intention.

A further problem is that through a misplaced courtesy, people often seek permission to ride along what they regard as a public path. This seriously weakens any case that the path is public. Such a person then has the permission of the owner and thus may well travel by permission rather than by right. In addition, it is necessary to show that the witnesses themselves believed that the path was public. It is difficult to establish this if they sought permission because no permission is needed to use a public highway, and if they realised it was public then why did they ask?

A common example of this problem arises when people claim to have used a path whilst hunting. Such use is rarely of any value as evidence. Hunting is not, of course, restricted to rights of way and is carried out with the permission of the land owner. It follows that the use of any particular path over the land is also by permission rather than of right.

Whilst it is important to be aware of these pitfalls, it does not necessarily follow that having witnesses known to the owner prevents a claim being made. Where the users have not sought permission and the owner has not sought to inform them that they used the route by permission only then it seems reasonable to argue that they did so as of right. Whilst it might be argued that if the owner knew all the witnesses then he could have implicitly given them permission, this should not be accepted as meaning that the users were not a sample of the public at large unless the owner can actually prove that he specifically gave permission to the individuals in question.

A similar argument applies to tenants of the owner. Some surveying authorities appear to take the line that evidence from a witness who is a tenant of the owner is not admissible. There may well be cases where the tenancy of a particular piece of land has associated with it a private right of way over another piece of land. Clearly if a witness has used an alleged right of way but proves to have a private right of way then his evidence is of little value. Where there is no evidence of such private rights then a tenant is also a member of the public and there is no reason to discount his evidence. The onus of proving a permissive use based on the tenancy should be on the landowner.

7.8. Collection of user evidence - a summary

There can be little doubt that when the original definitive maps were prepared many rights of way were left off or shown with fewer rights than actually existed, for example by showing bridleways as footpaths. In theory, at least, there is a vast opportunity for increasing the network of routes by the collection of user evidence. The reality has to be faced, however, that each path requires a great deal of effort and that in most areas there will be insufficient voluntary effort available for all of them to be fully researched. The sensible strategy is to concentrate on those routes where the evidence is likely to be strong enough for a claim to be successful.

To assist in deciding whether there is a basis for going forward, consider the following check list. It is necessary for all the following points to be true:

(a) There must be witnesses who can honestly state that they themselves have actually used the path in the appropriate way (that is they have ridden along a bridleway or driven along a byway), and they must all have followed precisely the same route.

(b) The witnesses must collectively have used the path for at least twenty years prior to the claim being made, or if the owner has challenged the right, for twenty years prior to the challenge.

(c) At no time during the twenty years must the owner in any way have indicated that he did not regard the path as of the status claimed, including by giving witnesses individual permission to use it.

(d) All the witnesses must have used the path believing that they had a right to use it as members of the public, and none of them must ever have asked the permission of the owner to use it.

(e) None of the witnesses must have any documented legal right to use the path privately.

(f) All the witnesses should be aware that their statements will be available to the owner and should not be liable to change their statements if approached by him.

(g) At least some of the witnesses should be prepared to give evidence in person at a public inquiry.

If all these statements are true then it is worth taking the matter further. If any of these are not true then it is unlikely to be possible to prove a right of way through usage alone. Unless there is evidence of reputation then the matter should be put in abeyance and resources devoted to other paths where all the above statements are true. However, any research carried out should be carefully recorded. Research into rights of way is a big jigsaw puzzle and some day the missing pieces may be found. This is especially the case if evidence of repute is later found and where the evidence of use may act as important supporting evidence.

Notes to chapter 7

1. O'Keefe v Secretary of State for Environment & Isle of Wight County Council (O'Keefe no 2) (1996) JPEL 42.

2. Until the Highways Act 1835, all new highways coming into use were automatically maintainable at public expense. From that act new carriageways did not become maintainable at public expense until they had been adopted by the highway authority. This rule was not applied to bridleways and footpaths until the National Parks and Access to the Countryside Act 1949.

3. North London Railway Company v Vestry of St Mary, Islington (1872) 27 LT 672. Here the railway company built a wide new street connecting two existing streets and providing access to a new station. Immediately it was opened it was freely used as a through route by general traffic and the courts held it to have been dedicated as a highway after only eighteen months of such use.

4. Rights of Way Act 1932. The relevant legislation is now contained in the Highways Act 1980, Section 31.

5. British Transport Commission v Westmorland County Council (1958) AC 126.

8
ADDING PATHS TO THE DEFINITIVE MAP

8.1. Introduction

This chapter deals with the procedures for getting additional paths added to the definitive map. It is important to remember that this can only be done if it is possible to prove that rights exist that are not shown on the definitive map; the procedure cannot be used where there is a need for additional paths but no evidence that such rights already exist.

Throughout this chapter it will be assumed that the necessary evidence has already been collected. Such evidence is likely to take the form of evidence from witnesses who have used the path, or of documentary evidence showing the status of the route; it is often a mixture of the two. The collecting of user evidence was dealt with in Chapter 7; documentary evidence is a large topic in its own right and will be dealt with later in Chapters 14 to 22.

The basic principle is that the surveying authority (normally the county council) has a legal duty to keep the definitive map up to date. On it becoming aware of evidence that a right exists that is not shown on the definitive map, then it should make a map modification order with its own relevant date (1). Subject to the order being confirmed, it adds the right to the definitive map and it has then the same protection as all the rest of the rights shown.

8.2. Preparation of a report of evidence

Before approaching the surveying authority it is important to have all the arguments for making the order properly assembled. It is necessary to convince the authority that a clear case exists and this should be more obvious if the evidence is set out in a cogent way. Assuming that the officers of the authority are convinced, then they will have to be prepared to justify the order to a public inquiry if necessary. This means that they would in any case have to present the evidence in a cogent fashion and will need to do less work if this has already been done. Clearly, the easier their task the more likely they are to make an order in a reasonable time.

It has been found useful at this stage to prepare a full report that summarises the case and explains clearly why an order should be made. The package should include:

because if it does decide to make an order then it needs to give notice again to the owners and occupiers and this saves the authority from having to find out who they are. If they were to make the order simply on the discovery of evidence and without a formal application being made, then the officers would have to find out themselves. This is probably the main reason why many authorities refuse to act without a formal application.

It can be surprisingly difficult to find the owners and occupiers. Where the route runs over farm land it will usually be known locally who farms the land. It is less likely to be known whether the farmer is the owner or only a tenant, and if the latter, who the owner actually is. In earlier times the owner was usually the lord of the manor but these days, the owner of tenanted land may be an institutional investor such as a pension fund.

One direct way of finding the owner is simply to inform the occupier that it is proposed to claim a right of way and ask for the identity of the owner. If the occupier wants to dispute the claim he will want to bring in the owner as soon as possible, especially if it is an institutional owner with much greater legal resources than an individual farmer. Thus there is no advantage to the occupier in trying to hide the identity of the owner.

Problems often arise in respect of woodlands. These have become particularly popular as investments and often belong to institutional owners. Generally, there is not a separate occupier as such and the land is managed by a commercial forestry company. If it is known who manages the woodland then it is possible to ask who the owner is and for the reasons stated above it is unlikely that the information will not be forthcoming. However, as forestry operations may only require infrequent visits by the managing company, the identity of the managing company may not be common knowledge in the vicinity.

There are also often problems on lanes that have hedges or walls on each side. It is not unusual for the owners on both sides to deny ownership on the basis that the plans attached to their deeds do not show ownership. There is a legal presumption that the owners on each side own the land up to the centre of the highway unless the contrary can be proved. However, it is not particularly unusual for another person to own the land under a road; for example, if the road was created by an enclosure award the lord of the manor may still own the land. Or where a road was originally created by a developer to serve individual plots which were conveyed without the land under the road, then it may still be owned by the original developer or his successor. The presumption that the frontagers own the land under the road would seem to be sufficiently strong to argue that the requirements of the law have been complied with if notice has been served on all the frontagers.

One can always take the pragmatic view that if there are additional owners or occupiers who are not known about and never come forward, then it does not matter anyway. If they do come forward then the mystery is solved and notice can be served on them. Where there is any doubt about the ownership of land between known people the best way is to serve notice on all of them. The legal requirement is to serve notice on all owners; there is no rule against serving notice on other people as well.

It is also possible to find the names of some owners through the Land Registry. The snag here is that there is quite a high fee which means that this tends to be used as a last resort. The procedure is set out in a leaflet available from the Land Registry. The first stage is to apply to establish whether the land is registered; by no means all land is yet registered. If it is established that the land is registered then a further fee is payable to find details of the property including the owner.

Finally, if all else fails the surveying authority may give permission for notification to be served by means of notices prominently displayed at the ends of the path in question. This is only allowed if all other enquiries have failed so it would seem only to be applicable to land that has been shown not to be registered. Clearly, it would not be permissible to put up site notices simply to avoid Land Registry fees.

8.5. *Making the order*

Once the surveying authority has received the certificate that all the owners and occupiers have been notified, it must then decide whether to make the order that has been requested. Although the decision rests with the council, the basis for the decision is not like most other council decisions where the members are required to make a value judgement on behalf of the public. Here the decision needs to be a weighing of evidence in the light of often arcane legal principles; a job that untrained councillors are hardly qualified for.

Thus one would expect the assessment to be made by the professional officers of the council who would advise the councillors accordingly. Although the councillors could make a different decision they could only do so the basis of their interpretation of the facts; they could not legitimately do so as matter of policy. For example, they could not have a policy that there were too many rights of way already and thus that all applications to add paths should be rejected.

The council has a duty to check whether the evidence produced is sound (3). Many councils adopt a policy of interviewing at least a selection of people who have made statements of evidence. This is why it is important that any statements produced can stand up; even if only one or two people interviewed say things that do not correspond with their statements it must throw doubt on all the other evidence. Obviously, checking these matters will take time and anything up to a year frequently elapses between the initial submission and the making of a decision.

Assuming that the council decides that the evidence supports the claim made, then the next stage will be for it to make the order. This has to be advertised and notice served on all the owners and occupiers (4). If nobody objects during a period of six weeks then the order may be confirmed and the map is amended to show the right claimed at a relevant date which is specified in the order.

If, however, an objection is made to the order then the council has to pass the order over to the Secretary of State for the Environment. He will normally call a public inquiry at which the objectors can put their case, and will then decide whether or not to confirm the order. It is important to note that at this stage the order is being made by the council and the original proposers of the order are now only supporters. This has the advantage that the council will normally provide its own legal officers to put the case to the inquiry; the other side of the coin is that if they make a mess of the job there is not a lot that can be done! Fortunately, this does not happen too often because however lukewarm the council may be over the whole affair, most legal officers take a delight in winning their cases. They will normally call the person who proposed the order as their key witness. In the unlikely event of them not doing so, an inspector at an inquiry normally allows anybody to have their say and so it is still possible to appear as a supporter of the order, including submitting any additional evidence if the council should have omitted it.

It should be noted that the right to object is not restricted to owners and occupiers of land and that any member of the public can also object. This often occurs where the evidence shows that byway rights exist over a path recorded as a footpath or bridleway and where members of the public, or user groups, object to the possibility of use by motor vehicles. These objections are often based on a misunderstanding of the law, with objectors arguing that the route would suffer from use by vehicles rather than the rights not existing. Whilst such objections are irrelevant and should be discounted by the inspector, it is far better if they can be avoided. It is certainly worth discussing the proposals at an early stage with other user organisations and attempting to persuade them not to object. It should be pointed out that the rights of all path users depend on the accuracy of the definitive map and if users seek to undermine the legal basis of the map for their convenience, they run the risk in the long term of undermining their own rights.

8.6. Changes to the order

If an order is made and there are objections, then the order can only be confirmed by the Secretary of State, who will normally hold a public inquiry. This is done by an inspector who will have delegated powers to make a decision. However, it is worth noting that the inspector may also vary the order as well as either confirming or rejecting it.

Except in very limited situations, if the inspector proposes to confirm a modified version of the order, then the changes have to be advertised and a further opportunity given for objections. For example, suppose a claim for bridleway rights is made where no path is currently shown on the definitive map. The inspector may find that whilst there is adequate user evidence on foot there is insufficient evidence of equestrian use. He may then propose to modify the order to show a footpath but before doing so he must allow a further opportunity for objection to the change; in this case people who had made the original bridleway claim might well object. This can then lead to another public inquiry dealing with the same path.

8.7. Enforcing the duty to make the order

What happens if the surveying authority will not make the order? We have here to distinguish between two different situations; firstly, where the authority takes an inordinate time in coming to a decision and secondly, where a decision is made not to proceed with the order.

If the council does nothing, then no action can be taken until a period of a year has elapsed from the formal application. After a year, a representation can be made to the Secretary of State who will consult the authority concerned. In theory, he can then direct the council to come to a decision. In practice, it appears to be accepted that progress is very slow and councils are expected to have some policy setting out the priorities they will give to different sorts of map modification orders. As long as the authority is sticking to its pecking order and is processing some orders, it seems that the Secretary of State is unlikely to intervene.

As in many areas of council work, the legal powers to enforce the carrying out of duties tend to be weak. In practical terms, it is usually better to proceed through lobbying of councillors rather than by legal enforcement methods.

However, suppose that the council does consider the matter but decides to take no action. In this case it is important to try and establish what went wrong. It is vital to obtain a copy of the officer's report to the council which should be available to the public.

Because the analysis of an application requires a specialist knowledge of the law of rights of way, it can reasonably be expected that the matters will have been examined by the council's legal staff who will have made a recommendation. If the councillors have made a decision different from that recommendation, there are likely to be good grounds for an appeal. The usual background is that councillors have not understood the rules and believe that they can make a value judgment, for example, on whether the adding of a path will affect the owner or other path users. This, of course, is not relevant and the recommendation of the legal staff that the evidence supports the application is a vindication of the strength of the case.

Where the legal officers recommend that the order should not be made, it is necessary to proceed with more caution. It will often be useful to arrange a meeting to establish why they took the line they did. Although officers are supposed to give the best professional advice that they can, it is not unknown for them to be pressurised by influential councillors to make recommendations that they want! Whilst officers are unlikely to admit this, if they cannot give cogent reasons for their recommendations then one may fear the worst. On the other hand, they may well have a great deal of experience in claims for rights of way and their professional judgement should not be minimised.

If it is decided that an appeal should be made, then it is necessary to apply to the Secretary of State within four weeks of the council notifying its decision not to make the order. The Secretary of State will consult the council and may then require it to make the order. It should be noted that where a council is required to make the order, this merely means that it is accepted that there appears to be a reasonable case. It will still be possible for people to object, a public inquiry to be held, and for the secretary of state not to confirm the order in the end.

Notes to chapter 8

1. Wildlife and Countryside Act 1981. Section 53 requires surveying authorities to keep the map up to date by the making of definitive map modification orders.

2. Wildlife and Countryside Act 1981. Schedule 14 sets out the rules for making a formal application to the council.

3. Regina v Isle of Wight County Council, ex parte O'Keefe (1989) JPL 934.

4. Wildlife and Countryside Act 1981. Schedule 15 sets out the rules for the surveying authority and the Secretary of State.

9
DELETION OF PATHS FROM THE DEFINITIVE MAP

9.1. Introduction

Although the definitive map is conclusive evidence at the relevant date, it can be modified. Rights of way workers need to know how to get additional paths added to the map; at the same time it is essential to understand that paths can also be taken off. This chapter explains the ways in which rights of way can be removed from the map completely or reduced in status. It emphasises the fact that very strict criteria apply and that, contrary to the views of some owners, it is likely that these will be met in only a very small number of cases. It is important that rights of way workers have a good knowledge of this aspect so that they can successfully oppose deletions that do not fit within the criteria laid down.

9.2. Background

The process for deleting paths is the reverse of the process for adding paths. It follows that the whole matter hinges on evidence of the existence or otherwise of the right of way. Just as a path cannot be added simply because it is needed, a path cannot be deleted from the definitive map merely because it is inconvenient to the owner. A path can only be deleted from the map if there is evidence that the rights shown do not, in fact, exist.

The other side of the coin is that if the rights can be shown not to exist then it is not possible to object to the deletion of the path on the basis that the path is useful or even essential. However, if an essential path were to be deleted on the basis that there was no right of way there would be a strong case for creating a path on the same line. This would replace the path on the map but would require the payment of compensation to the owner.

The effect of a current definitive map is to show conclusively the rights that exist at the relevant date. If a path had been put on the definitive map in error it did not create a new right of way but the conclusive effect means that as long as the map is valid the rights of the public are as if there really was a right of way. If the error is discovered and the path deleted, the right of way is not extinguished because it never existed. But once the map has been changed it is no longer possible to rely on its conclusive effect.

This means that if a right really does exist and it is deleted from the map in error, then as no formal extinguishment has taken place, all rights that previously existed still remain. If the error is discovered it is possible for the path to be put back again. It is, however, necessary to be able to prove that the right exists. It is not enough to be able to show that it was formerly on the map and its removal was a mistake, although evidence of this would help to support other relevant evidence.

9.3. *History of the deletion process*

It is of interest to look at the history of the law relating to deletions from the definitive map as it has had rather a turbulent history. Some knowledge of this is useful in understanding documents from earlier periods. It also gives an insight into why such cases are always contentious.

The definitive map system was introduced by the National Parks and Access to the Countryside Act of 1949. This set out the procedures for considering claims that rights of way existed. A complex process was laid down for coming to decisions where rights were disputed. It was intended that further reviews should be carried out every five years. The review procedure allowed both for the addition of paths that had come into existence since the original map or previous review and also any that had existed all the time but had been missed off previous maps. It also allowed for the removal of paths that had been legally closed since the date of the previous map. It did not allow for the deletion of any paths that had been put on by mistake, presumably on the basis that the very elaborate process for drawing up the map gave ample opportunities for objections by any owners who felt that rights being claimed did not exist.

Despite all the opportunities, it was not long before some examples came to light of obvious mistakes on the map where information gathered in surveys had clearly been misinterpreted or wrongly drafted onto the definitive map. The courts held that the public now had a right to use the route shown on the map and that there was no way that the mistake could be corrected (1). Applications could, of course, be made to have the path extinguished in the normal way but this would have to be treated as if the right had existed all the time. Landowning interests argued that this was an injustice and campaigned to have the law changed.

It is not really clear why the continuation of mistakes should be thought to be such an injustice. There are numerous processes to create, divert and extinguish paths which if not objected to become final even if the supposed reasons are not valid. For example, an order may extinguish a path on the grounds that it is not necessary. If users do not object, the closure will be confirmed and become final. Even if it can be subsequently proved that the path was necessary it will still not be possible to overturn the order. The preparation of the definitive map was arguably a similar process. There were ample opportunities for owners to object but once a right of way had been finally added to the map it would be perfectly consistent with other highway law if it were not possible for the designation to be overturned.

In the event, the law remained the same for almost 20 years, being eventually changed by the Countryside Act of 1968 (2). This did allow rights to be deleted from the map where there was evidence that there had not been a right of way, presumably at the time that the first map showing the right was prepared.

This legislation was replaced by the Wildlife and Countryside Act of 1981 which retained a power to delete rights but there was a subtle change in the wording (3). A right can be deleted where it can be shown that it does not exist; the use of the present tense implying that it is the state of affairs at the time of the order that is relevant. In 1987, in a case backed by the Ramblers' Association, it was held that a right could only be deleted if it had been extinguished or destroyed by natural causes since the relevant date of the current definitive map (4). This was because the definitive map is evidence of the existence of the right even if it did not exist prior to it having been first recorded on the map.

Landowners argued that this interpretation of the law flew in the face of what had been the intention of Parliament which in 1968 had clearly believed that it was necessary to have some mechanism for correcting mistakes. A case backed by the Country Landowners Association went to the Court of Appeal in 1989 where it was decided that the law did allow mistakes to be corrected (5). The rule now appears to be that the test is whether a right of way exists at the time the order is made, ignoring for this purpose the conclusive effect of the definitive map.

9.4. Circumstances in which deletions are allowed

There are two quite different circumstances in which it is legitimate to make orders deleting a path from the map, or reducing the status of a path, for example, from bridleway to footpath.

Firstly, a right can be deleted where the right properly ceases to exist after the relevant date of the definitive map. In one sense such orders are not necessary as conclusive evidence of the existence of a right at one particular date is of no real value if it can be shown that the right later ceased to exist. But if the definitive map is to be understandable it is necessary to keep it tidy by removing paths that no longer exist.

Secondly, rights can be deleted on the discovery of evidence that the rights recorded do not actually exist, or would not were it not for the map itself. This generally means the discovery of evidence that the right was wrongly recorded on the first definitive map on which it appeared. These are the sorts of orders that give rise to the greatest controversy. They are particularly difficult to resolve because the matter generally turns on events before the first maps in the 1950s and as each year goes by it becomes more and more difficult to get to the truth of the matter.

The procedure the authority uses for making such an order is the same as for an order adding a right to the map. The authority has a duty to make the order on becoming aware of evidence that the map is wrong. If it fails to do so, an owner can serve notice on the authority in precisely the same way as can a member of the public wishing to have additional rights added. Similarly, if notice has been served and the authority refuses to make the order, then the owner can appeal to the Secretary of State for the Environment (6).

9.5. Rights that cease to exist

A right of way can properly cease to exist through three different mechanisms: it can be extinguished or downgraded through the operation of the law, it can be destroyed by natural causes, or it can cease to be eligible for showing on the definitive map through it being upgraded to a higher status.

By far the most common way in which a right of way ceases to exist is through legal process. A path can be extinguished or downgraded by a public path order. Fortunately, it is far more common for paths to be diverted but it is important to note that a diversion is a simultaneous creation of the new route with the extinguishment of the old. Wherever a path has been extinguished or downgraded by a proper legal process then an order may be made to alter the definitive map accordingly.

Orders made as a result of a legal event such as a public path order may be made using the short-cut procedure in exactly the same way as where rights are being added to the map. It is not necessary to advertise such an order nor is there any right of objection.

In the very rare cases where a path is destroyed by natural causes, no legal event has taken place and thus the short-cut procedure cannot be applied. The authority can make an order on the basis of discovery of evidence that the path has been destroyed. This is open to objection in the normal way. Bearing in mind that whether a path has been destroyed is very much a matter of opinion there is clearly room for argument with cases of this sort. For example, land is rarely destroyed by the sea; erosion usually converts dry land to a tidal beach. As there can be rights of way along tidal beaches it is possible that where a coastal path is destroyed by erosion the effect is to create a new path along the resulting beach.

Finally, it should be noted that there can be circumstances where upgrading rather than downgrading leads to the need to delete rights of way. For example, suppose a new road is constructed along the line of an existing bridleway. Although equestrian rights still exist it will no longer be a bridleway and should be deleted from the definitive map. This can be done by means of a legal events order as the creation of the new road will be a legal event (7).

9.6. Alleged errors on the definitive map

Deletions from the definitive map because the rights have already ceased to exist rarely cause any problems and are clearly desirable in order to keep the map correct. Orders made on the basis that the right was wrongly shown in the first place are almost always controversial and complex. They are controversial because although the procedure was intended to deal with any obvious errors that were found, many landowners appear to regard the deletion process as one that can be used to challenge the whole basis of the definitive map by deleting paths wholesale. The rest of this chapter concentrates specifically on this threat and how it can be averted.

The work is complex for a simple reason. Under normal circumstances, that is if the definitive map did not exist, then disputes about rights of way would usually be resolved by considering the status and use of the route over a recent period, for example the twenty years necessary for dedication to be presumed. Where the assertion is that the right was wrongly shown when it was first recorded on the map, this usually means an allegation that a mistake was made in the early 1950s. It follows that the matter hinges on the status and use of the way during a previous period. As each year goes by, the events in question recede further and further into history and become more and more difficult to disentangle.

The matter is complicated by the way in which the original map was prepared. A survey was carried out by volunteers who prepared early drafts for each parish. These were then checked by the parish council or meeting and amendments made in respect of any suggestions made by them. This is an important point which is often glossed over by landowners who allege that the maps were prepared by rights of way activists without any local input or checking. On the basis of rights that were "reasonably alleged" to exist, the county council prepared a draft map.

Where landowners objected to rights shown then it would have been necessary for all the evidence available to be considered to see if it was strong enough to support the claim that the right of way existed. If this happened then it is usually possible to find some record of what matters were considered. In practice, however, most problems arise over rights that were never disputed at the time. In this case the proposals on the draft map went forward to the final definitive map. The parish council or meeting was never asked to substantiate the "reasonable allegation" that a right existed and so there is now no way of establishing whether the allegation was reasonable or not.

It has to be remembered that at the time the definitive map was prepared, and for nearly twenty years afterwards, there was no legal mechanism for challenging the map once it became final. There was no legal requirement for authorities to keep records of why right were recorded, nor at that time any logical reason why they should do so. It is hardly surprising that it is increasingly difficult to establish the basis on which rights were originally recorded.

9.7. The ground rules

Having looked at the problems, it is now necessary to consider the circumstances in which matters can be reconsidered. This is an important point because owners often appear to believe that all they need to do is to challenge the map and then the whole matter can be started again from scratch. Fortunately, this is not correct; the circumstances in which deletions can be considered are really quite limited.

To look at this it is necessary to consider the way in which the courts have interpreted the law. The leading case is that brought by the British Horse Society in 1975, usually known as the Hood case (8). This was a famous victory for the BHS which established the important principle that RUPPs could not be re-classified as footpaths simply at the whim of the authority; it could only be done if there was the same sort of evidence that would have justified downgrading a bridleway to footpath.

So much is well-known; what is less appreciated is that the judges went on to explain the sorts of circumstances in which this could be done. This judgment is so important that it is worth quoting at length.

Lord Denning, Master of the Rolls, said:

Under S33 of the Act of 1949 (as amended in 1968) there are circumstances in which a local authority can down-grade a way. But these circumstances are only when there is new evidence or evidence not previously considered by the authority...

These are the only grounds of review on a re-classification. There is no machinery to enable the local authority to reopen the whole question once more of whether or not the way was shown properly on the 1952 definitive map. I cannot think that Parliament ever contemplated such a reopening. The definitive map in 1952 was based on evidence then available, including no doubt, the evidence of the oldest inhabitant then living. Such evidence might well have been lost or forgotten by 1975. So it would be very unfair to reopen everything in 1975.

This was backed up by Lord Justice Browne who said:

It seems to me that the intention of the 1949 Act was that all questions as to the extent, nature and incidence of footpaths, bridleways and roads used by the public for other purposes should be fully investigated and decided before the definitive maps were drawn up under that Act, and that definitive maps should finally decide these questions...

It seems to me unlikely that Parliament intended in 1968 that the whole question of the nature and extent of public rights of way which had been settled by the definitive maps under the Act of 1949 should be reopened many years later when the evidence on which the definitive decision was made might well be no longer available...

It seems to me that when the authority or Minister is approaching the question of re-classification under the Act of 1968, one starts with the presumption that there was in 1952 a right of way for horses and on foot. In my judgment this presumption could only be displaced on the re-classification by such subsequent events as are specified in S33(1) and (2) of the Act of 1949 or by new evidence admissible under Part 1 of Schedule 3 of the Act of 1968.

Although this case referred to the 1968 Act which has been repealed, very similar powers were included in the 1981 Act which replaced it. Thus the salient points of the judgment are still equally valid. The most important point to note is the starting point for considering any changes that involve deletion of any rights. It is simply not open to the authority to treat the issue as if it were starting again, with the onus of proof being on those who wish to retain the right. Instead the starting point is that the map is right and it can only be altered if it can be proved that it is wrong. The onus of proof that the map needs to be altered rests on those who seek to change it.

Both judges quoted above laid particular stress on the fact that much of the evidence used to prepare the original map would be no longer available. At that time twenty five years had elapsed since the maps were prepared. Clearly after the passage of another quarter-century this point is now even more important. The presumption that the map is correct unless proved otherwise is of vital importance in avoiding the need to re-establish the fact proved originally. The ways in which this works in practice will be considered in more detail in succeeding sections dealing with different sets of circumstances in which deletions may be sought.

It is also necessary to consider the types of evidence that are eligible to set off the process of a change. Under the 1981 Act it is necessary for there to be the discovery of evidence that, taken with other evidence, shows either that there is no right of way or that the status recorded is incorrect (3). The use of the word "discovery" in the legislation is very important. This clearly indicates that there is a need for some element of evidence that was not known about before; you cannot discover what you already know. It is also important that the additional evidence "shows" that the map is wrong. It does not appear that the matter can be re-opened simply by the discovery of some fact which, although new, is essentially the same as some point already considered. The proper test appears to be that the new evidence should be such that it seems more likely than not that a different conclusion would have been reached had the evidence been available when the map was originally prepared.

It should be noted that the 1981 Act altered the criteria for what evidence could be considered and so the exact criteria described above by Lord Denning are now out of date. In particular, it is no longer necessary to show any reason why the additional evidence was not produced in the first place. The key point remains valid: the map is presumed to be right unless it can be positively shown to be wrong.

Having considered the basic ground rules, it is now proposed to consider how they ought to be applied to some of the common reasons that are brought forward to justify a deletion, namely evidence of lack of use, evidence of obstruction, and documentary evidence.

9.8. Evidence of lack of use

Perhaps the most common type of claim for the deletion of a path is based on lack of use. Such claims are usually those with the least basis and should be easiest to defeat.

The difficulty of establishing a case based on lack of use results from the reversal of the onus of proof and demonstrates how important this aspect can be. Under normal circumstances, for example where a claim is being made to add a path, then the onus of proving the existence of the path rests on those who allege the right exists. To prove a path through presumption of dedication it will be necessary to produce witnesses who have used the path over a long period of time. The owner may well dispute this by trying to show that the witnesses did not really use the path, or that they were not typical members of the public (perhaps using it by special invitation) or that he took steps to show the public that he had no intention of dedicating the path.

Where a right was recorded on the basis of use there will normally be no record of who used it, or even over what period. It must be assumed, as Lord Denning suggested, that information was obtained from the oldest inhabitants. For a map produced in the early 1950s it is not at all fanciful to assume that information was available back to the 1880s or even the 1870s. This would have given a great number of years prior to the watershed of the 1914-18 war. During the war years normal use was doubtless disrupted and the post-war introduction of early cars and buses started to make the first inroads into traditional patterns of travel on foot and horseback.

Some owners appear to believe that if they challenge a right, then the whole process can start again and that unless the rights can be proved then they should be deleted. There can be no doubt that if this were true, then large numbers of routes would be lost because evidence from earlier years could no longer be found. Fortunately, this is not the case. The key point is the starting presumption that the right exists. Anyone who seeks to overturn that presumption has to be able to prove that the map is wrong. It will be extremely difficult, if not impossible, to do this based on evidence of lack of use.

Firstly, it is always difficult to prove lack of use where there is no feature that physically prevents use. Use by the public is normally proved by witnesses who have themselves used the route believing that they do so as members of the public. If a reasonable number did so then it gives an inference that the owner dedicated it to the public. At the same time there will be millions of the public who have never even heard of the route, let alone used it. It must be obvious that producing witnesses who have never used the path does nothing to show that others did not do so.

Another approach is to produce witnesses who claim that they knew the path intimately and that nobody used it. But even when the owner or tenant can be found, it will be very difficult to prove that they kept the path under surveillance every hour of the day for many years. Or they may allege that people did use it but by permission. This would be a strong point where the alleged users were known. Given that the users are not now known, then the fact that certain people may have been given permission will not overturn the presumption that sufficient others used the path believing themselves to be members of the public.

The overwhelming difficulty of proving that the map is wrong through lack of use relates to the length of the period that would be required. Once a highway has come into existence, no period of disuse will extinguish it. In theory, therefore, in order to show no right exists it would be necessary to show that nobody had ever used the route at any time in the past; clearly an impossible task. At a more practical level, it might be arguable that if a path was put on the map on the basis of use or repute, then a mistake must have been made if it could be proved that no use had ever been made during living memory at the time the map was made. As indicated above, it is reasonable to assume that a map made in the early 1950s would have taken account of witnesses whose memory would have gone back perhaps to the 1870s. So to prove through lack of use that a mistake had been made, it would be necessary to show that the route had not been used at least as far back as that time. With the passage of years this becomes increasingly difficult; in practice, it is difficult today to find anyone who can testify to what the situation was earlier than the 1920s.

Finally, it should be self-evident that lack of use after the relevant date of the first definitive map showing the route must be irrelevant. If the argument was that a mistake was made when the map was drawn then anything that happened after cannot possibly assist in proving the point.

9.9. Evidence of obstruction

Claims for deletion are often based on the argument that the line of the path shown on the definitive map could never have existed because of obstructions. This is a particular problem with bridleways and byways. On a footpath one may expect stiles, and some stiles are little better than fences to climb over. Pedestrians can surmount most obstacles and so it is difficult to argue that a footpath could not have existed because of obstructions. A bridleway or byway can hardly be used if it has stiles or fences across it and claims for downgradings often allege just that.

If it can be shown that an obstruction of a nature that would prevent use existed during some period, then this could obviously be used to show that there was no public use during that period. The position would be similar to that described above in terms of evidence of lack of use, except that here there would be stronger evidence in that there would be no question of the route being used at a time when witnesses were not looking. Besides, a highway cannot be validly dedicated if it cannot be used. So not even an express dedication by the owner could be assumed if it were possible to prove that an obstruction existed before the path came into existence.

However, it cannot be emphasised strongly enough that the mere proof of the existence at some time of an obstruction does not necessarily show that the map is wrong. Once a highway has come into existence then no amount of obstruction will make it cease to exist. There is nothing inherently implausible in an obstructed path being shown on the definitive map. The starting presumption must be that those who originally drafted the map found that the right existed at some time in the past, and that it had later been obstructed but still remained as a legal right. This presumption can only be overturned where it can be positively shown that a mistake must have been made.

In theory, it could be argued that it would only be possible to show that a mistake had been made if it were possible to prove that the obstruction had existed right back to the time that the path had first come into existence. Evidence that the path had been obstructed for very many years prior to it being first shown on the definitive map might allow the inference that it had always been obstructed. For the same reasons that were discussed under evidence of lack of use, it seems arguable that obstruction would have to be proved well back into the nineteenth century. As the years pass it becomes increasingly difficult to do this.

On the other hand, evidence that a path existed and was not obstructed at some time in the past should be sufficient to overturn any case based on subsequent obstruction. If at some time in the past the route was usable, then it must be presumed that the showing of the route on the map was based on information from the period when it could be used.

It is only necessary to show that the route could have been used; it is not necessary to prove again that it was a public highway. This means that evidence that would be quite inadequate to prove a right of way can still be used to disprove allegations that a right does not exist. For example, local histories may well record that a particular route was used at one time by waggons or pack-horses. In a case where bridleway rights were being claimed, there would need to be a great deal more evidence than that, but such evidence should be adequate to prevent an inference being drawn that a route could never have been used by horses.

9.10. Information from OS maps

The other vital source of information is the Ordnance Survey large scale plans which in all areas show a great deal of detail from at least the mid-nineteenth century. The first thing to check is that the line shown on the map corresponds with a route shown to exist as a physical feature on the Ordnance Survey plans used at the time of the definitive map. If there is a slight discrepancy, the usual reason is a drafting error. These will be dealt with in 9.12 below.

Where the definitive map lines correspond with a physical route on the OS plans, then a study of earlier plans is important. The value of these is often under-estimated. Most plans carry a disclaimer that the showing of any route is no evidence of a right of way; even without the disclaimer it will be clear that a land-surveyor does not have the information to decide on the complex legal issues that concern rights of way. The surveyors did have the task of recording precisely what existed in a physical sense and this they did meticulously. For the OS to make a mistake in depicting a physical feature is virtually unknown and thus the plans must be very strong evidence of the physical nature of the countryside at the date the plans were prepared.

The Ordnance Survey large scale plans (1:25,000 and upwards) show all fences, walls and hedges as a single line. Where such a line crosses a track it means that there is some sort of barrier; it could be a gate or stile or simply a fence. Thus the existence of a line cannot prove that an obstruction existed at the time of the survey.

Where there is no line on the map it indicates that there could not have been any barrier. A study of plans of different dates often shows that field boundaries changed surprisingly frequently even in what are now thought of as more stable times. This means that it can sometimes be demonstrated that even if a particular obstruction existed, it could not have done so before a particular date.

A great deal of information can be obtained from the way in which tracks are depicted. The larger scale 1:2500 plans show everything to scale and thus the width of tracks can be scaled off. Not all areas are covered by 1:2500 mapping but earlier 6" to the mile maps are also true to scale, although a magnifying glass will be needed to accurately measure the widths. This gives a pretty clear indication of which routes were cart tracks as against mere paths; it is unlikely that a footpath would have been, say, twelve feet wide. This point is reinforced by the fact that paths usually had the letters FP (footpath) or BR (bridle road) placed against them. Effectively, the OS surveyors classified routes as being physically cart tracks, bridle roads or footpaths. This was done on editions between the 1890s and 1940s and was also shown on the very earliest 1:25,000 maps published in the late 1940s.

Although the plans are not evidence of public rights, they are evidence that the surveyor found that the routes shown were actually usable in the way recorded. For example, a path shown as a bridle road was not necessarily a public bridleway but it could be used on horseback. Thus there could not have been any obstructing stiles at the date of the survey. Similarly, for a route to be shown as a cart track means that there must have been field gates and although this would not be evidence of public vehicular rights, it must disprove the proposition that it could not have been used by horses or vehicles.

It is worth noting, that the opposite does not necessarily apply. The fact that a path was shown on the map as a footpath means that the surveyor was not aware of any use by horses at the time of the survey; it certainly does not mean that it would not have been possible for the route to be used on horseback.

9.11. Obstructions recorded on the definitive map

Particular significance is often attached to obstructions recorded as part of the preparation of the original definitive map. The first stage of preparation of the map involved the carrying out of detailed surveys of the alleged rights of way. Those carrying out the surveys were instructed to record the status that a right of way was believed to have, but also to record any obstructions. Thus where a bridleway was alleged to exist, but at the time of the survey was obstructed, then the clear instructions were to record bridleway status but to make a note of the obstructions. The original survey forms are normally preserved and form a vital record of the condition of the paths at that time. In many areas these descriptions of the paths also became part of the statement that accompanies the definitive map.

Owners today often claim that the fact that an obstruction was recorded at the time of the definitive map is good evidence that a mistake must have been made. However, this view is mistaken; the recording of an obstruction actually makes it much more difficult to establish a case for deletion of a right of way. This situation again arises from the starting presumption that the definitive map is right.

Where an obstruction is proved to have existed, but was not recorded at the time of the preparation of the map, it can at least be argued that those who prepared the map knew nothing about the obstruction and that had they done so they would have come to a quite different conclusion. Where the obstruction was recorded as part of the process of preparing the map then there can be no doubt that those preparing the map knew about it, and yet still recorded the route. There is, of course, no reason why an obstructed path should not have been recorded, provided that the authority was satisfied that the rights existed before the path became obstructed. Given the starting point that the map is right, it must be presumed that the authority examined the facts and came to that conclusion. Very strong contrary evidence would be required to overturn this presumption.

In addition, it is important to note that an order to delete a path can only be made where there is the discovery of evidence. This must mean that there has to be evidence that was not previously known about. Facts that were taken into consideration at the time of the original map clearly do not fall into this category. Even if additional evidence is found, it has to be such as to show that the map is wrong. To do this it must at the very least establish some facts that were not known at the time of the original map and would have been likely to have given a different result had they been known. Given that the path was known to be obstructed, it is unlikely that other evidence of obstruction would be sufficient. For example, evidence that there were additional obstructions or that the obstructions existed a few years earlier than the survey would not seem to establish any new facts.

9.12. Drafting errors on the map

A right of way wrongly shown on the map can come about as a result of two different types of mistake. There may be an error concerning the status of a route; for example, a route that is not a highway at all may be shown as a public path or a footpath may be shown as a bridleway. There may also be an error in the line of a path; a right of way with the correct status may exist along broadly the line shown on the definitive map but not in the precise location shown. Perhaps the path is shown on one side of a hedge when it should be a few yards away on the other side. Not surprisingly, in situations like this the definitive line is often found to be obstructed. Experience suggests that minor errors of this sort are quite common. There is every reason why errors of this sort should be corrected and the changes should be uncontroversial. However, there will always be greedy owners who try and get the definitive line deleted on the basis that it is wrong, but without admitting the possibility of another line.

Unfortunately, it is not possible to make an order that simply moves the path on the definitive map. The only way that the error can be corrected using map modification orders is to make two concurrent orders, one to delete the wrong line and another to add the right line. It is not clear what weight of evidence would be needed for this. One argument is that each separate order has to be justified by evidence that would stand up without reference to the other order. This creates some difficulties. In many cases the evidence for deletion would not stand up to the stringent criteria that have been previously described. On the other hand, there may well not be sufficient evidence to support the proposition that there is a public path along the right line. There is always the possibility that one order may fail but not the other, either leaving no right of way at all or two parallel paths a few yards apart.

The alternative argument is that it is not necessary to treat the two orders separately. Given that the two orders are concurrent, it seem likely that they could be justified together by a package of evidence supporting the proposition that the route of the path was in error but not its status. The package might include, for example, evidence of obstruction of the wrong route but not the right route, evidence that contemporary OS maps showed a path along the right route, plus witnesses that use was always of the right route.

It should be noted that in many cases a simpler approach to the whole problem of correcting the error would be to make a diversion order rather than a modification order and simply divert the path from the wrong route to the right one.

9.13. Claims based on documentary evidence

Most claims that paths were wrongly recorded relate to the time of the first map in the 1950s. As this date recedes further and further into the past it is likely that claims for deletion and downgrading will increasingly be based on documentary evidence. There will be some forms of documentary evidence that provide clear evidence that no right of way exists, but these are likely to be much less common than some owners seem to believe.

In some cases the survey documents for the definitive map record the reason why a path was recorded. If the reason was based on some documentary evidence and it can be shown that the facts relied on were actually wrong, then a deletion might be justified. There would need to be new evidence, for example that a document relied on had been found to be a forgery. It is not open to the authority simply to re-assess the previous documentary evidence in the absence of any new evidence. Such cases are likely to be very rare, if only for the reason that few paths seem to have been recorded solely on the basis of documentary evidence. Most paths appear to have been recorded because of evidence of repute or use.

Evidence for deleting or downgrading paths will generally attempt to show that at some time prior to the definitive map, there was no right of way as recorded. The strongest types of evidence are proof of extinguishment and proof of creation, although other types of evidence may be put forward.

The strongest case comes from documents that prove that a right existed but was later extinguished. If a proper legal extinguishment took place then immediately afterwards the right could not exist. Moreover, if it can be shown that the right recorded on the definitive map did actually exist at some time then it seems reasonable to conclude that the definitive map classification was based on that fact but without the knowledge that the right had later been extinguished. Documents proving an extinguishment include court records or orders made under various legal powers. Also some private acts for public works, such as reservoirs or docks, operate to extinguish all public highways over specified areas without having to list each one individually. Some enclosure acts operate in a similar way by extinguishing highways that have not been set out as part of the enclosure.

At first sight it might seem strange that evidence of the creation of a highway should be evidence that rights do not exist. Where there is a dispute over the types of rights along a highway then information from the time of creation may be illuminating. It is very unlikely that higher rights than those being created would have previously existed, or there would have been no need for any creation anyway. So evidence of creation of a footpath or bridleway provides strong evidence that at that time higher rights did not exist.

There are many other documentary sources that may be claimed to show that rights did not exist at the date of the document. Few of these are particularly conclusive. The key point is that there is a great deal of difference between knowing that there is no highway in a particular location and not knowing that there is one. Many people have good reason to know of the existence of certain highways. They may well be able to assert that they know of these highways and that they are not aware of the existence of any others. But it is quite another matter to assert that no other highways exist for how would they know anyway?

The courts have been prepared to accept plans of a proposed railway which did not record an alleged highway crossing the line as evidence that it did not exist (9). Here it was clearly of importance for the railway company to establish precisely what rights existed and it must be assumed that the surveyor carried out a reasonable amount of research. The position is quite difference from, say, a sale plan for an estate where it would clearly be in the interests of the seller to avoid references to rights of way that were not immediately obvious. The conclusion must be that, in general, documents describing highways can provide evidence of the existence of the specified highways but are very weak evidence of the non-existence of those not recorded.

Even where a highway can be proved not to have existed at a particular date, it is still possible that between that date and the date of the definitive map there was sufficient use for dedication of the route to be presumed. It would appear, therefore, that in the light of the starting presumption that the map is right then it would also be necessary to show that a right of way could not have been dedicated. Clearly the longer the gap, the more difficult it would be to prove this. On the one hand, if it could be shown that the right did not exist twenty years before the definitive map, then sufficient use to justify dedication would be unlikely. On the other hand, if it was shown that there was no right of way a century before then it would have been perfectly possible for a right to have been presumed to have been dedicated. A case for deletion would then have to show that over the whole period the owner either could not dedicate or made it clear that he had no intention of doing so.

Evidence of this is sometimes available. Before 1932 only the common law method of presumption of dedication was available. At common law, dedication cannot be presumed where the owner was not legally capable of dedicating, for example if the owner was a minor. Nor can dedication be presumed if the owner of the land is a statutory body whose purpose is incompatible with the dedication of a path. In addition, from 1932 it was open to owners to submit plans showing the rights of way that they acknowledged to exist over their land together with a statement that there was no intention to dedicate any more (10). These do not, of course, act to extinguish any rights that were not acknowledged and thus cannot be taken as proving that others do not exist. They do show that no other rights could have been presumed to be dedicated from the date of the submission.

9.14. Use subsequent to the definitive map

There is some doubt as to the effect of use of a path after the date of the definitive map. Suppose that a path can be clearly shown to have been put on the definitive map in error, but that the public have freely used it since that date. Can a new dedication be presumed which will prevent the right being deleted from the map despite it being shown to be an error? There are two different schools of thought on this matter.

Use by the public does not create a highway; rather it allows an inference of what was in the mind of the owner. If the public use a route, believing that they do so as of right, and the owner is aware of this use then it will be assumed that he either accepts a highway to exist or he is prepared to dedicate a new one. However, it is not at all clear that this will be the case where the right is recorded on the definitive map. In this case the public use the way as of right and, assuming the owner to act within the law, there is nothing he can do to prevent the use. It seems surprising that any conclusions can be reached as to the intentions of the owner when he clearly has no choice in the matter. Arguably, therefore, no dedication can be presumed once a right of way is recorded on the definitive map.

On the other hand, the Department of the Environment takes a different line in its published circular (11). This argues that a path can remain on the definitive map, despite evidence that it was shown in error, if twenty years of use as of right and without interruption can be proved. Although this interpretation would make it even more difficult for existing rights to be deleted, it does have the disadvantage of giving an advantage to the wrong-doer. It means that an owner who illegally prevents the public from using a right of way has a better chance of having it deleted than the law-abiding owner of a similar path who allowed the public the rights indicated on the definitive map.

Until a case concerning this aspect of the law comes before the courts, it is not possible to say which interpretation is correct.

Notes to chapter 9

1. Morgan v Hertfordshire County Council (1965) 63 LGR 456.

2. Countryside Act 1968. Schedule 3 contained amendments to the National Parks and Access to the Countryside Act 1949 and introduced for the first time a power to delete or downgrade paths on the definitive map. This has itself been replaced by the powers in the Wildlife and Countryside Act 1981.

3. Wildlife and Countryside Act 1981, Section 53(3)(c) dealing with the discovery of evidence.

4. Rubinstein v Secretary of State for the Environment (1988) JPL 485.

5. Regina v Secretary of State for the Environment, ex parte Burrows and Simms (1990) 3 All ER 490.

6. Wildlife and Countryside Act 1981. Schedule 14 sets out the procedures to be followed.

7. Wildlife and Countryside Act 1981, S53(3)(a)(ii). This is the short cut method for legal events and requires the authority to make an order on "the coming into operation of any enactment or instrument, or any other event, whereby a highway shown or required to be shown in the map and statement as a highway of a particular description has ceased to be a highway of that description". It is not clear whether there is here a parallel method on the discovery of evidence and it may be that there is no way that a member of the public can require an order to be made. It is also possible that there is no procedure for removing a byway from the definitive map if it becomes so busy that it no longer fits the definition of *byway*.

8. Regina v Secretary of State for the Environment, ex parte Hood (1975) 3 WLR 172.

9. Attorney General v Antrobus (1905) 2 Ch 188.

10. Rights of Way Act 1932. This has been repealed and the equivalent legislation is in the Highways Act 1980, Section 31.

11. Department of Environment Circular 1/83, Welsh Office Circular 50/81. Annex A, paragraph 16.

10
CLOSURE AND DIVERSION OF HIGHWAYS

10.1. Introduction

Although highways can only be closed or diverted through correct legal methods, there are nevertheless many ways in which this can be done under a variety of different laws. This chapter deals with the most common methods under highways and planning acts.

The Highways Act of 1980 contains a number of different methods of closing or diverting highways. The oldest method, dating from the era when parish surveyors were responsible, is by application to the magistrates court for an order. This method is still used and is dealt with in sections 10.2 and 10.3. It is still the only method available where a vehicular highway is proposed to be closed on the basis that it is unnecessary. But in more modern times highway authorities have been allowed to make their own orders covering the diversion or closure of public paths. This is by far the most common way of dealing with such changes, although some authorities persist in dealing with some public path matters through the magistrates court. In addition the Highways Act includes powers to close or divert highways to allow the construction of new roads, but this is a wider subject and is dealt with in Chapter 12.

With the introduction of town and country planning, parallel powers were introduced to deal with highways affected by developments that have been granted planning permission. These orders are similar in concept to orders under the Highways Act and are described in section 10.9.

It is important to realise that once a highway has been extinguished, the rights of the public cease and the land can be used by the owners as they please. It is not possible for the process to be reversed except by the creation of a completely new highway over the same line. It follows that the greatest care needs to be taken by rights of way workers to ensure that irreversible damage is not done to the network through closures and diversions.

10.2. Highways act - magistrates court orders

This is the traditional method of changing the network and is really a relic of the time before elected county councils when the magistrates had considerable responsibility for highways.

The basic principle is that the highway authority can apply to the court for an order stopping up a highway, reducing its status (say from bridleway to footpath), or for diverting it (1). It is also possible to apply for an order closing part of a highway, for example a grass verge. In recent years there have been increasing difficulties through councils seeking to close wide grass verges that they feel may be used by encampments of travelling people. These verges are, of course, very important to ridden horses and it is often necessary for such applications to be opposed.

The grounds for making the orders are limited. For a closure, the way has to be shown to be unnecessary. The courts have held that this means that the public as users do not require the right of way to be retained. It is not sufficient to show that its closure is in the interests of the general public, for example if the maintenance cost is argued to exceed its utility to users (2).

For a diversion, the proposed route has to be shorter or more commodious; in other words there has to be an improvement to users. A diversion that is less convenient to users but is better for the highway authority or for the owner is not permitted.

Orders made through the magistrates court can apply to highways of any status. In practice, however, they are mainly used for carriageways because councils can themselves make orders to close or divert public paths. Such orders offer greater flexibility and are generally preferred by authorities. They are also preferred by user groups because of a number of problems of the court procedure which will be described in the next section. Consequently, government advice to authorities is that the magistrates court procedure should not be used for public paths but, unfortunately, this is not always followed.

10.3. Magistrates court procedure

Before applying to the court, the authority has to advertise to the public its intention and the date and time on which the hearing will take place. Notices have to be put at the ends of the highway and adverts placed in a local newspaper and the official government paper, the London Gazette. This is monitored by the leading organisations representing rights of way users who will normally inform their local representatives. However, it is always useful for rights of way workers to keep an eye on the local press in order to ensure that court applications do not fall through the net.

The authority has also to consult the district council and the parish council or meeting where there is one. These bodies have an absolute veto; if they inform the highway authority that they oppose the change then the matter cannot be considered by the court. This may well represent the easiest way of defeating a proposal if it is possible to persuade the local parish council to apply their right of veto. This is one of the few real powers that a parish council actually has; sometimes the greatest difficulty is getting members to believe that they really can flex their muscles this time!

If the order is not vetoed, the hearing goes ahead as advertised. There is no need for objectors to make any written objection in advance of the hearing; they just turn up and speak. As most orders are uncontroversial it is usually assumed that the case can be dealt with in a few minutes and no time is allowed. If objectors do just turn up then the authority is liable to ask for an adjournment and the need to attend again. So it may well be worthwhile informing the magistrates' clerk and the authority that an objection will be made so that enough time can be made available.

The procedure appears to vary between courts depending on the attitude of the magistrates' clerk who advises the magistrates on legal points. It is often worthwhile finding out in advance from the clerk what the procedure will be. In particular, courts vary as to whether they will allow an individual who is not legally qualified to represent an organisation representing rights of way users.

This is not really a serious problem as any member of the public is entitled to object. Thus if the court will not accept the objector as a representative of a body then the objection can be made in the name of the individual. It should be noted that some magistrates appear to feel that the views of individuals who do not themselves use the route can be disregarded. This is not logical, but it may well be more helpful if the person making the objection is local and thus either uses the route or could reasonably want to do so.

In presenting the objection, it is important to remember that the authority is required to show that the order can be justified on the basis of the grounds laid down in the act. Thus the objector has to show that this is not the case and it is best to concentrate on this issue. For example, if the authority seeks to close off a verge because they fear it will be used by new-age travellers then this is not a valid ground; it has to show that the verge is unnecessary. The objector should concentrate on explaining to the magistrates how important the verge is to riders and the dangers of horses using the road. Do not be tempted to get into arguments about whether new-age travellers are a problem or not; simply point out to the magistrates that the issue is whether the verge is necessary.

Although many people find appearing in the magistrates court rather an unnerving experience, in practice magistrates are often sympathetic to the claims of ordinary members of the public; perhaps because they themselves are ordinary folk rather than lawyers. Experience indicates that objections in the magistrates court have quite a high success rate.

In the event of failure, there is not a lot that can be done. In theory an appeal to the crown court can be made but the legal costs are high. Only in very rare circumstances would an appeal be justified.

The question of appeal does introduce one of the problems of the magistrates court procedure. If an authority seeks an order in the magistrates court but this is rejected because of an objection, then it can appeal to the crown court and the successful objector becomes the defendant rather than the magistrates who have allegedly made the wrong decision. This grossly unfair system could potentially leave an objector facing substantial legal costs if the crown court were to reverse the decision of the magistrates. An individual who acts without the backing of some national body is clearly at some financial risk, albeit that the risk is in practice very small. It is, however, essential to seek legal advice if a local authority seeks to appeal against a decision of the magistrates.

10.4. Highways act - public path orders

The rather archaic system of orders through the magistrates court has been supplemented by orders which councils can make themselves. The power is available to both the county and district councils even where the latter is not the highway authority. They do, however, only apply to public paths, that is footpaths and bridleways. They cannot be used for byways. In theory orders could be made on RUPPs where no vehicular rights exist, but authorities generally play safe and seek a magistrates court order (3).

Councils first make the orders, that is to say they publish draft proposals. They then have to advertise them and there is a period within which members of the public can object. If there are no objections within the period then the council can itself confirm the order and the change in legal status takes place. If, however, there is an objection then the council cannot confirm the order which as to be passed on to the Secretary of State. He will normally hold a public inquiry following which the inspector in charge of the inquiry will make a decision as to whether to confirm the order. The complex business of how to object and present the arguments at a public inquiry is dealt with in Chapter 13; here we will examine the various types of order and the legal grounds under which they can be made.

Public path orders can be made to divert paths, to close them or to create new ones. A number of such proposals can be combined in concurrent orders; for example, a proposal to close a path may be concurrent with one to create a new path to replace it. Where there are proposals to modify a network of paths then the resultant package of orders can be quite complicated to understand.

The grounds for making the orders are much wider than for the traditional method of orders in the magistrates court. They are also more complex to understand in that they differ according to the purpose for which the order is being made. Even more obscurely, the grounds for making an order differ from those for confirming the order. The difference is that the grounds for making the order are more simple and relate to what appears at first sight to be a reasonable argument for making an order. The grounds for confirmation are normally more complex and usually involve a balance between conflicting factors that may have been raised in objection.

The grounds for confirmation often involve the introduction of the concept of expediency; for example that it is expedient to do so bearing in mind other factors. The word *expedient* is here being used in its more old-fashioned sense of being proper in the circumstances, rather than in the more usual sense today when the word implies more of a stop-gap solution to some unexpected problem. The principle of expediency allows a balance to be struck between opposing interests. For example, it might be expedient to divert a path in the interests of the owner, despite the fact that it is less convenient to the public; the council has to strike a balance between these conflicting claims.

The powers in the Highways Act were originally intended to modify the network of paths to try and reconcile the changing needs of owners and users. However, an additional problem was identified in the need to modify paths to improve safety at railway level crossings and in 1992 the Act was modified to allow this as well (4). As the grounds for this are different again, it is proposed to deal first with normal modifications to the network and then with level crossing orders.

10.5. Modifications to the network - diversions

Public path orders can close existing paths, divert them or create new ones. It is not at all unusual to have a concurrent set of orders of all three types when a complex set of changes is proposed.

The most common type of order is a diversion. This is actually a concurrent closure and creation; the old route of the path is closed and the new one created. There is an important proviso; the ends of the old and new routes have to be the same point except where the end of the new path is linked to the end of the old path by another highway. In the latter case the new end has to be "substantially as convenient to the public". For example, if two bridleways join a road opposite each other, then arguably it would not be as convenient if one was to be diverted to end some distance down the road.

Diversion orders can be made in the interests of the landowner or of the general public. Diversion orders are often requested by the owner and the council may only agree to an order subject to the owner meeting the costs of it. If the diversion reduces the value of any property, then compensation has to be paid. The effects of these rules are that almost all orders arise from requests by owners, as no compensation has to be paid and costs may be recovered. Orders made in the interests of the public may involve compensation as well as the council having to meet all the costs of the order. This is an extremely unsatisfactory situation in that the resources of a council should surely be directed towards the interests of the public rather than private individuals. Nevertheless, this is the reality of the situation and explains why rights of way workers tend to be on the defensive with diversion orders.

In coming to a decision on a diversion order a number of conflicting factors have to be taken into account. These are the convenience of the changes to the public, the enjoyment of the path by the public and the effect on the owner. In considering the last, account has to be taken of any compensation that has to be paid. Importantly, the whole is subject to an overall constraint that the route shall not be "substantially less convenient" to the public than the previous route.

This means that it is legitimate for a diversion to be made to suit the convenience of a landowner which provides a worse route for the public, so long as it is not "substantially" worse. On the other hand, a change that provides a better route for the public would have to be balanced against any adverse effect on the owner, after compensation had been paid. In theory at least, all adverse effects of a diversion should have been reflected in the compensation so that any residual effects should be quite small.

10.6. Modifications to the network - creations

A council can make an order to create a new footpath or bridleway. It is possible to make an order of this type to upgrade a footpath to a bridleway by creating a new bridleway along the line of an existing footpath. As in diversion orders, compensation has to be paid if there is any reduction in property values.

If a council can reach agreement with an owner that a path can be created in exchange for a payment of compensation, then an order is not necessary as the path can be formally created by agreement (5). If this is done then there is no opportunity for the public to object, the logic being that they can only gain by the agreement. This does mean, of course, that where a footpath is being upgraded to a bridleway it prevents any objections from walkers who may wish to prevent use of the path by horses and bicycles.

Creation orders may be appropriate where there is a proposal to replace one path by another, but where the old and new paths do not start and end at the same place and thus a diversion is not allowed. In this case it is possible to make concurrent creation and closure orders so that the two changes can be made to depend on each other.

A creation order will also be necessary where a new path is needed but the owner does not agree. An order can be made if the new path would add to the convenience or enjoyment of a substantial section of the public, or to the convenience of local residents. A balance has to be struck between this and the effects on the owner, but again this is after taking into account the compensation that would be paid. In practice, councils seem remarkably coy about making orders of this type, arguing that a compulsory creation should be very much a last resort. In a free society this should certainly be the case, but nevertheless the power is there to be used when required. Hardly any public projects would ever be possible without compulsory powers being available and used from time to time as a last resort; there is no reason why public paths should be any different.

10.7. Modifications to the network - closures

The most controversial types of public path orders are frequently those that seek to extinguish part of the network. It is important to note that the grounds for these are quite different from those for diversions and creations as these involve a balance between the needs of the path users and the landowners. A closure order can be made where a path is not needed for public use; the matter hinges simply on whether this is true or not and the question of any benefits to the landowner does not enter into the matter.

In deciding whether it is needed, it is legitimate to take into account other highways that provide a close alternative. If, for example, a new path has come into existence and provides a more convenient route than the old path, then it may be reasonable to close the old route on the grounds that it is no longer needed. The same logic can be applied to proposed paths and it is thus possible to have concurrent creation and closure orders where a proposed path replaces an existing path.

Another factor to be taken into account is the extent to which the path would be likely to be used by the public. This question normally arises where a path is proposed to be closed without any alternative being provided because it is argued that nobody would want to use the path. Such an argument is usually based on the fact that nobody is currently using the path; in practice it is often found that this is because the path has been blocked. In such cases there is a specific provision that any temporary features that prevent or reduce use should be disregarded. The courts have held that the term *temporary* includes any illegal obstruction, however permanent in actual construction (6). It is temporary in the sense that if it is illegal then the highway authority can, and should, secure its immediate removal. The implication of this is that in considering a potential closure of a blocked path, account has to be taken of the extent to which the path would be used if it were not blocked.

10.8. Level crossing orders

Most railways were constructed last century under the authority of individual private acts. These authorised the closure and diversion of highways, but only so far as was needed at the time. Many highways were taken across the line by level crossings, particularly on public paths as there was normally no requirement for these crossings to be provided with a crossing keeper. When the railways were built, few trains went faster than about 40mph. Now that trains are very much faster as well as quieter, some crossings that were originally quite safe are now dangerous in that visibility of oncomimg trains is inadequate.

Attempts to improve the situation were made difficult by there being no powers to close or divert highways for safety reasons, apart from the cumbersome method of a further private act. This led to changes from 1992 when additional powers were added to the Highways Act to allow orders to be made to close or divert public paths that go across level crossings (4). Note that these do not apply to vehicular rights of way which still cannot be changed by orders.

Orders can now be made by councils both to divert and close public paths in the interests of the safety of the public using the path. A path can be diverted onto land that belongs to someone other than the railway operator even if that person does not agree. If the diversion is approved then compensation will be payable to the owner by the railway operator. Given the high density of over and under bridges on railways in Britain it will often be possible to divert a path to another safer crossing point.

There are also powers to close a path. An order closing a path is not restricted to the section of route actually within the railway boundary but can also include sections on either side back to any junctions so as not to retain dead-end sections. There is a very important proviso that applies both to diversion and closure orders: the order has to be expedient bearing in mind whether it is "reasonably practicable" to make the crossing safe.

Under what situations is a crossing dangerous and how practicable is it to make it safe? Important guidance is provided by the Health and Safety Executive (HSE) who have produced standards for level crossings (7). These are based on an assessment of the crossing time and the warning time. The crossing time is the time needed to cross the line; the warning time is the time between a user first becoming aware of a train coming and it reaching the crossing. Simply enough, if the crossing time exceeds the warning time then the crossing is unsafe.

Users of the path are expected to look both ways, so the visibility along the line is important. In some cases, a crossing can be made safe simply by removing bushes that obstruct the view. The warning time can also be increased by installing signs requiring trains to sound their horn. Finally, there are red and green signal lights linked to the railway signalling system which indicate to the users whether it is safe to cross. The Executive accept these for speeds up to 125mph. As there are no lines in Britain authorised for speeds in excess of 125mph it follows that it is practicable to make any crossing safe if necessary.

The attitude of the HSE is that unsafe crossings are simply not acceptable. The options are threefold; to carry out works to make the crossing safe, to replace the crossing with a bridge, or to eliminate the crossing by closing or diverting the path. So although the making of the order starts from there being a crossing that does not meet the HSE standards, the decision as to whether to confirm the order is a balance between the cost to the railway operator and the convenience of the public. It is not a question of public safety against convenience to users.

Experience with the new powers is still limited and it is not yet clear how this balance will be struck in practice. A particular problem is the extent to which diversions will be considered rather than closure. A difficulty may be that in considering a closure it is necessary to take into account whether it is reasonably practicable to make the crossing safe, but not whether a diversion would be a reasonable alternative to meet the same objectives.

10.9. Town and country planning powers

In addition to the powers under the Highways Act, there are additional powers under the Town and Country Planning Act 1990. These are limited to situations where new developments are proposed on land crossed by a highway. The problem with this legislation is that the powers are considerably more draconian than under highways powers.

Orders under planning powers can be made by local planning authorities (normally district councils) to alter public paths (8). Orders for all highways can be made by the Secretary of State, normally on the request of the planning authority (9). This is necessary to close roads with vehicular rights.

The only reason needed is to allow a development that has been granted planning permission to be carried out; there is no need to consider whether a route to be closed is necessary, nor is there any requirement to provide an alternative. It should be noted that an order can also be made to allow developments by government departments which do not require planning permission and are thus treated as if they had applied and been granted permission.

The logic of this approach is that at the earlier stage when the decision was taken on the planning application, any necessary revisions to the highway network should have been taken into account. As the planning authority is supposed to be acting on behalf of the public, it should have balanced any effects on public use of highways against the wider benefits of the proposed development.

The fallacy is that in many cases rights of way are not even considered. The planning authority is usually a different council from the highway authority. It is required to consult the highway authority on all applications, but it does not have to take account of any response. In theory the highway authority ought to bring to the attention of the planning authority any rights of way affected but, in practice, this often does not happen. The problem for rights of way workers is finding out early enough about potential applications so that representations can be made to the planning authority about the need for rights of way to be properly considered. If representations are made but ignored, there is no appeal system. The whole development control procedure is arranged to favour development with a right of appeal to the Secretary of State for a potential developer whose application is turned down but no right of appeal for objectors to the application.

Once an application has been approved, an objection to the consequential order is on weak ground. Nevertheless, the courts have held that although the nature of the development cannot then be challenged, objectors may still challenge the merits or demerits of the order being made (10). The Secretary of State, in deciding whether to confirm an order, is not bound to confirm an order that adversely affects the public or a private individual such as the owner of neighbouring premises, even if it would not be possible to carry out the development without the order. The public may certainly object that an alternative proposal would have less adverse effect and would also allow the development to take place; for example, if a diversion is proposed then it is open to an objector to claim that a different diversion would be preferable.

It is also possible to challenge whether the change is needed to allow the development anyway. For example, the extension of a garden into a field is a development that requires planning permission. In a number of cases, inspectors have accepted the argument that this does not allow the closure or diversion of a path under planning powers as it is perfectly possible, and indeed not uncommon, for paths to run through gardens. It is not a contrary argument that the householder wants to fence off the garden as fencing does not require planning permission and thus does not allow the making of an order under planning powers.

10.10. Assessing proposals to change paths

The present network of public paths and byways is very much of an historical accident. It represents the vestiges of a much more extensive network that once existed, serving a completely different purpose at a time when farming practices were completely different. In the circumstances, it is perhaps not surprising that it is often claimed that this obsolete network could be modified in a way that would provide a much better system for users and owners alike.

In practice, these potential benefits are largely unattainable. The main problem with the rights of way network is that it is not continuous, and many sections can only be used if sections of motor road are used as well. The overwhelming need for improvements to the network lies in the creation of new sections of route to fill in key gaps and thus provide a more continuous system. If these links could be swapped for other sections of route that are either duplicated or in such a position that there is no real prospect of bringing them into a cohesive network, then the same total length of paths could be used to provide a much better service to the public.

This idealistic approach ignores many practical difficulties. The greatest is the fragmented nature of land ownership, which becomes increasingly so as the traditional big estates are broken up. Understandably, no owner is going to accept more rights of way on his land in exchange for a reduction somewhere else and there is no mechanism for the gainer to compensate the loser. It follows that most changes to the path network are relatively small in scale, generally affecting the land of only one owner. Rarely are changes of this sort capable of delivering the improvements that are sought by users.

At a more local level, alleged improvements often turn out to be illusory. This is because all too often, owners take as their starting point a path that they have already obstructed. Surely, they argue, a path that cannot be used because a building has been constructed on it must be inferior to a new path alongside. But this argument starts from the wrong basis. If a diversion is not made, then as the new building is an illegal obstruction it will have to be pulled down; thus the new path is really no better than the old. This is not to say that in these circumstances an objection ought to be made to a minor diversion, but it takes a rather curious logic to claim that the public have gained by it!

For reasons that were explained in 10.5, councils are generally reluctant to make orders except with the approval of owners. The consequence of this is that the whole process of altering the network is driven by requests from owners. Inevitably, their ideas are much more likely to reflect their own aspirations rather than any attempt to provide an improved network for the public. This means that rights of way workers dealing with public path orders tend to be on the defensive. It is important to remember that the process is one-way; a network of paths developed and protected over centuries can be wiped out overnight if a determined owner is allowed to exploit any weakness in the organisation of user groups.

A resolute defence of the public rights can lead to attacks by owners that user groups are uncompromising. However, the paths exist and people have a right to use them and to expect that they will not be obstructed or subjected to any harassment. Rights of way workers have to decide whether changes are an improvement or not from the point of view of users.

They may sometimes have to accept a deal which gives benefits to the owner without any benefits to users; but no proposals should be accepted that leave users worse off, however attractive such changes may be to the owner. Rights of way workers should always regard themselves as a species of trustee with a moral responsibility for the interests of path users. Just as real trustees have a legal duty to obtain the best possible deal for the beneficiaries of the trust, so rights of way workers should regard themselves as morally bound to obtain the best possible deal for other users. It follows that, morally at least, they have no authority to accept changes that worsen the position for users, however sympathetic they may feel on a personal level to any problems that this attitude will cause the owner.

The precise application of these principles will depend on the individual circumstances of each set of proposals. One clear implication is that a proposal to simply extinguish a route without any other proposals will always be unacceptable. An extinguishment should only be considered if part of a package of proposals including a creation at another part of the network. It is also important to remember that any offers to create permissive paths should not be regarded in any sense as an alternative to a legal right of way. This, of course, is because permissive paths can be closed at any time. They are always welcome, but never in exchange for a permanent path.

Beyond this it is difficult to lay down hard and fast rules. There is frequently a dilemma as to whether we are trying to maximise the total length of paths, or to create more direct routes. Suppose a diversion shortens a path by providing a more direct route; is this an improvement or a worsening of the path? There is no simple answer and rights of way workers will have to be prepared to consider each set of proposals on its own merits, always remembering their role as trustees determined to achieve the best possible deal for users of the network.

Notes to chapter 10

1. Highways Act 1980, Section 116.

2. Ramblers Association v Kent County Council (1990) JP 716. This is an important case in setting out the meaning of the criteria to be applied. Lord Justice Woolf said that it would be difficult for the magistrates properly to come to the conclusion that a way was unnecessary unless the public were, or were going to be, provided with a reasonably suitable alternative way. In deciding whether an alternative way was

reasonable, it had to be a way which was suitable, or reasonably suitable, for the purpose for which the public were using the existing way. Mr Justice Pill said that it was not open to the magistrates to decide that a way was unnecessary because they held the view that it was in the public interest that the highway should be closed.

3. Highways Act 1980. Section 118 deals with the extinguishment of public paths, whilst Section 119 covers their diversion.

4. Until the Highways and Works Act 1992, there were no powers to close or divert highways over level crossings. The Act amended the Highways Act 1980 by adding Section 118A dealing with the extinguishment of public paths and Section 119A covering their diversion.

5. Highways Act 1980, Section 25.

6. Regina v Secretary of State for the Environment, ex parte Barry Stewart (1980) JPL 175.

7. Railway Construction and Operation Requirements - Part F: Protection of footpath and bridleway level crossings. Health and Safety Executive. 1993.

8. Town and Country Planning Act 1990, Section 257.

9. Town and Country Planning Act 1990, Section 247.

10. K C Holdings (Rhyl) Ltd v Secretary of State for Wales and Colwyn Borough Council (1990) JPL 353. See also Vasilou v Secretary of State for Transport (1990) Times 16th July 1990.

11
TRAFFIC REGULATION ORDERS

11.1. Introduction

This chapter deals with traffic regulation orders made by highway authorities. These can be helpful to non-motorised users by restricting the use of roads by motor vehicles and thus making them more suitable for walkers, horse riders, carriage drivers and cyclists. On the other hand, orders can restrict the use of routes by all classes of users so they can adversely affect the use of highways by non-motorised traffic.

11.2. General points

It is first necessary to appreciate the important difference between traffic regulation and the closure of highways. Traffic regulation is effectively a series of rules made by a public body controlling the way in which the public may use highways and does not involve the owner of the land over which the highways run. If the public, through their elected representatives, decide to apply restrictions to the way in which they use a highway this does not affect the basic rights that the public enjoy of the owner. To give an example, a one way street has a traffic regulation order (or TRO for short) prohibiting traffic from going in one direction. But this does not affect the fact that the owner has dedicated a right for the public to go both ways and this basic right continues to apply.

If people disobey a valid TRO they commit an offence for which they can be punished. But the owner can take no action for trespass because the public right continues. This is quite different from the situation where a highway is extinguished. In that case anyone who continues to use the route trespasses against the owner but does not commit an offence.

It should be noted that it is possible to make a TRO to prohibit a use to which the public have no right. A common example is a TRO prohibiting the riding of horses on a footpath. Anybody breaking such a TRO would be committing an offence as well as trespassing.

The position of the owner should also be noted. The owner of a highway is perfectly entitled to use it on horseback or in vehicles even where the public have no such rights; obviously he cannot trespass against himself. But if a TRO is in force it applies to the owner just as much as anybody else, unless a special exemption has been made.

145

An important difference between a TRO and an extinguishment is that the former can always be rescinded and the owner has no comeback. This should be contrasted with an extinguishment where the status quo can only be restored if the owner re-dedicates it. This means that traffic regulation should always be preferred to extinguishment unless there is no prospect at all of the right being needed again.

TROs are made under powers in the Road Traffic Regulation Act 1984. However, the Town and Country Planning Act also includes powers to restrict traffic which are effectively traffic regulation; this aspect will be considered in 11.10. Finally, there are also some measures that are effectively traffic regulation although there are no actual orders and these will be described in 11.11.

11.3. Routes subject to traffic regulation

TROs can be made on any highway but also on any road to which the public have access (1). The first part is clear enough and as a highway includes a footpath or bridleway it follows that TROs can be made on these. The second part extends traffic regulation to roads to which the public have access, even if they do not have a right of way. Curiously, *road* is never defined but taking the normal meaning would suggest that the law applies to vehicular routes. Thus a TRO can apply to a private road which is used by the public, for example to a hospital or railway station. Although the matter is not entirely clear, it seems likely that a TRO cannot be applied to a path that is not a right of way.

Just as a TRO can be made on a private road to control traffic that has no legal right to be there, a TRO can also be made on a public path to control traffic that has no legal right to be there. For example, a TRO can be made to prohibit riding or cycling on a footpath even though there is no legal right for the public to use it other than on foot.

11.4. Classes of traffic subject to regulation

TROs are most frequently made to control the use of vehicles. It should be noted that orders can discriminate between different types of vehicles. Thus an order can prohibit motor vehicles but allow horse-drawn vehicles and pedal cycles.

Orders can also be made to control pedestrians, for example to exclude them from a high-speed road (2). For many years there was a curious anomaly that there were no powers to make TROs that affected ridden horses. This has been partly remedied but even now the law only allows a TRO affecting horses to be made on footpaths, bridleways and byways (3). A byway is defined as a highway with vehicular rights but which is mainly used on foot and horseback; it is not necessary for it to be recorded on the definitive map before a TRO can be made.

A key implication of this is that a TRO cannot be made to prohibit or restrict horses on normal roads, even where the road is a high-speed dual carriageway to near motorway standards.

11.5. Types of restrictions

Traffic regulation consists essentially of prohibitions applying to particular types of traffic in specified circumstances. These allow considerable flexibility. An order may prevent all traffic or it may make restrictions in the way traffic can move. For example, one way streets are examples of TROs that prohibit traffic from moving in one direction. Similarly, there can be orders which restrict certain movements, such as prohibiting turns at a junction.

Orders can apply to the whole width of a road or to just part; for example, vehicles can be prohibited from driving along the verge of a road. Orders can also apply only for part of the time; for instance, when shopping streets are closed to motor traffic during shopping hours only.

All these types of order could theoretically be applied to the use of public paths or byways. It is doubtful in practice if there are any one-way public paths or banned turns but they are possible in theory. In practice, the main use of orders on public paths is to restrict the use of footpaths by riders and cyclists. As there is no provision for making equestrian orders for normal roads it follows that one-way streets and banned turns do not apply to riders. Similarly, there are no powers to prevent horses being ridden along pedestrianised streets.

The law does provide protection for owners of premises adjoining a road affected by a TRO. An order may not restrict access on foot to any premises next to the road and having an access to it, or to any other premises to which there is no other way (4).

The rules are slightly different in respect of other traffic. It is possible to restrict vehicular access to premises for periods of up to eight hours in any twenty four, and this would also seem to apply to horse access to premises on footpaths, bridleways and byways. It is actually possible to prevent access for even longer but the conditions for making such orders are so stringent that they are rarely made and only under very unusual circumstances.

In order to avoid these problems, orders are often made with an exception for access. Alternatively, through-traffic may be stopped by a TRO affecting a very short length of the route with the dead-end sections on either side left for access.

11.6. Reasons for traffic regulation orders

Although the types of TRO that can be made are quite wide, the law does not allow orders to be made arbitrarily; there has to be some sort of reason for them. Basically, orders can be made for road safety, to prevent damage to the road or adjoining buildings, to enable roadworks to be carried out, to assist in the smooth flow of traffic, or to improve the environment (5). These five basic reasons can now be looked at in more detail.

The power to make orders for road safety is a wide one. The most common types are those that restrict the way that traffic uses the road so as to reduce potential conflicts, for example through prohibiting turns at junctions. It is also possible to promote road safety by restricting certain types of traffic. Orders prohibiting vehicular traffic from shopping streets are common enough and the same principle is equally applicable to rural roads if used extensively on foot or horseback. The same logic is used to prohibit horses from using footpaths, and could potentially apply to bridleways; fortunately the latter type of order is rare.

Restrictions to prevent damage to the road raise a fundamental question: is it legitimate to restrict traffic to avoid damage to a road when there is a clear duty on the highway authority to maintain the road to suit the traffic? It would probably be difficult to justify making an order of this sort for normal traffic under normal circumstances if the objective was simply to save maintenance costs. For example, it would be unreasonable to restrict horses from using a bridleway on the basis that they would damage the surface, as it is the duty of the authority to maintain the route by repairing any wear. On the other hand, potential damage would justify an order restricting horses from a footpath as in that case the horses would have no right to be there.

Orders are also sometimes made where unexpected circumstances make a road liable to damage by traffic. For example, a landslip might create a situation where use of a bridleway would cause further slipping and damage. In this sort of situation, whilst a restriction would be reasonable in the short term, it would be expected that the authority would take steps to repair the path so that it could be brought back into normal use.

148

There is a power to restrict traffic to allow works to be carried out on the highway, although this is only allowed on a temporary basis. This is increasingly used to close roads to motor traffic to allow repair if the method of working makes it impossible to provide a route. For example, the replacement of a bridge may require the old bridge to be removed completely before construction of the new one. Because of the restriction on the making of equestrian orders, where a normal vehicular road is involved there has to remain a route for horses. Orders of this sort are equally possible on public paths and byways, for example for bridge repairs. The authority is required to consider alternative routes and this usually takes the form of a signed diversion route.

Orders to help the flow of traffic usually apply to vehicular traffic and this justification can apply to orders to ban certain turns or to restrict parking. It would seem difficult to justify on this basis any restrictions on use of public paths or byways.

There are a number of different reasons for making TROs relating to the environment. Restrictions can be placed on vehicles (but not horses or pedestrians) where the traffic is unsuited to the existing character of the road or has an adverse effect on adjoining properties. Although these seem intended to allow restrictions to be made to vehicular traffic in urban areas, for example to prevent through traffic in a residential area, they could presumably be applied to rural roads as well.

In addition, an order can be made to preserve the character of a road where it is specially suitable for persons on horseback or foot. Although obviously intended to restrict vehicles, it would seem possible to use this power to restrict horses on public paths.

There are additional environmental grounds available in areas of special interest comprising national parks, areas of outstanding natural beauty, country parks, National Trust land and official long-distance paths (6). In these areas there are powers to make orders to conserve or enhance the natural beauty of the area or to enable the public to better enjoy the area. This part of the legislation was added later in response to a concern that the normal reasons did not give sufficient powers to restrict motor traffic in order to protect the general ambience of a popular area.

11.7. Duration of orders

A so-called permanent TRO has no termination date and thus lasts indefinitely. It is not really permanent as it can be rescinded at any time by the authority that made the order. The public have a right of objection to a permanent order; the procedure will be set out in the next section.

Experimental traffic management schemes are sometimes introduced to find out how an idea works in practice. The experiment has to have a fixed duration which cannot be more than eighteen months. During the period a decision has to be made either to scrap the experiment or, if it is to be continued as a permanent feature to make a permanent order. An experimental order can be made for all the reasons set out in 11.6, other than for repairing the road.

Temporary orders are intended to cover temporary situations. They can be used to close a road to carry out repairs, and indeed orders for this purpose can only be made on a temporary basis. They can also be made to avoid danger or serious damage to the road but not for traffic flow or environmental reasons. Like experimental orders, they can be introduced with only seven days notice to the public and there is no right of objection. Temporary orders have a maximum duration of six months for public paths or eighteen months for other roads; this can be extended but only by permission of the Secretary of State.

Orders can also be made without any advance notice at all, but only where danger or serious damage to the road is involved. Such emergency orders have a maximum duration of fourteen days during which the authority is expected to make a temporary order as above. This procedure is clearly intended to deal with unexpected events such as a landslip or a bridge being washed away.

11.8. Making a traffic regulation order

To make a normal TRO the authority has to give notice in newspapers and by notices posted at the road in question giving the public the opportunity to inspect the order and if not satisfied to lodge objections. The authority then has to consider the objections, but it may then overrule them. The authority may hold a public inquiry but it is not forced to and, in practice, such inquiries are rare. Nor is there any appeal, at least in the sense of questioning the justification for the order.

It is, in theory, possible to apply to the High Court to have the order set aside but only if it can be shown that the order is outside the powers of the authority or there has been a failure to carry out the proper procedures. In practice this is hardly an option because if the case were lost the costs would run into thousands of pounds. In any event, the normal reasons for objection are that the order proposed is not justified by the circumstances rather than being outside the powers of the authority, and in this situation the courts would have no remit to interfere.

It follows that if it is desired to prevent an order being made, the best approach for an objector is likely to be through political rather than legal action. The approach required is to create a strong public opinion against the order and to lobby councillors not to accept it. It should be remembered that even if the campaign does not succeed at first and the order is implemented, it may be worth continuing to lobby the authority to rescind the order. Unpopular measures often become more unpopular once they are introduced and the public have the opportunity of seeing the effects in reality rather than in the abstract.

Experimental and temporary orders can be introduced with even less formality and with no provision for any objection. As there is no formal channel for objection it is clear that the only practical way of opposing a temporary or experimental order is by means of lobbying councillors.

11.9. Enforcement of traffic regulation orders

Once a TRO has been properly made then it is a criminal offence for anybody to break it. However, action may only be taken by a police officer in uniform or a traffic warden; there is no power for the highway authority or an owner to take any action to enforce the order. As the police have limited resources for this type of enforcement it is often necessary to devise physical measures by which orders may become self-enforcing.

It is an offence to disregard a TRO only if the proper signs as in the official Signs Manual have been erected. For example, where vehicles have been prohibited on a byway then it is necessary to erect proper signs at each end and at any point where another vehicular route joins it. This will be costly and in addition the signs may well be regarded as eyesores in a rural area.

Even where the signs exist, they are only likely to be observed if there is some kind of police presence. In a rural situation this is unlikely to be the case. Also, even if the police are present they have difficulty in enforcing a prohibition where there are exceptions for access. Most routes are likely to give access to some premises or other and anyone stopped can simply claim that they are using the route only for access.

In many cases, particularly in rural areas, it is more effective to rely on physical measures. Once an order has been made the authority is allowed to put up barriers to prevent illegal use. If this is done it may not be necessary to put up signs; if it is impossible to use the route then it does not matter that it would not be possible to prosecute anybody who did use it.

151

Of course, barriers are not allowed to prevent the legitimate use of exempted traffic. The most common solution is a point closure. In this the order simply prohibits the use of a short length of road on which there are no accesses. No exception need be made for access which then allows a barrier to be put across the road. All traffic can continue to use the two dead-ends of the route which effectively restricts it to local access traffic.

Point closures are frequently applied to vehicular roads with a prohibition of driving order over a short distance. Highway authorities often need to be reminded that such an order cannot prohibit equestrian use and that any barriers must allow horses to pass as well as pedestrians.

11.10. Traffic regulation through planning powers

In addition to normal traffic regulation powers, there is an additional power in the Town and Country Planning Act that allows the pedestrianisation of highways (7). This is normally used in shopping streets although it could in theory be used in the countryside as well.

The wording of the legislation is a little obscure. An order made under these powers is said to *extinguish* vehicular rights. However, unlike a normal extinguishment it is possible to simply rescind the order and restore these rights. In this respect it is more akin to traffic regulation than an extinguishment of rights.

The order process is started by the planning authority rather than the highway authority, although the latter must be consulted. The actual order is made by the Secretary of State and, unlike normal TROs, a public inquiry will be held if there is any objection made. Although described as a pedestrianisation order, and thus implying the downgrading to footpath standard, the order only prohibits vehicles and so actually creates a bridleway. However, as vehicular rights are suspended there is no right to ride a bicycle unless these are specifically excluded from the prohibition in the order.

11.11. Traffic regulation without orders

There are also some long-standing forms of traffic regulation that do not require any orders. Since 1835 it has been possible to set aside a footway at the side of a road for the use of pedestrians. It is an offence to ride a horse or drive a vehicle on a footway and this, of course, includes bicycles (8). However, it is possible to incorporate the footway back into the vehicular part of the road, or, in other words, to rescind whatever process created the footway. Thus we have all the characteristics of traffic regulation but without any order being made.

The situation has been made less clear by more recent laws that also allow facilities to be provided within a road for horses and cyclists. Whilst it is normally assumed that a margin for horses will be grass and a footpath or cycleway hardened, this does not necessarily follow. It is arguable, therefore, that the existence of a path alongside a road does not necessarily mean that it is an offence to ride along it unless there is a specific resolution of the highway authority that it is a footway.

Where a margin is provided for the use of horses, there is no law prohibiting use by vehicles (9). So unlike the provision of a footway, the provision of a riding margin does not involve any element of traffic regulation.

A highway authority can also set aside part of a carriageway as a cycle track (10). This is defined as a right of way for cycles with or without a right for pedestrians. It is an offence to drive any other sort of vehicle on a cycle track and so this is a form of traffic regulation.

It is not entirely clear what the effect of designating part of a carriageway as a cycle track is on riders, or indeed on walkers if the track is designated for cyclists only. As it is not an offence to walk or ride a horse on a cycle track, there is no element of traffic regulation. It appears that rights on foot or horseback are suspended, as are those for vehicles other than cycles, but are capable of coming into existence again if the authority rescinds the cycle track designation. In practice, the main effect of the suspension of riding and walking rights is that nothing can be done if the authority takes any action that obstructs the path from a riding or walking point of view.

Notes to chapter 11

1. Road Traffic Regulation Act 1984, Section 142.

2. Road Traffic Regulation Act 1984. Section 2(3) extends the powers of the act that regulate vehicular traffic to include pedestrians.

3. Road Traffic Regulation Act 1984. Section 127 further provides that powers to regulate pedestrians on footpaths, bridleways and byways also extend to horses.

4. Road Traffic Regulation Act 1984, Section 3.

5. Road Traffic Regulation Act 1984, Section 1.

6. Road Traffic Regulation Act 1984, Section 22.

7. Town and Country Planning Act 1990, Section 249.

8. Highway Act 1835, Section 72.

9. Highways Act 1980. Section 71 requires highway authorities to provide a grass or other margin for the use of horse-riders where it feels that this is necessary.

10. Highways Act 1980, Section 65.

12
PATHS AFFECTED BY NEW ROADS

12.1. Introduction

This paper deals with the special problems that arise when the line of a proposed road intersects an existing public path or minor road used by non-motorised users. The law allows existing highways to be modified to fit in with the proposed road; this is done by orders under the Highways Act known as side road orders. In recent years there have been increasing problems through road schemes that fail to take into account the needs of pedestrians, cyclists and horses. This chapter is intended to assist rights of way workers to understand the complexities of road schemes and to show how to achieve a better final result for non-motorised users.

12.2. Background to road proposals

Until the 1960s the main roads of Britain remained largely as they had been since the turnpike age, apart from the provision of a tarred surface. With the substantial growth of car ownership it was felt necessary to improve the network by the creation of new motorways and by improvements to existing all-purpose roads.

Motorways were an innovation and provided for the first time routes available only to motor traffic. This meant that other traffic was not allowed to cross on the level (or *at grade*, to use the jargon). Although some minor highways were closed, the 3000 km motorway network built in the 1960s did retain most minor highways by the provision of over and under bridges.

The improvement of other roads caused more problems because in most cases grade crossings were retained. In retrospect, far too little attention was paid to the effects of increased traffic nor was the possibility of speed increases allowed for. The building of the motorway network has encouraged the development of vehicles that can cruise effortlessly at the motorway speed limit; indeed recent surveys have shown that 60% of motorway traffic is exceeding the limit. This motorway mentality has led to much faster driving on all-purpose roads and to these roads being designed to allow higher speeds. In the early 1960s even major trunk roads like the A1 were still being designed for traffic travelling at 80kph; today such roads would be designed for speeds in excess of 120kph. It is hardly surprising that such roads have come to be regarded as no-go areas for walkers, riders and cyclists. Yet this point has still to be properly recognised in the design of new roads where impossible grade crossings are still being built.

Another assumption of the 1960s has also turned out to be flawed. At that time there was a belief that growth would tail off in the 1990s because most households would have a car; current projections show growth continuing strongly for at least another thirty years, unless action is taken to contain it. The problem arises partly from the modern aspiration of a car for each person rather than for each family, but more from the increase in travelling that a motorway mentality encourages.

Although most people have a perception that urban congestion is the real problem, the fact remains that by far the greatest growth is in inter-urban travel, or in other words along the main roads in the countryside. The growth in motorway traffic is around twice the national average which is itself around twice the growth rate in towns. This is because people are tending to make longer trips as well as more trips. In the future inter-urban traffic growth may well replace urban traffic congestion as the primary transport problem.

Projections in the late 1980s of traffic growth of up to two and a half times by 2025 led initially to government proposals to substantially increase road-building. But this immediately led to concern both among transport professionals and many of the more environmentally-aware public that this is not really a feasible way forward. A consensus has developed that it is not appropriate to build a way out. Instead policies try and maintain a combination of some road building, some traffic management and control, some public transport development and so on.

Although many people may have doubts about the logic of further road building, nevertheless this paper is not intended to give guidance as how to object to roads as such. Rather it assumes that roads will be built but concentrates on how to obtain the best possible deal for non-motorised users. With the correct approach it is possible to secure improvements over the present situation, in particular where improvements are proposed to roads that are already difficult to cross. However, the fact that road builders are everywhere on the defensive cannot but be useful to us in that they will tend to be much more ready to accommodate our needs so as to effectively buy-off at least some of the opposition!

12.3. Types of new road

There are around 360,000 km of surfaced road in Britain of which only 51,000 km are motorways and A class roads. But this 9% of the network carries more than

60% of the traffic and it is these types of road that are most likely to be improved or replaced by newly constructed roads.

The most important roads are described as trunk roads and the highway authority for these is the Department of Environment, Transport and the Regions (DETR) who act through their agents the Highways Agency. The trunk roads are regarded as being the key national network and the cost of them is met from national funds. The trunk road network amounts to about 11,000 km which includes almost all motorways. The remainder of the A class roads are known as principal roads and are the responsibility of the local highway authority.

Because trunk roads carry the greatest volumes of traffic and in view of their national importance, they are the most likely to be altered. However, local highway authorities often have quite extensive programmes of new construction on principal roads, particularly in terms of the construction of bypasses to towns and villages.

12.4. The planning process

To lobby effectively for proper facilities, it is necessary to understand the processes that go on during the long period of planning that precedes the construction of a new road. This section is intended to give a brief overview of the various stages.

The starting point is normally the identification of a problem, for example traffic congestion or damage to the environment. Then traffic surveys will be carried out to give a basis for any analysis. Based on this, possible road solutions will be derived but at this stage will only be lines on a map.

Estimates can then be made of the travel times between different points with and without the new road. Computer traffic models are used to predict traffic flows for what is known as the design year, fifteen years after the expected opening date. As predictions so far ahead are obviously difficult, two separate predictions are made. These are known as high and low growth predictions and are supposed to represent the possible extreme values; the truth is expected to lie somewhere between. These predictions allow the type of road to be determined (for example, single or dual carriageway) it being assumed that the road should be able to accommodate the high-growth travel in the design year.

Once the type of road has been determined, it is possible to make a first approximation to the cost. This will be based on unit costs obtained from other similar roads. At this stage no specific allowance will have been made for the cost of accommodating other highways crossed apart from the fact that the unit cost should have allowed for similar problems elsewhere.

At this stage there are still likely to be a number of options. Two questions need to be answered: which is the best option and is even the best option worth doing? To answer these questions a simple cost-benefit analysis is carried out with each option being compared with the effect of doing nothing. The analysis evaluates the effects of each option on the highway authority and on motorised road users. For the authority, the analysis considers the cost of building the road and maintaining it into the future. For the road users, it estimates changes in the operating costs of vehicles, in the number of accidents and in the travel time of users. The normal effect is that the authority has extra costs but the users gain extra benefits. Using a technique known as discounting it is possible to convert all the costs to an equivalent capital cost. The difference between the value of the benefits and the cost of the road gives a sort of social profit of the road, at least as far as those who use and pay for the road are concerned.

Taking the simple case where all the options cost the same, that which gives the greatest benefit is regarded as the best. Sometimes the benefits from even the best option are not as high as the cost; this means the road is simply not worth building.

This sort of analysis does not, of course, take any account of the effect on other people. In particular, it fails to take any account of environmental effects or of the effect on non-motorised traffic such as horses and pedestrians. As such effects differ between options they have to be considered outside the cost-benefit framework. As at this stage the details of crossing points have not been worked out it must follow that the effects on minor road users cannot be realistically allowed for.

Once a decision has been taken as to which option, if any, is worth building then the detailed design starts. The designer prepares plans showing the layout of the new roads and hence the areas of land which need to be bought. At the same time he will work out what to do with minor highways that enter the line of the new road and decide whether he wants to maintain them on the same alignment making a connection with the road, divert them to a new alignment which may involve bridges over or under the road, or to close them.

Having worked out the details, the legal orders are drafted both for the compulsory purchase of the land and for the side roads. These are advertised giving the owners and the public the right to object. If any objections are received then a public inquiry will be held. On confirmation of the orders, construction can begin.

It will be clear from this that by the time the orders are made, most of the detailed design work will have been completed. If orders are not confirmed then there will be a substantial amount of wasted work. If it is necessary to alter side road proposals, not only will the road have to be re-designed but it is likely that this will lead to changes in the area of land to be acquired. This will almost certainly mean starting all over again with the various orders and hence serious delays to the start of construction. It is hardly surprising that road designers will strongly defend their proposals at a public inquiry. Given that the final decision is made by the Secretary of State for Transport, even for a road promoted by his own Department, it must be clear that the cards are very much stacked against the objectors at a public inquiry.

However, this does not mean that it is impossible to get what we want. The trick is simply to try and influence the designer from the time that detailed design starts. Because the possibility of a successful objection has such serious effects on the construction programme, designers are often quite amenable to making provision for non-motorised users and thus avoiding a potential objection. It should be remembered that engineers do not pay for the roads they design out of their own pocket; on the contrary the prestige of an engineer is measured by the cost of the project that he is working on and he will often be only too pleased to add extra features. The more bridges on a road, the more fun it is to design and build!

12.5. Public consultation stages

Given the great importance of getting to the designer early enough, how does the rights of way worker find out what roads are proposed? The key to this is the public consultation stage which varies according to which body is responsible for the road.

The national trunk road network is the responsibility of the Department of Environment, Transport and the Regions. Since April 1994 the work has been split between the Department proper which deals only with policy issues and the Highways Agency which effectively acts as a consultant and deals with all the detailed work of designing and building the roads. The Agency has to know what roads it is supposed to be working on and this is set out in the roads programme.

Governments have always taken the rather high-handed view that the question of which trunk roads should be built is a matter of national policy and not something on which they will consult the public. At intervals, Parliament has approved a roads programme which is the list of roads which are supposed to be in preparation. Formerly, the process was very long-winded with trunk roads regularly taking more than fifteen years from first appearing on the programme to being opened to traffic. A problem to rights of way workers was that the Department appeared to work in a rather desultory fashion on a wide variety of schemes and it was difficult to find out which ones were really active.

Since the formation of the Highways Agency, a different approach has been adopted. The roads programme has been reviewed with a number of unlikely or unpopular schemes having been dropped entirely. The remainder have been classified into three categories. Those in category 1 and 2 are actually been worked on whilst those in category 3 are intended to be built sometime but are not actually in preparation. The intention of this is that with work concentrated on the category 1 and 2 schemes, it will be possible to complete them more quickly. This makes it much easier for us to tell which schemes are actually in progress and to target our efforts more effectively. It follows, of course, that rights of way workers must be aware of which category 1 and 2 trunk road schemes exist in their area.

Although the Government adopts the approach that the need for a road cannot be challenged, it does consult on the line of the road. This takes place after the stage of identifying options and determining their approximate costs. The Highways Agency will normally produce a leaflet setting out the options and will hold a public exhibition where staff are available to explain them. For example, if a bypass round a town is proposed then options may be displayed of a number of different lines for the bypass, perhaps passing on each side of the town. The public will be asked for their views on which option should be proceeded with. The Highways Agency normally consults with the national bodies representing rights of way users, who can then consult their local organisations.

At this stage rights of way workers should identify the effect of the various lines on public paths and other minor highways. If one line seems to be preferable in this respect then the Agency should be told so. But perhaps more useful is the fact that the consultation is an opportunity for us to lay down a marker that we expect proper consideration to be given to minor highways and for us to specify the conditions under which we would not object to the line of the road. For example, if a dual-carriageway is proposed that crosses a public path then the Agency should be made aware that an objection may be expected unless a route over or under the new road is provided.

After the consultation stage, the Agency will make an announcement as to which of the options it intends to proceed with; this is circulated in the same way as the original consultation. This is the time at which the Agency gets down to the detailed design; it is also the trigger for us to get involved. Find out who is the project manager for the scheme and make an appointment to meet. At a meeting it is possible to expand on our requirements and to drop hints as to how much trouble can be expected if they are not met!

Roads promoted by local highway authorities follow a similar pattern. Authorities prepare a document known as the Local Transport Plan (LTP). This document is published every five years and should be available for inspection at council offices and perhaps at local libraries. This includes the proposals for roads for at least the next five years with at least a broad picture of what can be expected in the following fifteen to twenty years. The LTP is subject to public consultation and this allows rights of way workers to make clear their requirements for facilities at an early stage. Again, it is necessary to meet the project manager and to start to discuss requirements as early as possible.

12.6. The legal framework

Before starting the negotiating stage it is important to be clear as to the law relating to the building of new roads. The key point is that just as existing highways cannot be interfered with by private interests, they equally cannot be interfered with by road builders except with specific legal authority. That authority comes by way of a side roads order made by the Secretary of State for Transport (1).

A side roads order can be made where a new road is to be constructed or an existing road to be improved. It allows side roads, that is existing highways including public paths which cross or join the main road, to be altered. They can be diverted or their levels changed or they can be stopped up completely. An order can also allow the construction of a new section of road. Taken together, these give wide powers to alter roads in the vicinity of the new road. It is worth noting that there is actually no limit as to how far the alterations may be from the line of the main road; any changes have only to be on a road that intersects the main road and presumably have to arise from changes on it.

The law requires that the Secretary of State may only make an order closing a highway if he is satisfied that a "reasonably convenient" alternative exists or will be provided. The phrase "reasonably convenient" is at the heart of the problems of side road orders because there are different interpretations of what it means.

Rights of way groups argue that it means that the alternative must provide broadly the same facility to users as did the old. As the two are different there must be an element of judgment as to which is best, but it may be argued that the meaning of the requirement is that a reasonable person would view the two routes as broadly similar. The essence of this approach is that it is an absolute test of the alternative route; the result is not altered by either the number of people who use the route or the cost to the road builders of providing it.

Unfortunately, officers of the Highways Agency tend to try and apply a different interpretation. They argue that the phrase means as convenient an alternative as can reasonably be provided. Thus, they claim, they can allow for the number of people using a route and the cost of alternatives. They argue that it is legitimate to provide an alternative that is demonstrably very much less convenient than the route closed if few people use it, or a proper alternative would be costly. What effectively is being proposed is the use of cost-benefit criteria with the implication that routes can be closed if the disbenefits to users are less than the costs of providing a proper alternative.

The reason why the agency argues this way will be obvious. Modern roads are being made wider and wider, with the latest proposals for the M25 being a quadruple-carriageway motorway of no less than fourteen lanes. Bridges over or under such roads would be extremely costly. Assuming the user groups' interpretation of the law would mean that bridges would often have to be provided; a strict application of cost-benefit criteria would result in almost all routes being closed.

The technical arguments against the agency's interpretation are beyond the scope of this chapter and it is only possible to give the broad outlines. The key point is whether it is equitable to treat all users of highways as a single whole and thus offset disbenefits to local walkers and riders against benefits to vehicles on a main road. Our argument is that the two groups, although both subsets of the public, are really quite separate and that the rights of the local non-motorised users ought to be recognised as being on a par with owners of private property rights. If, for example, a new road requires one hole from a golf course then the invariable response is for the club to be provided with a replacement hole. No engineer would even consider applying cost-benefit criteria to the problem of whether the disbenefits of a seventeen hole course would be less than the cost of providing the new hole.

Not only is the approach to rights of way different from that applied to private property rights but the latter is increasingly applied to environmental impacts. As a result of strong pressure from the environmental lobby, new roads construction now often involves substantial costs to ameliorate any adverse effects. Again the approach is to assume that the effect of the road should be as neutral as possible; certainly cost-benefit criteria do not seem to be applied. This has given rise to the bizarre situation that underpasses are provided for toads and badgers but not for members of the public!

12.7. Forming alliances

Whilst we believe that the approach of the Highways Agency is technically and legally flawed, we do have the problem that the Secretary of State has the final say, even for trunk roads where he is judge and jury in his own case. It follows that to actually get our own way requires some careful planning.

To get a good deal it is often helpful to form alliances with other bodies with similar aims. This makes it more difficult for road builders to weaken the opposition by playing off one group against the other. Which groups to ally with will depend on the local situation. However, it will usually be better to avoid getting involved with groups who are opposed totally to the new road; they are likely to be on the losing side and this will not help to get the concessions we want. It will generally be best to ally with groups concerned specifically with rights of way. In previous cases, groupings of the British Horse Society, Ramblers Association, and Cyclists Touring Club have successfully put the case for proper consideration of non-motorised users (2).

In addition, it is worth establishing whether county or district councils are prepared to become involved. Where the new road is a trunk road that affects local highways, the views of the highway authority responsible for those roads tend to carry more weight than those of ordinary members of the public. Where the main road is not a trunk road the highway authority for both the new road and existing paths will be the county council, but it may still be worth lobbying the district council to see whether it will be prepared to take up the matter on behalf of the residents of their area. However, it has to be recognised that councils are often so carried away with the supposed benefits of the new road that they may not be prepared to argue for proper provisions for non-motorised users in case this affects the case for the new road.

12.8. Preparing the ground

The legal position seems clear enough; the test of whether an alternative is convenient or not is an absolute one and the result should not depend on how much the existing route is used. However, in practice the DETR appears to ignore this requirement unless a need for the route can be established. The approach does, in fact, appear to be the pragmatic one of considering whether there is likely to be significant public concern over the closure. Given this unsatisfactory starting point, rights of way workers need to be clear that to obtain a good deal they will have to establish a good case for the retention of the existing route.

To succeed in this requires some pre-planning. The process starts as soon as any potential road lines are made public. The lines need to be checked to see if they intersect public paths, byways or local roads used by non-motorised traffic. It is particularly important to check whether there are any routes that are believed to have a status different from that recorded on the definitive map.

Where routes are recorded and in use, it is necessary to lay down markers for the designers at the earliest possible stage. As many local people as possible should be encouraged to respond to consultation documents and to comment on potential problems. For example, suppose a village bypass crosses a bridleway leading out of the village. As many people as possible should be persuaded to take part in any consultation process, to point out the importance of the bridleway and to say that if that line were to be chosen then they would expect the bridleway to be taken over or under the new road. In this way, the designer is made aware at the earliest stage of the importance of taking the route into account.

The situation is more difficult where the path is recorded but not used due to obstruction. Again it is necessary to lay down a marker at the consultation stage, but there is certainly a risk of the road designer taking the line that no replacement is needed because the route is not used. Because of the long period taken to design a road, all is not lost. The best approach is to take firm action to persuade (or if necessary force) the local highway authority to carry out its duty and make the path available. If this can be done relatively quickly, it may then be promoted to local users such that by the time design gets seriously under way there will be reasonable use of the path.

Even greater problems arise where a path is not properly recorded, for example a bridleway may be recorded as a footpath. The first difficulty is that road designers, not being rights of way experts, frequently believe that the definitive map is definitive in the sense that no rights can exist if they are not recorded. Even if they can be convinced that they have a legal duty to take account of all highways, they still have a defence for not doing so if a route cannot be proved to be a highway. In some cases, for example byways that are recorded as highway by the local authority, it will simply be necessary to point out the existence of the additional routes. However, where the status is disputed the only real way forward is to make an application for a definitive map modification order. The difficulty is that these often take a long time to be processed by the local authority. However, where there is an important reason for deciding an application then it should be possible for any queues of orders to be jumped. In any case, the very fact that an application has been lodged will itself lay down a marker to road designers that the status of the route is not necessarily as shown on the definitive map.

Experience has also shown that designers tend to take more account of paths that form part of some coherent network. For example, they will be more likely to respect a long-distance route or a circular route which has been promoted to the public. This obviously opens the way to tactics of trying to be one step ahead of road-builders and ensuring that promoted routes are in place before the threat to the route materialises.

12.9. Grade crossings of main roads

Where the line of an existing minor highway is crossed by the line of a new road other than a motorway, the designer may well try to maintain the existing route and simply form a crossing on the level. In these circumstances, it is normal to make a side roads order to extinguish the old route within the boundaries of the new road, with the grade crossing of the new road forming the alternative. As the public must take a new highway as they find it, they cannot complain that the new road has obstructed the old. However, this procedure does allow an objection to be made to the side roads order on the basis that the grade crossing is not a reasonably convenient alternative to the previous route.

This is an issue that causes a good deal of argument. The basic cause of this is that the DETR advice to road designers completely fails to recognise the problems of crossing high-speed rural roads. Instead, the methods suggested by the department are based on research carried out on urban roads with intense but relatively slow-moving traffic. Results from research of this type indicate that with a traffic flow of

2000 veh/hour a pedestrian (or presumably a rider) would face a mean wait of around 19 seconds for a gap long enough to cross the road (3).

The reality is quite different. Drivers tend to proceed on main roads at high speed and on the assumption that there will be no obstacles in their way. This means that people wishing to cross the road have to treat roads rather in the way that they treat railway level crossings. Applying the same safety logic as the Health and Safety Executive applies to railway crossings (4) indicates two types of problem: inadequate sighting distances and excessive waiting times.

Roads are designed such that drivers can see along the road a sufficient distance to be able to stop from the assumed design speed of the road if they see an obstacle in their path. But where non-motorised users assume that vehicles are not going to stop, the sighting distances required by them exceed the normal stopping distances needed by vehicles. It follows that there may well not be a sufficient safe sighting distance even where a road has been designed according to normal rules. Problems arise especially with wider types of roads which, of course, need longer crossing and sighting times. There are good reasons for suggesting that roads wider than the standard 7.3m single carriageway design are inherently unsafe for crossing; this includes the 10m wide single-carriageway designs often specified where traffic levels are higher.

If the crossing times can be determined, it is possible to calculate statistically what is the average wait for a gap of sufficient length to come along. The theory is beyond the scope of this chapter, but it is sufficient to note that the wait increases dramatically with either the required crossing time or with traffic flow. Taking a 10m road for example, the mean wait with a traffic flow of 2000 vehs/hour is in theory almost an hour rather than the 19 seconds claimed by the DETR! Looking more practically at the maximum flows which would allow a mean wait of no more than 2 minutes, this can be shown to be 1150 vehs/hour for a 7.3m single carriageway or 900 vehs/hour for a 10m road. As a 10m road would not be used for flows as low as this, it again points to the fact that grade crossings of wide single-carriageway roads should not be used. It should, of course, be clear that grade crossings of dual-carriageway roads are totally out of the question except in rare cases where the carriageways are so far apart that it is possible to wait safely in the space between; then the carriageways can be treated as if they were separate roads.

Predictions of traffic on new roads are normally in terms of Annual Average Daily Traffic (AADT for short). As a broad rule of thumb, a flow of around 10% of the AADT flow can be expected in each of the busiest two or three hours each day. This leads us to our own rules of thumb; grade crossings on high-speed roads are only acceptable on 7.3m single-carriageway roads with AADT flows of less than 10,000 vehs/day.

It should go without saying that the flow used is for the design year with high growth assumptions. The whole idea of different assumptions and a design year is to allow a robust design that performs satisfactorily in the design year under the full range of traffic assumptions. The point is made here because it is not unknown for designers to try and persuade rights of way workers into accepting designs that work only in the opening year, or with low growth assumptions for traffic. So be prepared to refute this argument!

12.10. Grade-separated crossings

Where it is found that a grade crossing is not practicable then it will be necessary to argue for a route passing over or under the new road, or a *grade-separated* crossing to use the engineers' jargon. Whilst we will be arguing that a reasonably convenient alternative route must be provided, it does not follow that the best option will be simply a bridge or subway precisely on the line of the existing path. There may well be other options that are cheaper and will still be reasonably convenient; clearly the designer will be looking for these. We ought also to be interested in whether we can identify ways of actually improving the network as part of the new road. Clearly, there is great scope for a constructive dialogue with the engineer responsible, and this makes it all the more important that it is started as soon as possible. To get the most out of the negotiations it is important to understand some technical points about the design and construction of roads.

On a modern road designed for high-speed traffic, there are stringent rules about the profile along the road. These are necessary to avoid excessively steep gradients, sudden changes of gradient that would give a roller-coaster effect, and humps that would restrict visibility. To achieve this it will rarely be possible to follow the profile of the natural ground surface and many sections of the road have to be in cuttings or on embankments. This creates further problems in that earthmoving is expensive, particularly where the material taken out of the cuttings does not balance that required for the embankments. Even where a balance can be achieved, it will still be important for the engineer to minimise the movement of earth from one part of the road to another as this is also very expensive.

To achieve an alignment which meets all these requirements is not easy, and these days it is usually done by computer. The significant aspect from our point of view is that when an optimum solution has been found, any changes to the levels of a road can have very substantial costs. It will rarely be possible to revise levels to fit in rights of way crossings and it will usually be necessary to regard the profile of the road as fixed.

The best way of forming grade-separated crossings will depend on whether the road is above or below ground. As a general rule, the cheapest place to cross a new road will be where the road is on an embankment and a subway can be provided through it. This will be constructed by building the subway box first, and then placing the earth of the embankment around it. However, there are practical aspects to consider. A subway is no good if the bottom fills up with rain and to avoid this it is necessary to provide drainage. This means that the floor level of the subway cannot be any lower than the level of local ditches and so on, or it will be impossible to provide the drainage without expensive and unreliable pumping.

This effectively means that the subway has to fit in between the constraints of the fixed road alignment and the fixed water level. In many cases, of course, the difference between these two levels will not create any difficulty. If there is plenty of depth it may well be possible to provide a subway of the corrugated steel type which will generally be cheaper than the concrete box type, but does require a reasonable depth of embankment above to spread the load. It is inevitable that there will be situations where it is simply not possible to fit in a subway of standard height, although in some cases a sub-standard subway would be possible. This point is looked at again in the next section.

Bridges over the road will generally be more expensive. It is often not appreciated how large a structure is required. For example, consider a bridge which carries a path over a 8m wide road in a cutting 6m deep. Although the road itself is only 8m wide it will have 1m wide hard strips together with 2m wide level verges before the start of the cutting sides. The cuttings sides will be typically at a gradient of 1 in 3 giving a further width of 18m on each side. This means that although the bridge structure crosses a road only 8m wide, it will have a total length of no less than 50m. In any case a cutting is the best possible situation. Where a bridge is needed in flat country, it will be necessary to have long approach ramps which means either more structure, perhaps with zigzag ramps or preferably approach embankments. These, of course, substantially push up the cost of the crossing.

In view of the high cost of separate crossings, designers will often look at combining path crossings with other routes. It will often be possible to combine a public path with a farm accommodation route, that is, a private access for agricultural traffic. It may also be possible to use a grade-separated route being provided for a minor road. If these are little-used then such an approach might be acceptable; obviously we would look askance at sharing a route with an A or B road.

More worthy of consideration is the use of bridges carrying the road over railways, rivers or canals. It will often be found that increasing the length of a bridge span costs relatively little as the extra cost of the bridge is offset by reductions in the cost of the embankment. By an increase in the span of the bridge it may be possible to squeeze in a path parallel to the railway or watercourse.

Another possibility that should not be ignored is the joint use of culverts carrying the road over streams. Most new roads will be found to have a large number of culverts, often of surprisingly large cross-section. The reason for this is that culverts have to be designed for a flood flow which very rarely occurs. In some cases the culvert could be replaced by a rather larger subway at little cost. The stream would then be piped beneath the path or in a channel alongside. On the rare occasions of flood conditions the path would also be flooded but this could be a small price to pay for the provision of a subway under a busy road.

12.11. *Planning rights of way crossings*

It will be clear from the above that the cost of a route over or under a new road can fluctuate considerably according to the circumstances. Most importantly, the cost of crossing the same road could vary greatly between different potential crossing points only a short distance apart.

This fact is clearly of significance in planning rights of way crossings. It may well be that if it is assumed that paths cannot be diverted then the cost of providing bridges and subways at all crossing points will be prohibitive. If, on the other hand, paths are diverted so as to cross at suitable points then the cost could be acceptable.

Whilst road designers are aware of this they are generally reluctant to consider diversions other than those immediately adjacent to the new road. Typically such a diversion consists of stopping up only the section of path under the new road and providing new paths along both sides of the road to, say, an accommodation bridge. Obviously, there is a limit to how far a path can reasonably be diverted in this way.

A much more satisfactory solution is to consider all the rights of way within a corridor of, say, 1km on either side of the proposed road. Often a diversion starting further back is more readily brought to a suitable crossing point without excessive additional distance or sections alongside the new road. There is no legal reason why diversions needed for a new road cannot start some distance away; the normal reason for designers ignoring this possibility is a reluctance to become involved in the complexities of public paths.

12.12. Design standards

As negotiations proceed on the provision of facilities, consideration often needs to be given to the design standards to be employed, particularly in respect of structures carrying paths over or under new roads. At first sight it might seem sensible to press for the highest possible standards. However, this can be counter productive and a measure of caution is required.

Any process of design involves taking into account a large variety of different factors and coming up with the best solution within certain constraints. An engineer with flair will rise to the challenge of the problem; but for the mediocre the whole thing becomes too mind-boggling. The only way a solution can be found is to introduce constraints that are not really there so as to limit the number of possible solutions. Hence the popularity with engineers of design standards or rules which they like to believe are absolutely rigid, even when they are not. This means that suggestions as to standards that we regard as desirable may very well be taken as rigid rules, and perhaps not always to our advantage.

A good example is the height of a subway to carry a bridleway under a new road. The point was made in 12.10 above that there may be limits on the available height created by the road alignment and the water level in nearby streams. A rigid adherence to a fixed standard height may lead to the conclusion that a subway at a particular location is not possible. This in turn may well lead to the conclusion that no provision should be made. If, on the other hand, a less rigid approach had been followed then it might have been possible to have achieved a crossing but with a slightly sub-standard height.

The DETR specification gives the absolute minimum height for a subway as 2.7m. The BHS, on the other hand, suggests an absolute minimum of 2.8m (the metric equivalent of the standard height of 9' for overhanging structures that was applied throughout the Middle Ages!) But in any negotiations, great care needs to be taken to avoid our higher standard being used against us to justify a subway not being provided.

We should hold in reserve the possibility that even lower subways could be used. Many subways built to pedestrian dimensions (2.3 - 2.6m depending on length) are regularly used by people on horses. Remember that the majority of riders are children on ponies who may well be able to ride through safely. Adults might have to dismount and lead their horses through; an inconvenience but better than having no crossing at all.

Similar arguments apply to overbridges. It is important to note that bridges for footpaths, cycleways and bridleways all use the same design loadings; hence a bridleway bridge of the same width as a footbridge does not need to be any stronger. In the past, footbridges were usually built with steps but pressure from the lobby for people with disabilities has meant that as far as possible such bridges are provided with ramps with a maximum gradient of 1:10. Such ramps would present no difficulty to horses and with a minimum width of 1.8m there should be no difficulty in getting a horse over such a footbridge.

The BHS recommend a width of 3m with an absolute minimum of 2.2m. Whilst this is a useful starting point for negotiations, it is important not to give the impression that this is an entirely rigid standard. In at least one case where an authority has provided a footpath rather than a bridleway alternative to an existing bridleway, the additional cost of providing a bridge to the BHS standard has been quoted as justification.

Finally, the questions of bridge parapets is of importance. The types of parapet normally used on footbridges have been found to create problems for riders. It was thought to be not high enough, and riders feared that they might fall over. In addition, the use of open parapets caused some horses to shy from the appearance of high vehicles that seemed to be heading directly for them. After a great deal of negotiation between the BHS and the DETR, a revised equestrian parapet was agreed. This is 1.8m high, with the bottom 0.6m being in the form of solid infilling to prevent the horses seeing vehicles approaching. This should always be asked for on bridges that replace existing bridleway routes.

It should be noted that even the new standard appears to have given rise to some problems through horses still shying at traffic seen through the upper 1.2m of the parapet. The DETR has resisted solid infilling over the whole height of the parapet on the grounds of cost and aesthetics. In practice the cost implications appear negligible, and indeed many bridges carrying motorways over local roads have had solid panels fitted already to reduce noise levels. Whilst the desire of the DETR to maintain the appearance of its bridges is praiseworthy, there seems something wrong if this prevents them being used by the traffic for which they were designed. Thus there would seem to be a case for bridleway workers to press for solid parapets, but again it is important not to give the impression that a bridge without solid parapets is the same as no bridge at all; if you do there is a fair chance of finishing up with the latter!

Notes to chapter 12

1. Highways Act 1980. Section 14 covers side road orders for all-purpose principal roads, that is A roads other than motorways. Similar powers for new motorways are in Section 18. There are also powers in the Town and Country Planning Act 1990, Section 248. These apply to all highways but only where closures or diversions are needed to prevent danger to traffic on the main road, or to facilitate its free flow.

2. Breaking point - the severance by road schemes of routes used by cyclists, equestrians and ramblers. Metropolitan Transport Research Unit. 1993.

3. Transport and Road Research Laboratory. Report SR 356.

4. Railway Construction and Operation Requirements - Part F: Protection of footpath and bridleway level crossings. Health and Safety Executive. 1993.

13
LEGAL ORDERS AND PUBLIC INQUIRIES

13.1. Introduction

An important part of rights of way work is dealing with the various legal orders that either alter the network or modify the definitive map. This chapter describes the legal processes that have to be gone through in making an order of this sort, and how they can be successfully opposed. The steps needed to make a formal objection are set out with advice on how to mount a challenge to an order at a public inquiry if need be.

Although it is probably more common for rights of way workers to be on the defensive at public inquiries, this will not always be the case. If a local authority can be persuaded to make an order to create a new path or add one to the definitive map, there may well be objections from owners or other members of the public leading to a public inquiry. In this case the authority may well want a rights of way worker to present evidence in their support. Many of the skills needed to oppose orders that we do not want are equally useful in support of those we do.

13.2. Orders affecting public paths

There are a number of legal orders that can alter the network of public paths. The processes that are gone through and the opportunities for opposing them are similar and so will be dealt with together. There are three main types of orders:

(a) Public path orders. These may be made under both highways and planning powers and create, divert or extinguish public paths. These are by far the most common orders that will be met with.

(b) Definitive map modification orders. These orders do not themselves alter the path network but seek to record on the definitive map changes that have already happened or claims that the definitive map is wrong.

(c) Side roads orders. These are orders made to modify the network of all highways, including public paths, as a result of proposals to construct a new main road.

Whilst these are the types of order most commonly met with, it should be noted that there are a number of other types dealing with such matters as military land and open-cast mining. In the event of such orders being met with it will be necessary to

173

establish what the opportunities are for objection. In most cases the procedure will be found to be similar to that for the common types of order listed above.

It is important to understand the stages of making an order, particularly as the terms used tend to be confusing to beginners. The first formal stage is the *making* of an order. Although this sounds as if it is final, it is in fact only a draft. The order is then advertised to the public and there is an opportunity for objection during a specified period. If there are no objections then the order may be *confirmed* by the body making the order, that is to say it becomes final. If an objection is made then the order cannot be confirmed until the matter has been fully considered by an independent inspector. This process often involves a public inquiry.

Most orders will be made by local authorities and this chapter will generally be written as if this were the case. However, there will be circumstances in which orders are made by Government departments. Most commonly these will be side roads orders for trunk roads but there may also be some orders made under planning and highways powers. The process for making and confirming the order, and the opportunities for objection, are the same as for orders made by a council.

13.3. The making of the order

Although the making of the order is the first formal stage in the process, many councils have introduced an earlier consultation stage. Knowing that most objections to public path orders come from bodies representing path users, they first circulate drafts of any orders to them. If user bodies indicate that they have no objection, then the council can go forward with some confidence that the order will be able to be confirmed. It will, of course, still be necessary to go through the various legal processes and individual members of the public may well put in their own objections.

If, on the other hand, user bodies indicate their intention to object to the real order, this may well dissuade the authority from even making the order. Public path orders are often merely for the convenience of landowners, and councils may well feel disinclined to go to all the trouble of a disputed order with no benefit to them at the end of it.

The system of advance consultation is clearly of advantage to everybody and authorities should be strongly encouraged to follow the practice. Public path workers on their part should show their support for the system by replying promptly, even where no objections are being made. This can be easily done by preparing standard forms, one of which can be quickly filled in for each draft order.

The making of an order involves drawing up a legal document which is then sealed on behalf of the authority. Public notice has to be given in a local newspaper and in notices posted on site. Importantly to rights of way workers, notice has also to be sent to various national bodies that represent path users. These bodies will normally pass the orders on to their local representatives for action.

It will be appreciated that this system is not entirely safe. If a council forgets to send an order to the national body then it will probably not be known that the order has been made. Similarly, the order might be sent on to the wrong person or lost in the post. Obviously, anybody receiving an order wrongly should immediately send it on to the right person. To play safe, it is helpful if path workers keep their ears to the ground so that they know which orders to expect and can take action if they are not received.

The public notice of the order will specify a period within which objections can be made. It is vital that a decision is made during that period and that if an objection is made, it is made in time. If no objection is made during the official period then the authority will simply confirm the order and nothing more can be done. If, on the other hand, any objection is made then the process is stopped in its tracks. The order cannot be confirmed unless either all objections have been withdrawn or the full process of arbitration has been gone through.

13.4. Should an objection be made?

The period during which an objection can be made is quite short and this may pose problems. A difficult decision may be involved and more time may be required to consult others or to visit the site. There is a simple rule - if in doubt, object!

If no objection is made and it is later decided that one should have been then it will be too late. But if an objection is made, then the whole process stops. Because public inquiries are expensive and time-consuming, authorities faced with an objection will invariably commence negotiations to see if there is any basis on which the objector will withdraw. There is no difficulty at all in withdrawing an objection and this is very frequently done. So if there is any doubt at all about the situation the right approach is to make an objection but to be prepared to withdraw it later.

Particular care should be taken with packages of concurrent orders. For example, a deal may be made with a landowner to extinguish some paths in exchange for others being created and a set of orders made to achieve this. Although the orders may be presented in this way, there is nothing to prevent the authority confirming some orders but not others. So paths could be lost without others being provided to replace them, particularly if members of the public were to object to the creation elements.

The way to play safe is to put in a holding objection to the extinguishments. Once the objection period is up then it is known whether there are any objections to the creations. Assuming that there are none, then the objections to the extinguishments can be withdrawn but subject to the condition that confirmation of the whole package takes place.

It is necessary that any formal objections should be made in writing to the person specified in the advertisement. It is preferable to object as early as possible within the period of objection and to request a confirmation in writing that an objection has been made. Then the authority cannot claim that it has not received the objection.

In making an objection, reasons should be stated. This is so that it can be seen that the objection is relevant. However, it is not necessary at this stage to give the whole case away. For example, if an order was made to remove a path from the definitive map on the basis of evidence that a mistake had been made, then an objection might be made on the grounds that "the evidence is insufficient to justify the making of the order". This would establish that the grounds were relevant unlike, for example, a claim that the path was needed. At the same time it would not give away the details of the case that might ultimately be presented at a public inquiry.

13.5. *Negotiations*

Once a formal objection has been lodged, the council cannot confirm the order itself. It then has three avenues open to it. It may simply give it up as a bad job and abandon the order, particularly if the order is primarily for the benefit of an owner and gives no real benefit to the council. If it wants to persevere with the order it will need to be passed on to be dealt with by an independent inspector. However, this will rarely be done immediately. The normal practice is to commence negotiations with the objectors to see if some agreement can be reached by which they will formally withdraw their objection. Once all objections have been withdrawn, then the council can itself confirm the order exactly as it would have done if there had been no objections in the first place.

In some cases it will be possible to reach an agreement that will allow objections to be withdrawn. This may be unconditional, for example where the authority is able to provide additional information that was not previously clear. This may also be the case where a holding objection had been made to allow time for further enquiries. In other cases it may be possible to withdraw the objection but on certain conditions. The case of concurrent orders has previously been pointed out. Where there were no objections to the creations and the authority undertakes in writing to confirm all the orders together, then a holding objection can be withdrawn.

Another situation where a conditional withdrawal might be appropriate concerns side roads orders. It may be that a diversion of a path would be acceptable subject to certain constructional details. For example, it might be acceptable to divert a bridleway across a bridge over a new road if the parapets are to the equestrian standard. Such details are not normally specified in the order. In these circumstances a formal objection could be made to the diversion on the grounds that the new route would not be a reasonable alternative. This objection could then be later withdrawn if a written undertaking was given that the parapets would be provided.

In many cases the proposals will be simply unacceptable and it will not be possible to withdraw if they remain unaltered. However, it is sometimes the case that proposals are broadly acceptable but that one or two details are not. In these circumstance it may be that agreement can be reached that a modified set of proposals would be acceptable.

A local authority is not allowed to confirm a modified order, even if all the objections have been withdrawn. This is because the modified order might become unacceptable to someone else who would then want to object. Thus if a modified set of proposals is agreed, the correct procedure is for the authority to go back to the start, abandon the original order and make a new one.

If agreement cannot be reached and the authority still wants to press on with the order, it must then forward the order to the Secretary of State for a decision. He appoints an independent inspector who will arrange for all the parties to have a full opportunity to put their views. This will usually mean holding a public inquiry, or in some cases the matter can be dealt with by written representations. The inspector will hold the inquiry or receive written representations and make a report. In most cases he will have delegated powers of the secretary of state to actually make the decision as to whether the order can be confirmed. In some cases, for example side roads orders, the inspector will make a recommendation but the final decision is made by the Secretary of State. In practice, it is quite rare for the advice of the inspector not to be followed.

13.6. Public inquiries - what are they?

Objecting to orders often leads eventually to a public inquiry being called. It is important for rights of way workers to gain experience in presenting cases at these inquiries, and thus it is necessary to understand the background to inquiries and how they differ from courts of law.

Courts of law are essentially places of conflict. It is not too fanciful to argue that over the centuries they have developed from the mediaeval system of trial by conflict. In those days, when people were in dispute, they hired muscular champions to battle it out at some agreed venue. In our less violent times the arena has moved to a court of law and the champions are skilled in verbal rather than physical battling, but the principle remains the same.

A judge is really in the position of a referee, to see fair play between the combatants and to decide who wins. It is not his job to establish the truth of the matter; he is there to assess the evidence. To some extent at least, the role of a judge tends to be to assess the technical skill of the lawyers rather than the inherent merits of the case.

All this means that a court of law is essentially for lawyers. Courts operate according to obscure rules, which the layman might well suspect are a form of restrictive practice to prevent non-lawyers becoming involved. In any case, the way in which courts operate means that it is difficult for ordinary individuals to present their own case without legal representation. Because of the system of the loser having to pay the winner's costs, someone conducting their own case is still at risk of having to pay heavy costs for the other side. This means that conducting one's own case in a court of law is usually a false economy; if one does become involved in lawsuits it is more or less essential to employ a lawyer.

For all these reasons, courts are not really places for non-lawyers. If all disputes arising from public path orders had to be resolved in the courts, there can be no doubt that most people would be intimidated into not objecting. Fortunately, this has been recognised and the forum for resolving such disputes is a public inquiry. The whole basis of a public inquiry is that members of the public should be able to put their own case without any intimidation.

It is arguable that the concept of public inquiries is also derived from a long-standing tradition of British life, that of commissioners. The idea was that the King would appoint commissioners to enquire into a particular aspect of life and then report back, or even take decisions on behalf of the King. Commissioners had a duty to find the facts and would normally take evidence from people who had knowledge about the matter being looked into. Unlike judges, there was no rule that commissioners could only consider formal evidence or that they could not take into account their own knowledge. Indeed, the contrary was the case; commissioners were, and still are, chosen specifically because of their specialist skills in the area being considered.

Although public inquiries are a modern concept, the approach closely follows that adopted by commissioners. The inquiry is run by an inspector who is independent. He is not a civil servant, although obviously his wages have to be met from public funds. Inspectors are rarely lawyers which means that they have no vested interest in maintaining obscure procedures that only lawyers understand. Like commissioners, they are charged with finding all the information that they can and are not limited to a consideration of evidence.

For example, suppose that an order has been made to divert a path but an objection has been made on the grounds that the new route is less attractive to the public. The inspector will hear the views of both sides as expressed at the public inquiry, but will also walk the routes both in the company of the two sides and on his own. His decision will obviously take account of what he has been told at the inquiry but he can also apply his own judgment and experience and take into account what he has actually seen, even if no one has pointed it out. This is quite different from the approach that a judge would be obliged to follow.

The most important role of the inspector is to conduct the public inquiry. There are no rules laid down as to how this should be done but the key thing is for him to ensure a fair hearing for anybody who has a point to make. Public inquiries are very much in the British tradition of free speech and fair play. Inspectors invariably lay great stress on allowing people a fair hearing and will be particularly on their guard to avoid any unfair intimidation.

The rules allow any person to be represented by any other. It follows that it is not possible to keep lawyers from getting in on the act if individuals decide that they want to have legal representation. Inspectors will generally keep them in their place; it is a public inquiry and they should have no privileges over other members of the public. Beginners are often concerned about being pitted against professional lawyers, but within the rules of a public inquiry, amateurs can often give them a good run for their client's money.

The high cost of lawyers is, in fact, where we have an advantage. A landowner who wants to be represented by even a solicitor is likely to have to pay more than £100 an hour for his services. Barristers of course cost a good deal more. This means that nobody can really afford to pay for a lawyer to really get into every detail of a case. Amateurs can, and often do, spend weeks preparing a case and thus have a good start on the professionals. If rights of way workers can learn the necessary presentational skills, there is no reason why a good success rate should not be achieved.

Although public inquiries are much less formal than a court of law, it is important to be aware that there are rules. These mainly relate to the great importance attached to people being able to speak without intimidation. It follows that people are only allowed to put their points when invited to by the inspector. Others are required to keep quiet whilst people are speaking. This is not a political meeting and interruptions, cheering, clapping, heckling and so on will not be tolerated. To ensure this the inspector will make it quite clear that he is in charge. By convention the inspector is addressed as "Sir" or "Madam" as appropriate. As inspectors can exercise a great deal of personal judgment in coming to a decision, common sense dictates that they should be treated with particular respect.

13.7. Applications for costs

A very important difference between the procedures followed by courts and public inquiries is in who pays the legal costs. In courts of law the costs of both sides have to be met by the loser. This means that getting involved in lawsuits is a risky business. In public inquiries the normal practice is for everybody to pay their own costs. The main exception to this relates to path creation orders where owners whose objections are overruled are entitled to their legal costs as well as compensation for loss of value.

However, it should be noted that the Secretary of State has the power to order the payment of costs where a person has behaved unreasonably. In practice this will only be the case where somebody has deliberately disrupted the process. An example might be if somebody objected to an order, insisted on their being a public inquiry and then failed to turn up without any reason. It should be emphasised that public inquiries are precisely for the public to object to proposals that concern them and if this is done in a reasonable way there is no question of costs having to be paid. This is true even if the nature of the objection might be regarded as unreasonable.

It is sometimes argued that it might be held to be unreasonable to make an objection which is not relevant to the order and to refuse to withdraw it even when this has been pointed out. An example might be an objection to a definitive map modification order based on need rather than evidence of the existence of rights. It is doubtful whether an order for costs would be made in these circumstances. The difficulty is that the question of what is an irrelevant objection may be a rather obscure one that the inspector has to decide. Whilst the authority making the order might well tell an objector that his objection is irrelevant, the objector is entitled to disbelieve what he has been told by a body with a vested interest in the withdrawal of the objection.

The point is not of too much importance to skilled path workers who, of course, do not waste their own valuable time in making objections that are irrelevant and thus can only fail. However, the downside of this is that little can be done to prevent members of the public, or even organisations representing walkers, from objecting to modification orders upgrading footpaths to bridleways on the grounds of the effect on walkers. This tends to waste a lot of time but it is the price we have to pay for our own freedom to object.

Occasionally one finds owners or their legal advisors who try and take advantage of objectors' inexperience by telling them that if they persevere in their objection the owners will apply for costs on the grounds of unreasonable behaviour. This, of course, is just bluff. As indicated above, members of the public have a perfect right to make objections, given that this is done in a proper way. If this is done then there is no risk of having to pay costs. However, where rights of way workers act as representatives of national organisations, then their advice should be sought if any concern is felt about risks being run.

13.8. Procedure at public inquiries

In theory, the inspector can adopt any procedure that he likes, so long as it is seen to be impartial. In practice, most inquiries follow a fairly similar pattern.

Care is usually taken to try and have the inquiry as close as possible to the site of the issue being discussed. For public path inquiries, this usually means the local village hall. Inquiries concerned with road orders tend to be bigger and go on longer and for these the venue is often an hotel or public hall in a nearby town.

The layout of the room is deliberately kept informal. There will be a table and chair for the inspector, and one each for the promoters of the order and for the objectors. The two sides are of equal status and there should be no question of superior facilities being provided for one side or the other. There will also be a

181

space allocated for the current witness and there should be seats for any members of the public who come along.

The inspector will open proceedings by giving his name and saying what the purpose of the inquiry is. He generally asks if any members of the press are present; this is so when he has made a decision he will be able to send a copy to any press representatives who have reported the proceedings at the inquiry.

He will then make a list of appearances, that is to say all the bodies who will be speaking, who their representatives are and whether they will be calling witnesses. The difference between a representative and a witness is an important one. A representative (often described as an advocate) is a person who presents a case but does not produce any evidence himself. He can call witnesses who produce the evidence. The witnesses are subject to questioning by the other side. The representative can be questioned only by the inspector if there are points in the presentation which he has not understood. Bodies making orders will normally have a representative (probably a solicitor) who will call witnesses. Voluntary bodies, on the other hand, are often only represented by one person who combines the role of advocate and witness and is thus subject to questioning by the other side.

The inspector will first ask who represents the body making the order. The advocate will give his name and list any witnesses that he is going to call. The inspector will then ask those bodies who have put in formal objections to identify themselves. Now is the time for the representatives of the objectors to give their names and say whether they will be calling any witnesses. The inspector will then ask whether there are any other people who will wish to speak. He is not obliged to listen to anyone who has not made a formal objection but in practice inspectors invariably give a hearing to anybody who has a point to make. This can sometimes be useful, for example if rights of way workers wish to support an order that an authority is making even if the authority does not wish to call them as witnesses.

It is normal at this stage for the inspector to explain in which order he will be asking people to speak. The usual practice is for the body making the order to make its case first. This will be followed by any other person who wishes to support the order. Next the objectors present their case, followed by any members of the public who support the objection. Finally, the advocate for the order-making body will make a final statement in support of the order.

In simple cases the inquiry will be completed within a day, and it is usual for all parties to stay for the full period. Where an inquiry is expected to last longer, a different approach is normally adopted. Everybody is expected to attend the first session when the inspector compiles his list of people wishing to speak. A timetable will then be drawn up setting out the times at which people can attend to make their points. This means that it is not vital to attend at other times. Inspectors will usually try and accommodate people who are only able to attend at certain times and try and fit the inquiry timetable around these.

Having set the scene in this way, the inquiry proper gets under way with the proposers of the order setting out their case. The advocate will make an opening statement where he explains what he is intending to demonstrate. He then calls witnesses. The main witness will probably be an officer of the authority who will describe the reason why the order is being made. This may well be followed by other witnesses. For example, if an order is made to divert a path in the interests of the landowner then the first witness is likely to be a council officer who will explain why the council thought it appropriate to make the order. He might then be followed by the landowner himself to explain precisely why he would like to see the path diverted.

Normally, the witness will give a prepared statement. In a public inquiry it is allowable to read the statement which is referred to as a *proof of evidence*. It is normal for the proof to be distributed to the other parties at the inquiry. If both sides are working from proofs it is sometimes possible to negotiate an exchange of proofs before the inquiry but this may depend on tactics and whether either side wants to spring a surprise on the other.

When a witness has finished his proof of evidence his advocate may ask a few questions to bring out points of importance. When he has finished, the witness is then open to cross-examination. This means that the advocates representing the objectors may ask questions. The techniques of cross-examination are dealt with later; at this stage it is sufficient to note that the advocate will attempt to ask questions that show the evidence of the witness in a poor light.

When the objectors have finished asking questions, the witness may be asked some supplementary questions by the advocate on his own side. This is so he can try and repair the damage if the witness has made any damaging statements under cross-examination. As the other side have no opportunity of asking any further questions, the witness will not be allowed to bring forward any more evidence (that is statements of facts) that were not in his main evidence.

The above process is followed for each witness that the order-making authority wishes to call. When all the witnesses have given their evidence, the advocate will probably sum up the implications of all the evidence and why it supports the case that he is trying to make. As the advocate is not subject to cross-examination he is not allowed to bring forward any evidence himself.

The inspector is not forced to allow members of the public who have not formally objected to have their say. However, most inspectors take the line that they should hear from anyone who has anything to say. Usually, those supporting the order are allowed to speak after the authority making the order; those opposing the order speak after the formal objectors have put their case. Members of the public who do speak are treated as witnesses and are subject to cross-examination.

Now it is the turn of the objectors. Each objector will be allowed to present a case as to why the order should not be made. The procedure for the objector will be exactly the same as has been described above for the authority making the order. An opening statement can be made, witnesses called and cross-examined and a closing statement made. In practice, most objectors tend to be their own advocate and will simply give evidence and be questioned on it.

When all the objectors have made their case, together with any other people the inspector allows to speak, the advocate of the order-making authority will give a closing statement. He cannot bring any more evidence but will sum up for the authority and will try and argue why the inspector should disregard the objections that have been made.

The inspector will then close the formal part of the inquiry, thank participants for their attendance and announce any arrangements for a site inspection.

13.9. *Preparing the ground*

Let us now consider how a rights of way worker can set about preparing a case for a public inquiry. It will be assumed that the case is in the form of an objection to an order; occasionally the boot will be on the other foot but the broad principles remain the same.

The most important point to be aware of is that winning requires meticulous preparation. It is no good simply going to an inquiry and hoping that it will all fall into place. Good preparation can lead to amateurs gaining a significant advantage in that the other side is unlikely to have been able to afford the costs in professional fees of preparing the ground as fully as we can.

The first step must be to find out as much as possible about the arguments that are going to be put in support of the order. The simplest way of finding out is to ask.

If an order is made by a public body such as a council then it is accountable to the public; it cannot make orders arbitrarily nor refuse to explain why it is doing so. In practice, as was explained in 13.3 above, orders in draft form may well have already been through some sort of consultation process and at that stage the rationale for the order will have been explained. Usually the making of the order will have been approved by councillors and the reasons for making the order will have been explained to them. Remember that any reports made to councillors have to be available for inspection by the public. In some councils the making of orders is delegated to an officer but such decisions have to be recorded and open to public inspection. One would expect that the reason for the order should also be recorded.

This can give objectors another advantage over the authority making the order in that we can work out pretty well what their case is going to be whilst remaining fairly vague about our own case. This is not always the best tactic. It is always better not to have a public inquiry by persuading the authority not to make the order at the consultation stage. This will usually mean having to make it clear what our objection is, although not necessarily precisely what evidence we are going to produce. In addition it helps detailed preparations of the questions to be asked if a copy of the other side's proofs of evidence can be obtained in advance. It will usually only be possible to obtain this in exchange for the objector's proof. It is worth remembering that a professional advocate is used to thinking quickly and that he is much less likely to be put out of his stride by something unexpected than would be an amateur. So whilst something up the sleeve may be useful, it will not be so at the expense of allowing the other side to spring surprises on us.

This brings us to an important point; it is always best to try and reach agreement on as many things as possible before an inquiry. It reduces the risk of situations that are difficult to cope with, it speeds up the inquiry and thus saves our valuable time and, not least, puts the inspector in a better frame of mind! These points will not be lost on the other side who will usually cooperate to resolve as many areas of disagreement as possible, particularly on matters of fact.

Having decided what arguments to advance, it is now necessary to write out the statements to be made. In principle, there can be two of these: the proof of evidence of the witness and the advocate's closing statement. Even if only one person presents the whole case, they do so first as a witness and then as an advocate. It is not essential to have a closing statement but it is often useful. If the proof of evidence of the witness is to be circulated in advance then it will only be possible to refute in it those parts of the other side's case that they have already made public. It may well be that other points arise during the inquiry which can be refuted during the closing statement.

At first sight, it might be thought difficult to work on a closing statement of this type when it is not known what points will be made. In practice it is often possible to guess what the points will be and to work out in advance what response will be required. Again, careful preparation pays dividends.

Having written the statements it is necessary to check them very carefully for errors. Then it is necessary to try and put yourself in the position of the other side. What awkward questions would they ask? And would you be able to answer them? Looking at the proof in this way may very well enable it to be changed to avoid some potential questions. And even if they cannot be avoided, it is useful to work out a list of the sorts of questions that might be asked and to rehearse the answers.

13.10. *Presenting the arguments*

If the preparation of the case has been done thoroughly, the actual inquiry should not present too many difficulties. This section looks at some of the techniques which help to put forward a convincing case on the day.

The authority making the order will do its best to appear slick and professional. There will be an unspoken message that the objectors, whilst decent people, are really an uneducated rabble whose views need not be considered too seriously. We have to overcome this by making sure that we give as professional an air as possible. It is useful to dress in a vaguely legal style; male lawyers usually adopt a dark suit, whilst lady lawyers appear to have a uniform of dark skirt and white blouse.

It is useful to arrive sufficiently early to obtain the best seats, but remember that neither side is more important than the other and both should have equal facilities. Introduce yourself to the advocate on the other side; that is what real lawyers do and it is as well to set the tone right from the start that we expect to be treated in a professional way. It is perhaps worth pointing out here the need to adopt a detached professional air and not get worked up; getting upset will cloud your judgment and may lead to mistakes happening. It also gives an unprofessional impression. Real lawyers do not get emotional about the case they are presenting; they don't need to because they earn fat fees win or lose! They maintain the convention that the advocate on the other side is not really their competitor; rather that they are both there to assist the inspector to come to the proper decision.

As explained in 13.8, the body making the order will have the first go. It is necessary to make careful notes of the points being made. If the preparation has been done properly then there should be no unexpected points made and the responses should already have been prepared. But if anything new does come up then make a note and try and work out how best to deal with it either in the evidence to be given or the closing statement.

After each of the witnesses for the order has given evidence there will be an opportunity to ask questions. There is, of course, no obligation to ask any questions. Cross-examination is something of an art and if done badly it will hinder rather than help. It is probably better for beginners to avoid cross-examination for the first few inquiries so as to give an opportunity to study the techniques of other advocates.

If it is proposed to ask questions, this is another area where meticulous preparation helps. If you have previously established what the case for the order is, then it should be possible to work out all the weaknesses and hence which questions to ask. The aim is generally to get the witness to make conflicting statements that throw doubt on his credibility. It is also useful to get the witness to agree statements of fact that will be used in your own case. Your own witness can make the same point but there will be more impact if it has also been accepted by the other side. The objectors have an advantage here in that the witnesses for the order may not be able to guess how the objector's case is going to be developed and it is difficult for them to avoid potential traps!

When all the evidence for the order has been given, it is time for the objectors to put their case. If there are several objectors they will normally agree among themselves who will go first. If the preparation has been done properly, giving the evidence is really the simplest part of the whole process. Remember to give a copy of the proof to the inspector so that he can concentrate on what is being said rather than having to take notes. Then read the evidence as clearly as possible, resisting the temptation to gabble. It is customary to also give the opposition a copy of the proof. After the evidence has been given the other side can ask questions. Here again, preparation is important. It should be possible to anticipate the questions that are likely to be asked and thus have a slick answer ready. Again, take your time and think before giving a reply. However, it is important not to give the impression of being evasive as this may suggest that you have something to hide. It is best to answer in a firm and positive manner but without saying too much as there may be some sort of trap. Having said that, most inquiries do not hinge on allegations that people are not telling the truth and cross-examination has hardly the excitement that some people expect from watching movies of American criminal courts!

13.11. The site inspection

In public path inquiries a site inspection is usually arranged after the close of the formal part of the inquiry, and is attended by the inspector and the various parties involved. The idea of the inspection is for the inspector to see on the ground those features that have been described to him at the inquiry. As the inquiry has by then been closed there is a strict rule that no new information can be put forward.

It is important to go along to the inspection and to point out to the inspector salient points that have been brought out in the proof of evidence. To make sure that nothing is missed it is useful to prepare a check-list of things that need to be seen. It is useful to do this at the same time as preparing the proof. The thought process can often help to identify items that need to be added to the proof.

Although new evidence cannot be presented, the site inspection can be used to throw doubt on the other side's evidence if they have exaggerated anything. For example, suppose it is alleged that a right of way could not have existed because there has always been a large ditch there. If on site it is seen to be much smaller then this can be pointed out to the inspector. It would be new evidence to allege directly that the witness was lying but the point can be made obliquely; for example "look, Sir, there's the ditch that Mr Bloggs said was three feet across".

13.12. Written representations

It is at the discretion of the Secretary of State whether a public inquiry is held. There are two other options; a hearing or written representations. A hearing is similar to a public inquiry except only the promoters of the order and those who have formally objected are invited to appear. The methods described for a public inquiry will be equally applicable here. In practice, hearings do not seem to be generally used, presumably because they have no real advantage over an inquiry and are open to the objection that in an open society such things should not be conducted behind closed doors.

The other option is to have written representations. The idea here is that the same sort of matters that are considered at a public inquiry are dealt with in writing. The missing element is that it is not possible to question witnesses. But where the facts are not disputed and the argument hinges on interpretation of facts or on a value judgment of their significance, then written representations can save a lot of time. They may also favour the amateur in that no advantage is gained through having a quick-thinking advocate. In an exchange of representations there is time to weigh carefully the merits of points made by the other side and the possible implications of various responses.

In theory, the Secretary of State has the discretion to decide on written representations whenever he wants. In practice, he will consult the various parties and will only go forward if they all agree. It gets too complicated if there are many parties involved; written representations are normally only suggested if the issues appear relatively simple and there are only one or two objectors.

13.13. The results

Once the inquiry is over then it is only necessary to wait for the decision letter. This will normally be completed within three or four months of the inquiry and will be sent to those who have appeared at the inquiry or made written representations.

Waiting for the decision is perhaps the right time to reflect on the right philosophy about winning. Whilst it is necessary to play to win, it is important not to get obsessive about individual cases; this can lead to becoming disheartened if the decision goes against us. It is worth remembering that even the average barrister loses as many cases as he wins!

Besides, an individual inquiry is only one skirmish in a much greater campaign and the impact made by a well-conducted objection to a public inquiry may be much more important than the result. This is because a campaign of objection can often cause immense inconvenience to order making authorities even if they are ultimately successful. The more difficult we make it for them, the more likely they are at other times to try and accommodate us. For example, there is no real benefit to a council in making orders downgrading bridleways to footpaths. If a council believes that there will be no opposition then it might well agree to a request from walkers or an owner to do just that. If the council knows from previous experience that such an order will be resolutely opposed right through to a public inquiry, then it will probably conclude that it is not worth the hassle. The success of an objection may not be measured in terms of whether it succeeds or not; in the longer term the key point may well be the amount of trouble that it causes to the authority.

If the case goes against us then there is little that can be done apart from analysing what went wrong and looking to see how similar cases could be better presented in future. In theory, there is a right of appeal to the courts but only on points of law. The cost of doing so is huge and in almost all cases the resources will be far better spent on dealing with other paths. Even if the decision is quite clearly wrong in law, as these decisions are not legal precedents the loss of one inquiry will not prejudice the results of others.

Very occasionally, there will be an issue which comes up repeatedly and which may need a court decision to establish a new legal precedent. As the costs of this are high, it is only likely to be possible where this is backed by a national body such as the BHS. Even national bodies have only the resources for a few milestone cases and assistance will inevitably be selective. The normal principle adopted will be to go to the courts only where an important principle is at stake affecting many other paths. Policy decisions of this sort have to be taken quickly as any appeal must be lodged within six weeks of the date of the decision letter.

14
DOCUMENTARY EVIDENCE OF
PUBLIC PATHS AND BYWAYS

14.1. Introduction

For more than a thousand years from the withdrawal of the Roman forces, inland movements of both people and goods in Britain depended largely on pathways. People travelled either on foot or on horseback and goods were mainly carried by pack-horse. Although there were always horse-drawn vehicles, for centuries they were only of limited use due to poor roads, and the public path system of today represents to a considerable extent the vestiges of a system on which the economy of the country once depended. So as well as a recreational resource, these ways are also historic features worthy of preservation for their own sake.

Because of the historical significance of pathways to the life of the countryside, researching their history is a fascinating task and adds significantly to our knowledge of local history. There is another side to the task that looms large in the minds of rights of way workers. We believe that very many of the historical paths were either not recorded on the definitive map or else were recorded with the wrong status, for example bridleways or byways being recorded as footpaths. The correcting of these errors is seen as a key task, and researching historical documents plays an important part in this work.

14.2. The importance of documentary evidence

It should be appreciated that the whole business of proving a right of way through historical research rests on two important legal principles. First, it has been established law for many centuries that a highway cannot cease to exist through disuse. Thus if a highway can be shown to exist at some time in the past and that it has never been legally extinguished, then it must still exist at law however long it has been out of use. Secondly, the courts have held that if it can be proved that a highway existed at some past date, then it must be presumed to still exist unless it can actually be shown that it has been extinguished. Thus the onus of proving that a way was legally extinguished rests on anyone alleging that that the route is no longer a highway.

191

Although these legal principles make it possible to have a route added to the definitive map purely on the basis of historical evidence, nobody should fool themselves that it is easy. The test is a balance of probability; in other words we have to show that it is more likely than not that the route existed. But it is important to understand that we do have to prove our case; we cannot simply go on guesswork or assumptions. It has to be appreciated that the sort of evidence that would be acceptable in local historical work is often far too weak for legal purposes. This is a fundamental point and the main purpose of this chapter is to give an overview of the problems and the requirements of proving the existence of public paths or byways through the use of documentary sources.

It is worth noting that historical research is more often a factor in considering bridleway and vehicular rights than for rights on foot. There are two main differences which bring about this situation.

Most claims for footpaths are based on evidence of use leading to a presumption of dedication. It tends to be more difficult to do this for bridleways or byways because the usage is lower and more local and can be easily prevented by obstructions. As the years go by it becomes increasingly difficult to find cogent evidence of use from the period before 1940, and there was very little horse use over the period 1940-1960.

On the other hand, although footpaths and bridleways tend today to be lumped together, historically they had quite different origins. Byways and bridleways, or bridle roads as old documents tend to describe them, were formerly important routes and the skeleton around which the countryside was made. Footpaths generally seem to have been much more ephemeral, developed and changed to fit in with local circumstances. It follows that there tend to be many more documentary references to bridleways and byways, and thus a much better chance of establishing their status through research than is the case for footpaths.

14.3. The nature of documentary evidence

It is important to be clear about the true nature of documentary evidence. Unfortunately, many people fall into the trap of assuming that any document that is old must be true. This, of course, is a fallacy!

Any piece of writing is a form of communication between the writer and the reader. In principle, it is an alternative to the writer making the same statement verbally. Writing has the advantage that the writer can communicate with more people, including those alive many years later, but it has precisely the same drawbacks as verbal communication, namely that the statements made may not be true. In terms of evidence, documentary sources are less valuable than the same statement made verbally for two reasons. Firstly, it is always possible that the document is a forgery and that the claimed writer never made the statement that he is credited with. Secondly, it is not possible to ask supplementary questions to ascertain that the writer is telling the truth.

In considering any documentary evidence it is necessary to ask three key questions:
- Did the writer really make the statement alleged or is the document a forgery?
- Did the writer really believe what he said or was he lying?
- Assuming that the writer honestly believed what he wrote was the truth, are there good reasons for accepting that he would be likely to know the true position?

It is now proposed to look at each of these aspects in turn.

14.4. Is the document a forgery?

This is obviously a potential problem where a modern dispute may hinge on an old document. The question then arises as to whether the document is genuine or whether one of the parties to the dispute has forged it to prove his point. A document from an official records office is obviously of value here in that its history is known from the time that it was deposited and during that period it should not have been possible for it to have been tampered with.

It should not be forgotten that a records office can have had no control over documents before they were deposited. It is thus theoretically possible that a document that has been in a records office for many years is actually a forgery. However, any forgery would not have been for the purposes of the current dispute and it would normally be accepted that the document was genuine in the absence of any evidence that the contrary was the case. In particular, where a document was deposited as an official record of some event at the time it happened, then it is very unlikely that anyone would be able to successfully challenge its authenticity.

14.5. Was the writer telling the truth?

Assuming that a document is authentic in the sense that the person alleged to have written it actually did so, it does not follow that he was telling the truth. In general, a written statement carries less weight than a living witness because it is not possible for the person making the statement to be questioned. Whilst it might be thought reasonable to assume that a statement is true unless there are grounds for the contrary, it is often possible for those on the other side to put forward reasons why the writer may have tried to mislead his readers. If the document is to be given any weight it is necessary to show reasons why it would have been difficult for the writer to have lied.

The most useful sources in this respect are those where the writer had a duty to make an accurate statement and where the resulting document was a matter of public record at the time that it was prepared. For example, the clerk to a body such as a borough council has the job of accurately recording the resolutions of the council. Because the minutes are read and checked by the councillors, inaccuracy would have been spotted immediately. As his employment depended on him performing properly then he would obviously have made sure that the records were accurate. Thus, the official minutes of a council may be relied on to give a true record of what the council decided. Compare this with, say, a private document such as a letter or a diary where there would have been no real check and thus it is far less certain now that the statements made are true.

In some cases, there were criminal sanctions against those who made untrue statements. This includes statements made on oath or by statutory declaration. There are also instances where information is supplied to official bodies, such as the Inland Revenue, where giving an untrue statement is an offence. Written statements made under such circumstances are likely to be accepted as true, unless there are cogent reasons for believing that the writer was lying.

14.6. How did he know that anyway?

Let us assume that it is accepted that the alleged writer did actually write the document and that he honestly believed what he wrote to be true. We still have to get over the biggest obstacle of all in that it is necessary to be able to show that the writer had some good reason for knowing the true position.

The best way of understanding this is to imagine that the issue that the writer was describing is happening today and the writer is giving verbal information. Would his evidence hold much weight?

It very much depends on the nature of the information supplied. If the information relates to facts that anybody present would be aware of then there should be no problem. If someone says today that many people drive from Manchester to Birmingham via the M6, we believe them. Similarly, if someone in 1800 said that coal is delivered to his village by packhorses along a particular track, then we also should have no difficulty in accepting it.

It is necessary to beware of information that depends on a legal or historical assessment of other facts. Someone (like us) who asserts today that a particular highway exists and bases that view on an assessment of other information may well be correct, but the bald assertion does not make it so. This is at the bottom of most disputes over rights of way. What is not always properly understood is that the same must apply to people who in the past made similar assertions.

For example, in the early nineteenth century there was quite a vogue for local histories. The writers, like antiquarians today, had to assess the information that was available to them and make judgments. In some cases at least, they got it wrong! The trap to avoid is assuming that guesses made 200 years ago have now acquired the status of truth; the reality is that they are still guesses with the added problem that we cannot now ask the writers what sources they used to justify their views.

14.7. Official documents

It should by now be appreciated why official documents are particularly valuable in proving rights of way. Ideally, the document would have been prepared specifically to act as a record of the matters described and would have been required to be lodged in a records office and hence no question of forgery could arise. It would have been prepared by a person with specialist knowledge of the matters recorded and should record a process which the public were party to and to which they had some recourse if the document was thought to be wrong. This makes it very unlikely that the writer lied or was mistaken because, if so, surely someone would have noticed at the time.

There are, perhaps, no documents that display all the ideal characteristics described above. There are, however, many official sources that display some or most of these characteristics and these tend to be the best sources for proving rights of way. For this reason further consideration of documentary sources will concentrate on a limited number of types of official document with a separate chapter devoted to each. The types of sources to be considered are as follows:

- Books of reference for private Acts of Parliament
- Tithe maps
- Ordnance Survey maps
- Enclosure award records
- Court records
- Highway authority records
- 1910 Finance Act records

14.8. Interpretation of records

The most important point to understand is the great variation between the potential values of different documents. In practice, they range from being virtually conclusive to virtually useless. The problem is how to tell which is which.

Researching routes from documentary sources is not just a matter of visiting a records office and looking at documents. The real art is in interpreting the documents. This is a skill that can only be acquired over time. To interpret documents requires knowledge in two different areas. Firstly it is necessary to understand the background to a particular class of documents. The main sources listed above were not one-off documents but were at the time of their preparation being produced all over the country. They were written for professional people who knew what they were for; without this knowledge the reader may well have difficulty in understanding the document and would certainly not be able to appreciate the value of the information in terms of evidence.

In addition to understanding the background to the type of document being examined, it is usually very helpful to have a feel for the local history of the area being studied. The documents represent a record of events that took place and these will normally be linked in relating to the same physical features. For example, an enclosure award may convert a common into separate fields, which are later the subject of tithe records and still later are modified to accommodate a railway. The common thread is the gradually evolving pattern of the field boundaries which may only be fully understood by considering all three sets of records.

The following chapters are intended to give the reader an introduction to the main features of the types of records set out in section 14.7 above. However, it must be emphasised that it can be no more than an introduction to the topic and those who wish to understand the documents involved will need to read more deeply and, most importantly, study actual documents.

This all points to the fact that it is very difficult for one person to pick an individual route and fully research it. It would be necessary to have a very large body of knowledge in order to interpret all the different types of documents found. Besides, documents tend to be poorly indexed and it is very time-consuming to find those for a particular path among all the similar documents relating to other routes. The reality is that if a problem suddenly rears its head on any specific route and historical research is started, then in most cases the result will be a great deal of hard work ending in disappointment.

14.9. A systematic approach

Given the difficulty in finding and interpreting the evidence for a route, the reader may wonder how it is possible to make any progress. The answer is that a systematic approach is required with three key elements; the researching of a whole area at a time, the proper recording of information discovered and the training of volunteers with specialist skills.

We believe that in most areas there are significant networks of public paths and byways that were left off the definitive map or wrongly classified. It has to be accepted, though, that in most cases it will not be possible to find sufficient evidence to justify their inclusion on the definitive map. Until a great deal of research has been carried out it is not possible to determine which routes could be added and which not. For this reason it is generally unproductive to start with a particular problem path and look for evidence; it is generally better to start with the main sources and see where they lead.

It is important not to do work that has already been carried out. Local history is becoming a very popular study, and in many areas local societies, individuals or schools will already have checked the main sources. For example, rather than pore over hand-written documents in a records office, it may be possible to obtain a transcript from someone who has already done so. It is also worth checking whether other rights of way organisations have already checked out routes in the area; even if they can tell you that there are no leads, this at least saves a lot of fruitless effort.

If the information found is properly recorded, it is not critical in which order the various documents are checked. It is always heartening to have some early successes or volunteers will become discouraged. For this reason the ideal is to check all the sources for one area at a time, establish the paths in that area, then move on to another area. In practice it will not be quite so simple because the areas covered by each document differ and in any case it may not be possible to locate them all at first.

The most important part of the task, and one often neglected, is the proper recording of the information found. It is of importance to realise that arguments about the evidential value of documents often hinge on obscure points of wording; even if all the research is done by one person at a time it is impossible to remember all the subtleties. In practice, it is unlikely that one person would do all the research; the amount of work to be done is far too large and a team will be needed. It is also unlikely that all the information will be located at the same place. Sources are often spread around different records offices and other collections, and are often poorly indexed. Valuable information may be found by accident when looking for something else. Without a systematic approach to recording the information it will be impossible to match all the pieces of the jigsaw.

Precisely how to record the information can be a problem. One approach is to obtain photo-copies of all the relevant documents. Unfortunately, this is frequently difficult in that the documents are awkward sizes or are too fragile to be copied without damage. Thus copying might well prove impossible. It is also worth remembering that the volume of information thus obtained might be so huge that it became difficult to find the relevant sections. Almost certainly, some form of indexing would be necessary if the accumulated information was to be used.

A better alternative might be to prepare a summary of the relevant information to be found in each of the key sources. The summary would have to include sufficient information such that when all the relevant information had been collected, it would be possible to see for each potential route whether there appeared to be a basis for a claim. In the relatively few routes where there was such a basis, then copies of the relevant documents could be obtained. It will be clear from this, that the summary will have to include precise details of the reference and location of all the documents used such that they can be found again!

It should not be forgotten that the successful collection of documentary evidence requires a lot of time and effort. It is likely that to cover an area effectively a team of volunteers will be needed to carry out the work. Use of a team has the further advantage that individual members might make themselves expert on one particular type of record and then specialise on that type. For example, one person might examine all the enclosure records for a wide area, another all the tithe records and so on. It will, of course, be particularly important that proper summaries are made of the information discovered such that the work of all the teams can eventually be brought together.

The management of a team of volunteers is a large subject in its own right which will be dealt with in Chapter 24. It is worth noting, though, that the complexities of researching documentary evidence are such that it will be very useful to ensure that each member of the team has some sort of mentor to help them with any difficulties, and to encourage them when problems seem insoluble. This will be particularly important where new volunteers are just starting and may have an over-optimistic view of how fast progress will be.

It is vital that proper arrangements are made for safeguarding the summaries as work progresses. All too often volunteers carry out very useful work and then lose interest or even die before recording what they have found. Or perhaps the work is documented but then lost before it can be brought together with the rest of the work; remember that researches of this type may well be spread over a number of years. It is suggested that a useful way round this is to have a coordinator of the team who ensures that each member records their findings and that copies are circulated to the other members. This adds interest to everyone's work as they can see the dossier of evidence gradually being collected and it provides a stimulus of competition by showing what other members of the team are actually achieving. By having duplicate copies it minimises the risk of vital information being lost.

14.10. The dossier of evidence

It should by now be appreciated that a team which has successfully assembled sufficient evidence for a path claim will not only have carried out a great deal of work but will also have become expert in some fairly arcane aspects of social history and law. This can lead to a problem: in that it is necessary to convince other people of the significance of the evidence that has been assembled and volunteers who themselves have specialised in historical work may forget that most other people, including many professionals in the field, will have no idea what they are talking about.

The majority of claims for the addition of rights of way to the definitive map tend to be made on the basis of evidence of use and professional rights of way staff tend to be more expert in this area than in the analysis of documentary evidence. Similarly, local authority lawyers who may be brought in to assess the evidence will normally be general practitioners with a wide body of knowledge about the law affecting local authorities, but not necessarily a very deep knowledge of highway law. Even experts on modern highway law are unlikely to be fully conversant with the proper interpretation of laws that may well have been repealed more than a century ago.

It follows that in presenting the arguments for adding or upgrading a path it is necessary to prepare a detailed written statement setting out the argument. This dossier will need to include copies of the relevant documents on which the case is based. It is important that a commentary is also included which explains the background to the documents included and the reason why they are significant in a way that can be understood by someone without specialist knowledge. To assist in preparing this, Chapters 16 to 22 discuss in more detail the background and significance of the main types of document. These need to be set within a framework of the historical development of highways which will be covered in Chapter 15.

14.11 The time capsule

However carefully the dossier of evidence is prepared, there will always be the possibility that an application will fail. If this should happen then the position is worse than before the work started because unless additional evidence can be found it is not possible for a further application to be made. Thus an amateurish approach will handicap anyone coming later with a more carefully prepared case. This emphasises the importance of taking great care in preparing the case; it also points to the fact that there may sometimes be advantages in not making an application for an order.

Where an owner denies that a path is public and prevents it being used, then the only risk in making an application is the loss of time in carrying through the case and the possibility of preventing a future case that is better prepared. However, the public is not always prevented from using a path which is disputed. It is not unknown for an owner to dispute that a path is public but at the same time to declare that he is happy for the path to be used for the time being but only on a permissive basis. This presents the rights of way worker with something of a problem.

It is necessary to consider why the owner might want to take such action. The key point is that a true permissive route is very much less of an evil to the owner than a public path. A permissive path can be closed at any time and thus does not provide any constraint to future development. Importantly, it means that a permissive path does not depress the value of the land because any subsequent purchaser does not have to honour the permissive arrangement. Of course, not having a permissive path would be even better but the owner has to consider the risk that an application to add the path to the definitive map might succeed. If he believes that an application would have a reasonable chance of succeeding, and hence reduce the value of his land, then he might well feel that it would be preferable to retain a permissive path rather than take the risk. Of course, the question of whether an application is made is outside his control but he may suspect that allowing a permissive path would make a formal application less likely.

Let us now consider the matter from our side of the fence. If the owner is prepared to offer a permissive path then it probably indicates that he believes an application might succeed. Nothing is certain however, and if users called his bluff and actually made an application then it might fail. Having reached that point the owner would then have nothing to lose and would have no reason for maintaining the permissive path. Thus, whilst the owner continues to allow the public to use the path, making an application carries the risk that it may cause the path to be lost to the public without any immediate gain should the case be won since people were using the route beforehand anyway.

The main advantage of having the path included on the definitive map is, of course, that it is not then possible for the existing or future owners to prevent use of the path. If this were to happen then an application could be made at that time and the case would not be any weaker assuming that the appropriate evidence could be preserved. On the basis that this could actually be done, the tactical case for not making an application must be quite strong.

This points to the importance of what might be regarded as a *time capsule*. In essence this would be the dossier of evidence. However, it will be necessary to take the greatest care that the dossier is complete and understandable without any assistance from the person who compiled it. Extra care will also need to be taken with references to other documents. Ideally, the documents to be referred to should be those in official custody which should still be available when needed. If other documents need to be referred to it may be safer to include copies within the dossier of evidence, but in this case there ought to be some other evidence of the authenticity of the document. Again, it is important to work on the basis that the evidence must be capable of standing up without the intervention of the person who has collected it.

Once the dossier has been prepared, it is necessary to establish where it should be stored. This should not be under the control of a private individual as such documents are notorious for being lost. A possible option would be to deposit a copy with the rights of way department of the highway authority with a request that the dossier of evidence should remain on the files. However, this is open to the objection that the authority has a legal duty to act when they discover evidence, and not only when a formal application is made. Thus, strictly speaking, the authority would be obliged to act on the deposition of the evidence and would not be allowed to let the matter remain on file even if requested to do so by the person depositing the evidence. In addition, it is by no means unusual for rights of way departments to lose evidence of this sort, so they cannot be regarded as safe places for our time capsule.

The best solution would be for the information to be deposited with the county records office. The records offices are properly set up for preserving documents for all time and have a special responsibility for maintaining records relating to the work of the county council. As recording highways is a county responsibility, evidence that might potentially be used to resolve a highways dispute should be regarded as properly the responsibility of the records office.

There is no point in trying to keep the collection of the evidence a secret from the owner. On the contrary, one of the main advantages of the time capsule approach is to impress the owner with the strength of the case. Once the dossier of evidence has been deposited in the records office, a copy should be sent to the owner. It is likely to be the fear of a potential order that prevents the public from being excluded from the path.

However, although secrecy should be avoided there is no reason for trying to secure any agreement with the owner. A rights of way worker has no power to make an agreement on behalf of other users so it is impossible to give an undertaking that no application will be made by anybody. For his part the owner is very unlikely to give an undertaking that he will allow permissive use for as long as no application is made; the advantage of having a permissive route is the avoidance of the possibility that it could otherwise be closed. The best that can be hoped for is a sort of stand-off where the owner is made aware that the retention of permissive use will reduce the possibility of an application being made.

Although the time capsule approach is particularly valuable where the evidence is essentially documentary, it can also be used where some or all of the evidence is based on use leading to a presumption of dedication. However, it should be noted that this leads to additional problems. The evidence of use will have to be for the period prior to the deposit of the evidence; obviously as the years go by it becomes increasingly difficult to check the details of such use. Normally, it is desirable to be able to produce in person at least some of the people who claim to have used the path, but this will become increasingly difficult as the years go by. This makes it particularly important to ensure the quality of the evidence as set out in Chapter 7. There will be particular advantage in securing some statutory declarations. As challenges to witnesses often hinge on the suggestion that they used the path by special invitation of the owner, it would be helpful if any declarations specifically stated that this was not the case. This points to another advantage of giving the owner a copy of the evidence. It gives him a chance to dispute matters of this sort; if he does not do so at the time it would be very difficult for him or a subsequent owner to later argue that the witness used the path by invitation.

15
THE HISTORICAL DEVELOPMENT OF ROADS

15.1. Introduction

This chapter is intended to provide a brief account of the way in which the highway system of England and Wales has developed over the centuries. It is important to realise that despite the impressions which may have been gained at school, there is no such thing as a true or correct history. Instead, the historian describes a very small proportion of the events over the centuries and attempts to show how they have influenced each other; another historian may marshal a completely different set of events and come to a very different conclusion.

This history presents the author's personal selection of events. As far as possible, the conclusions set out are those that the majority of experts subscribe to; where there is a significant divergence of opinion then both views are set out. Obviously, no guarantee can be given that future research will not lead to the accepted wisdom being overturned - that is the very nature of historical research.

The intention is to give particular emphasis to events that gave rise to the documents that are described in later chapters. It must be emphasised that this can only be a brief introduction to the subject and the reader who wishes to research a particular type of document is urged to read more detailed works; to assist in this, some ideas for further reading are given at the end of each chapter.

15.2. Prehistoric and Roman roads

Most accounts of the historical development of he road system take a great deal of account of the roads built during the Roman occupation of Britain. However, evidence of the existence of Roman roads, or even earlier roads, is of little value in proving the existence of highways today. So it is only proposed to look very briefly at road development in this period, mainly to set the historical context for later developments.

Before the Roman invasion, what is now England and Wales was inhabited by relatively primitive Celtic tribes. They used horses for transport, including to pull chariots, so they must have had some roads although there is only scanty information about where they ran. The development of iron ploughs in this era had allowed the cultivation of lowland areas, but in earlier times users seem to have preferred to follow ridges where there was less boggy ground and dense vegetation. Thus some of the oldest surviving routes such as the Berkshire Ridgeway follow the high land.

The Romans first invaded Britain in 55BC. The local tribes were eventually overcome and England and Wales as far north as Hadrian's Wall remained firmly within the Roman Empire for some 400 years. The Celtic people were not expelled but stayed on to enjoy the benefits of Roman civilisation including central heating, hot baths and paved roads; all benefits which Britain was not to enjoy again for fifteen hundred years.

Our interest is in the roads. It is well-known that the Romans built superb roads, having developed the techniques for building paved roads as well as being skilled engineers in the construction of bridges and even road tunnels. What is less well-known is that the Romans also introduced many administrative and legal concepts. Our legal system still includes many features derived from Roman law. In particular the common law classification of highways into footpaths, bridleways and carriageways is derived from a similar classification within Roman law.

The Romans also introduced concepts of town planning, with towns arranged in the grid-iron pattern, as adopted many centuries later in the settling of North America. They even anticipated future growth by laying out spare blocks on the outskirts of towns to accommodate expansion. And, of course, the main roads were laid out to link the towns in what was a truly national or even European network. In those days a traveller could ride from Carlisle to Jerusalem not only in safety, but also without being bothered by any frontier controls.

However, although the Roman era in Britain was the start of important technical and legal innovations, the lines followed by the Roman roads are of little interest in proving the existence of highways today. This is because when the Roman Empire crumbled, Britain was overrun by new invaders who pushed the original inhabitants back into the western hills of Cornwall, Wales and Cumbria. The new inhabitants started afresh and certainly did not recognise any of the laws or customs of those who had lived there before. In any case, the new society was essentially a rural one that saw no value in towns or main roads. In some cases they were abandoned or used as quarries. Others continued to be used and survived for centuries; indeed some of our own main roads follow Roman alignments and have been in continuous use for almost two thousand years. There is unlikely to be any dispute over the status of such routes. Where it can be shown that a road existed during the Roman period but it has subsequently disappeared, this will not prove any status today unless there is also evidence of more recent use.

15.3. The Dark Ages

The period following the Roman occupation was one of instability as successive waves of invaders from North Germany and Scandinavia occupied what is now England, but which was then a series of small nations frequently at war with each other. Raiders first began to appear during the period of the Roman occupation and it was necessary to strengthen coastal defences and to maintain a battle fleet in the North Sea. With the withdrawal of the Romans the attack intensified with the Celtic people being pushed steadily westwards. A spirited defence said to have been led by King Arthur held up the advance for a generation but by the middle of the sixth century the invaders had succeeded in colonising all England except Cumbria and Cornwall. The new inhabitants were from a number of racial groups, but are normally referred to today as the Anglo-Saxons.

Three centuries later there was another invasion, this time by the Danes or Vikings. For some time they came only on isolated raids on coastal communities, but in 867 they launched a major invasion capturing most of eastern England between the Tees and the Thames. The Anglo-Saxons led by King Alfred prevented them from capturing the rest of their territory and eventually peace was restored with what were effectively two separate countries: the Anglo-Saxons with their capital at Winchester and the Danes with a capital at York.

In this era there seems to have been relatively little travel and no new roads were made, but at least the more important Roman roads continued to be used. Late in the period it became established that there were four great roads or royal roads: Watling Street, Ermine Street, Akeman Street and the Fosse Way. These roads alone were under royal protection and this appears to be the origin of the idea of the King's highway, a concept which only very gradually spread to include all public routes.

Although the Dark Ages were a period of instability in the sense that there was no single nation or centralised government, nevertheless it was a period in which many of the foundations of our national life were laid down. The Anglo-Saxon and Danes were the last invaders to come as settlers, sweeping out the previous people. The later invasion was different in that a small group seized power; the descendants of the settlers of the Dark Ages went on living as before, as did the Celtic refugees in the western hills. Consequently, the physical form of the countryside is still strongly influenced by the way in which it was laid out by the settlers of the Dark Ages.

It is important to appreciate the importance of the village community in this era. Much of the countryside was still uncultivated, or waste. In many areas there were dense woodlands, although a lot of these had already been destroyed by primitive slash and burn farming techniques. Whatever the type of land, much back-breaking work would be needed before cultivation could start.

This work could only be carried out by the collective action of a number of families, pooling their effort, equipment and livestock. For example, the normal plough of that era was drawn by eight oxen and in many cases this represented the combined resources of eight families. This communal way of life made it sensible for people to live together in villages rather than scattered around the fields being worked. It is probable that in many cases the villagers were largely the descendants of the original settlers and formed a sort of extended family or tribal grouping.

These village communities have proved extraordinarily stable over many centuries. They became the manors of the Norman era as recorded in the Domesday Book of 1086. In most country districts the villages of today correspond almost exactly with those recorded more than 900 years ago. These manors became the hamlets, townships and parishes which remain the basic building blocks of our local government system. Of course, our rural society of today is still very much rooted in the community life of the same villages.

The Norman settlers probably brought with them from Europe what became known as the feudal system. In those lawless times it was necessary to have a system of protection which worked through a pyramid of power. At the head was the King, then various nobles who owed allegiance to him. Other lesser people such as local lords or village headmen owed allegiance to the main nobles, and so on down to ordinary villeins who were the lowest class to hold land. In addition there were many landless people who were virtually slaves.

The King was the only person who actually owned land. Everyone else who had land did not actually own it but held tenure of it from somebody higher up. Thus an ordinary villein would hold the land of the local lord of the manor, who might hold the whole manor of an important nobleman who held a vast area of the King. The point of this system was that each layer was under a duty to protect those underneath who, in return, had to perform certain services. The most important service was that of providing military service in times of war.

The effect of this system was that all land was held by somebody, even if it was not really in use. Often the territory of a village would include a large area of *waste* that was not cultivated but might be used for rough grazing or to gather turf or sticks. Such land would be held by the lord of the manor, together with the cultivated area. Ordinary people would hold of the lord their own areas of cultivated land, together with a right to use the waste lands. The waste lands were thus used in common by the people of the village and thus became known as *commons*.

This hierarchical system developed into a system of government where control passed down from the King through important nobles to local lords of the manor and hence to ordinary people. The change to a more democratic system was only accomplished in the Victorian era when most of the remaining powers of the lords of the manor (acting as justices of the peace) were done away with. In legal theory, ordinary people still cannot own land; instead a freeholder still holds a tenure of somebody else, normally the lord of the manor. As the right to use the land is irrevocable and can be bought and sold, in practice the point is immaterial.

The gradual development of land ownership since the feudal system explains the confusion that surrounds the ownership of common land. It is widely believed that common land belongs to the public. In legal terms this is incorrect; it actually belongs to the lord of the manor (or somebody else if he has sold the rights). It is difficult to avoid the conclusion that the misconception is at least morally and historically more correct. After all, nobody seriously suggests that the lord of the manor owns all the manor, even though the freeholder still has the tenure of the lord. The continued role of the lord in common land has no more logic and only survives because of an anomaly in land law which insists that land cannot be owned by a group of people in common.

The appearance and layout of the countryside is still influenced by the work of the early settlers. Where the land was suitable for arable farming, the open fields system was widely used. In this a village had only two (or sometimes three) very large open fields. Within each field the various families had strips of land, nominally 22 yards wide by 220 yards long and containing an acre. To share out the good and bad land, the holdings of a family were not all together but scattered around the fields without any fencing between neighbouring strips. Each year one of the fields would be fallow and animals could be grazed in it; the other field or fields would be cropped with animals allowed in after harvest time.

The working of the open fields system required a substantial community involvement with little potential for individual initiative. The people lived together in a village, with their houses grouped around a green. The original purpose of the green was so that livestock could be herded there at night for protection and to prevent them from straying. As the normal grazing on the fallow field or on the commons beyond was unfenced, the stock would have to be watched through the day otherwise they could wander away. To move animals between the green and the commons, wide strips of common were often left to form a communicating route. These routes often seem to have been arranged to narrow towards the village, presumably because this made it easier to herd the stock together.

With self-contained villages there would be little need for travelling. Each village would be likely to have paths to its neighbours and the few people who wished to travel longer distances would have to pass from village to village, unless they were lucky enough to find one of the surviving Roman roads. The normal pattern was for paths to radiate out from the village green, passing through the fields and then across the waste land which usually separated the villages. Where a broad strip had been left for moving stock between green and common, this was often used as the path out with the route then continuing across the common to a similar way into another village.

The overall framework of the countryside has often survived for more than a thousand years with the houses of a village still clustering around a green with a radial pattern of roads preserving the system of paths from village to village. Although strip fields disappeared during the era of the enclosures, their location can often still be seen marked by long narrow fields which replaced the old strips or by ridge and furrow grassland where the arable fields were anciently converted to pasture. Unfortunately, modern farming methods are rapidly destroying a thousand years of history and such indications are becoming less and less common.

The pattern described above was common throughout those areas where arable farming was possible. With much land in the lowlands still unclaimed from the waste, there was less need for farming hill country which often remained uninhabited until after the Norman conquest. However, where hilly country was used, a different pattern often applied and this was particularly true in the Celtic areas. As there was less scope for communal farming methods, there was less emphasis on villages and more on isolated farms. Over the years, the rising population often led to the original farms being divided among a family leading to a small cluster of farms together. Even today there tend to be fewer villages but far more hamlets in the West Country and Wales than in the more eastern areas of England. The road patterns also tend to be different with more complex twisty roads, as are seen in the little lanes of Devon and Cornwall.

15.4. The Norman Conquest

Few children can have gone through school without learning the importance of the year 1066 - a pivotal point in English history. In many ways, though, it has more importance in political history than in the sort of social history which we are looking at.

In that year William, Duke of Normandy, mounted an invasion of England. He planned the operation like a business venture, with a well-organised army of no more than about 8000 adventurers, each promised a share of the spoil. William took advantage of one of the periods of instability which were all too common; the new King Harold was not accepted by the leaders in the North who wanted to split away from the South and join with Norway. Harold rushed north to destroy the invited Norwegian army at Stamford Bridge only to learn that his own territory had been invaded by the Normans. By the time he was able to return, the invaders had consolidated their position and the King and most of his army were killed at Hastings, thus allowing the South to be occupied without further resistance.

The occupation of the North proved rather more difficult because of continued resistance by local guerrilla fighters. These were eventually overcome by the total devastation of large parts of the North with the murder of the population and the destruction of livestock and crops. William never attempted to carry the invasion into Scotland which remained a separate country for more than six centuries until in 1707 England and Scotland agreed to a merger to form the United Kingdom of Great Britain. This separate development led to English and Scottish common law developing differently which has important implications for rights of way even today.

However, the Normans did have ambitions to the west. Initially, William occupied the territory formerly controlled by Harold which excluded Wales, then a collection of small states operating to a quite different system of Celtic law. It was not long before the Norman barons took over South Wales from whence in 1169 they invaded Ireland. North Wales was gradually brought under the control of the Normans and in the thirteenth century Celtic law was arbitrarily replaced by English common law. This led to a rebellion which was suppressed in 1282, after which Wales was brought under the control of the English parliament and laws. Finally, an act of union in 1536 made the two countries one and the development of the law relating to highways has since been the same in both England and Wales.

Although outside the scope of this book, it is interesting to note that a similar replacement of Gaelic law by the English common law also took place in Ireland. This has resulted in most aspects of the basic law of highways in Ireland being as in England. For example, the principle "once a highway, always a highway" applies throughout Ireland (including the Republic of Ireland) even though it does not apply in Scotland.

Our interest, though, is not in the political changes that arose from the Norman conquest but the social changes that spread from them. The immediate effects were limited, apart from those parts of the country that William destroyed as a reprisal. Unlike earlier invasions, no great wave of new settlers came over to push refugees still further west. Instead, William's army consisted of a relatively small number of adventurers who now formed a new aristocracy. The basic structures of the Anglo-Saxon, Danish and Welsh communities were retained with the simple substitution of a Norman lord of the manor in place of the former village headman. As the communities were largely self-contained and governed according to different rules which had developed through long custom, in the early days of Norman control different laws applied in each manor, it being one of the responsibilities of the lord to operate a manorial court to enforce the law and to resolve disputes.

15.5. The Middle Ages

As the years went by, society gradually became more prosperous as the population expanded and more and more waste land around each village was reclaimed for agriculture. An important result of this was that villages became less self-contained as there was now more being produced than was necessary to supply the inhabitants. This gradually led to the development of market towns where the villagers could take their surplus produce to sell and to use the money to buy specialist goods. This led to the growth of craftsmen producing these goods, who were usually based in the market towns.

The growth of market towns led to roads becoming of some significance for the first time since Roman times. Routes were needed to allow villagers to take their goods to the local market. It was reckoned in those days that people could reasonably travel up to six and two-thirds miles to a market; this odd figure arose because a day's journey was reckoned as twenty miles with a third of the day necessary for trading and a third each for going and coming back. It was laid down as a rule that where there was already a market operating under a royal charter, no other market

211

could be established within this distance. This is still the law today and has led to the pattern of market towns generally around ten miles or so apart.

Roads were also needed to link market towns so that merchants could travel around the country from market to market. At a very early stage a distinction was being made between the roads running from market to market and the local roads used by villagers to reach their local market. The concept of a road hierarchy has been with us ever since; even today the network of A roads broadly corresponds with the network of roads between market towns.

Traders were only part of the traffic between market towns which grew up during the Middle Ages. There was a growing business traffic of officials of church and state. Surprisingly, there were also tourists. As early as 1390 Chaucer described the adventures of a group of pilgrims travelling from London to Canterbury. This was clearly a short trip if we judge from one of his characters, a widow who has already been on pilgrimages to Spain, Italy, Germany and three times to Jerusalem!

During the Middle Ages the legal system was reformed such that justice became the responsibility of the King rather than individual barons through their manorial courts. This involved replacing the individual customary law that applied in each manor with a uniform or common system, hence common law. Major progress was made during the reign of Henry II from 1154 to 1189 and the latter date is now regarded as the starting point of the English legal system. From that date new customs could not come into existence, but local customs that already applied were to remain. This means that if it can be shown that a highway existed in 1189 then it is assumed that it existed through ancient custom; there is no need to assume, as for a later highway, that somebody must have dedicated it.

This will obviously apply to Roman roads that had continued to be used as highways up to 1189. But where a Roman road had already disappeared, perhaps centuries earlier, then its use would not constitute a valid custom and hence a highway at 1189. Although by 1315 the courts were accepting that highways could not cease simply through disuse, this can hardly apply to those that were already long-gone by the time the common law started. Where the evidence is that a road existed in Roman times but was later lost at some unknown date, then it is not possible to argue that it must still exist through the "once a highway, always a highway" principle.

As well as the introduction of a common system of unwritten law, this period also saw some of our earliest recorded statutes applying throughout the whole country. There were laws about highways as early as 1285 when the first statute of Winchester required roads between market towns to be maintained by the manors through which they ran, and for brushwood to be cut back on either side to reduce the risks to travellers from robbers. It seems from this that the concept of a royal road or King's highway, in the sense of a road under some degree of national control, had by then spread from the four great roads to all roads between market towns.

It is worth noting that although the different rights of pedestrians, riders and vehicles have been recognised since the earliest times, the relative importance of these have altered over time. Roads were so poor in the Middle Ages that vehicles could only be used on limited routes and then only in good weather. Waggons might be used in a village in summer to bring the harvest in, but for normal traffic the saddle-horse was the main mode for travellers and the pack-horse for goods. Even the King rode on his travels rather than having a coach; indeed there were no coaches until Tudor times when Queen Elizabeth was the first monarch to acquire one in 1565. It follows that for many centuries bridleways were the vital arteries of communication on which all trade and commerce depended.

15.6. From Tudor to Georgian times

In that timeless classic *The Making of the English Landscape*, Professor Hoskins described the period between 1570 and 1770 as the flowering of rural England:
Before that time life had been hard and comfortless, with little or no margin to spare beyond the necessities of living: what little there was went to the adornment and beautification of the parish church. After that time we witness the break-up of the village community, the degradation of most of the rural population, and the flight into the towns. But for those two hundred years - seven human generations - rural England flowered. The exhausting labour of colonization was over, except in small patches here and there. There was now enough people for an agricultural country at least, and there was time to rest and play.

Although in political terms these two centuries were turbulent days, they represented a period of considerable stability in the development of the countryside. As far as can be judged, the same applies to the roads and paths of the countryside which may be regarded as the starting point for the changes after 1770 that have led to the network of today.

Although many records survive from that period, it is often difficult to understand what they mean because we cannot always be sure of the meaning of the terms used to describe different types of route. Thus we may find the King's Highway, common highways, public highways, customary ways and private ways. Unfortunately, even the experts fail to agree completely as to what they all were.

It is clear that there were highways which operated in the same way as now; this is to say that all members of the public could use them and there was an obligation to maintain them that could be enforced by the courts. In those days each parish was responsible for highways and the maintenance was carried out by what was known as *statute labour*. This meant that every inhabitant was obliged personally to work on the highways; later it became possible to make a money payment in lieu.

In addition there were customary ways, which may be regarded as belonging to the parish. At common law the inhabitants of each parish were obliged to maintain them, but the right to use them was restricted to the inhabitants plus anyone else who needed to use the roads to visit the village or its inhabitants. This meant that if the inhabitants failed to maintain the roads properly it was purely a private matter and there was no power for outsiders to intervene, for example through the criminal courts as in the case of a highway. This seems to have been the practical implication of the limited number of people who had a right of way. There is no evidence that the wider public were ever excluded from using customary ways; merely that there was nothing that they could do if the ways were out of repair.

We do not know the extent to which the different types of routes existed at different times. Presumably all routes were originally customary ways in that when each village was a self-governing community there can have been no system to allow outsiders to interfere. The four great roads of the pre-conquest period must have been the first highways and the idea must have been accepted as applying to more and more routes. As customary ways are now virtually extinct, it seems clear that they were gradually absorbed into the expanding network of highways. What is not clear is how and when. To a significant extent, our problem in establishing this relates to the meanings attached to *common* and *private* ways and thus to understanding contemporary documents.

15.7. Common and private ways

The word *common* means pertaining to more than one person. Thus a customary way is a common way in that it is common to all the inhabitants. So is a highway, in that it is common to all the public. By contrast, *private* means pertaining to one or more individuals, that is to say, not public. So a customary way could properly be described as a private way as could a route available only to one individual, that

214

is to say, a private road in the modern sense. It follows that the meanings of *common* and *private* do overlap, and that a customary way may be correctly described both as common and private. However, despite the overlap, the two terms do not necessarily mean the same.

Our understanding of the types of roads in the seventeenth century relies heavily on two key sources: Lord Coke's law reports written between 1572 and 1616 based on previous legal authorities (1), and a judgment of Sir Matthew Hale in 1672 (2). Both these sources are important in classifying ways into different categories.

Coke described carriageways as being of two types: *regia via* (King's way) or *communis strata* (common street). The distinction between these is not entirely clear, although it seems evident that the former comprises the more important routes used by all members of the public whilst the latter are more local. In addition to these two types of carriageways Coke identified bridleways and footpaths.

Hale, on the other hand, had a three-fold classification of ways: great roads, highways and private ways. Great roads were not explained but were presumably the most important routes. The difference between the other two classes was described by Hale:

If a way lead to a market and were a way for all travellers, and did communicate with a great road etc, it is a highway; but if it lead only to a church, to a private house or village, or to fields, there it is a private way. But 'tis a matter of fact and much depends upon common reputation. If it be a publick way of common right, the parish is to repair it, unless a particular person be obliged by prescription or custom. Private ways are to be repaired by the village or hamlet, or sometimes by a particular person.

It is often assumed that Coke's common streets correspond with Hale's private ways, but this is by no means certain. It is noteworthy that Coke did not describe either of his classes of road as private or public. Hale, on the other hand, did not refer specifically to common streets and, indeed, describes public ways as being of common right. It seems quite plausible that Coke's King's highways are Hale's great roads, and that Coke's common streets are Hale's highways or "publick" ways. On this interpretation, Coke does not refer to Hale's private ways, possibly because the whole context of his description is the different public ways.

This fits in with other law reports which use the word *common* in the sense of *public* (3). By 1717 the courts held that *regia via* and *communis strata* were synonymous expressions (4). We seem to have lost the secret of what the distinction ever was; one can only speculate that perhaps the King's highways or great roads may originally have been only the routes between market towns, with the common ways being the more local access roads, which were nevertheless public and which each parish had an obligation to the public to maintain.

Whilst the concept of a common way seems to have gone by the eighteenth century, Hale's private way seems to have continued for at least another century. Importantly, the concept was still alive through the period of enclosures, and it will be seen that the use of the term by enclosure commissioners poses many difficulties for us in understanding what they meant.

The context of Hale's judgment was whether the criminal courts could intervene where a way was obstructed or out of repair. The conclusion was that this was so where the way met his definition of a highway, but not in the case of a private way. Hale's words continued to be quoted in legal works on the criminal law until well into the nineteenth century, and so it appears that this requirement continued. Unfortunately, we have very little information as to precisely how the private ways worked.

It is important to note that these private ways were very different from the modern concept of a private road in at least one important respect; Hale said that private ways were to be maintained by the local community. Hale's distinction between the different maintenance regimes of parish as against village is rather obscure. The most likely explanation is that highways were to be maintained by the parish under statute, whilst the private ways were to be maintained under common law by the manor. In very many cases, though, the two areas were the same and doubtless the different maintenance regimes would have been blurred.

The most difficult point to establish is who had a right over the private ways. Hale's definition makes it clear that a highway had both to be open to all the public and to be of more than local significance; it does not necessarily follow from this that a local access route that did not meet the criteria for a highway could not still have rights for all the public. As we know that customary ways existed and that they met Hale's criteria for private ways, we must accept that at least some private ways did not have rights for all the public. So there seems no basis for assuming that all Hale's private ways automatically had public rights. On the other hand, it seems equally rash to assume that all the private ways were customary ways open only to those requiring local access, if for no other reason than the historical fact that many private ways are known to have come into existence long after 1189 and thus could not have existed by custom.

We will probably never entirely solve this problem. The true answer may be that there was no simple universal pattern. Perhaps some private ways were customary ways open only to local access traffic, whilst others were for use by all the public. The key point is that Hale's private ways were maintained by what we would regard today as a public body, and the real issue is what happened to this maintenance obligation. We will take up this point again in Section 15.12.

15.8 The enclosure period

During the eighteenth century there were developments in farming methods which allowed more to be produced from the same area of land. New rotation methods replaced the old system of leaving land fallow, and produced new crops such as turnips that could be fed to animals. A combination of new crops and improved methods of managing permanent pasture land allowed substantial increases in the livestock that could be kept. At the same time selective breeding methods were developing better breeds such as much heavier sheep and beef cattle. Taken together, these innovations had the potential for dramatically increasing food production, particularly important at a time of rapidly increasing population.

It was impossible to introduce these methods where the communal farming methods of the pre-Norman period still lingered on. Where common field systems survived, new rotations could not be introduced because there were not enough fields to rotate nor anywhere to keep stock if there was no fallow field. Nor was it possible to introduce improved breeds where all the stock was kept in a single field.

The solution was a re-distribution of land. By dividing the common fields and commons between those who had rights in them, it was possible to create farms in the modern sense with a compact block of land under the control of one farmer. As well as allowing farmers to introduce whatever new methods they wanted, it also allowed the farm buildings to be situated in the land being farmed, rather than in a remote position in the village. The process of re-distribution was known as enclosure in that the open landscape of the large fields and commons was replaced by what we have come to regard as the traditional rural landscape; a pattern of relatively small fields enclosed by walls and hedges.

A change like this could only be introduced if everyone agreed, and enclosure by agreement was carried out in many places even as early as the sixteenth century. The problem was that even one owner could prevent the whole process. So in the eighteenth century, the system of enclosure by private act was started. If those who wanted enclosure could secure a private Act of Parliament authorising an enclosure, then it could be carried out even where some individuals were opposed to it.

Most parliamentary enclosure took place between 1750 and 1850. More than 2500 acts dealt with over four million acres of common fields. In a great swathe of country from East Yorkshire to Dorset, and including most of the Midland counties, around a third of the entire area was subject to enclosure. So complete was the process that only a few hundred acres of common fields survived. In addition the high food prices brought about by European wars of the early nineteenth century encouraged the enclosure of moorland and mountain commons with some 1800 acts enclosing around two million acres. However, the process was never completed as falling prices from the middle of the nineteenth century made further enclosure uneconomic.

Such major changes to the rural landscape required substantial changes to the network of roads and paths. The commissioners who carried out each enclosure were authorised to close and divert existing routes and create new ones. The fashion of the time was for straight roads, and these were used extensively. It is often possible to identify which areas were the subject of parliamentary enclosure simply by looking at the map for areas with straight roads and squarish fields.

Our main interest in the enclosure process is that it was meticulously documented at the time and many of the records still survive. In many cases they represent the earliest comprehensive record of the status of the various routes and as such are key historical documents. Their interpretation is not always easy, as will be described in detail in Chapter 19.

15.9. The turnpike roads

For centuries highways had been maintained by the inhabitants of the parishes through which they passed. In times when traffic was mainly local and repair methods simple, this approach was adequate. But as trade developed, more and more traffic moved between the main towns and more effort needed to be directed towards the more important roads. The parish system proved quite inadequate to achieve this. With an amateur surveyor, unskilled workers and a legal limit on the resources that could be applied, the parishes would have been unable to maintain the main roads even if they had wanted to. They had no incentive to do so. Having good roads between major towns benefited the merchants of those towns who paid nothing towards the roads; a parish that was unfortunate enough to lie between two towns gained nothing from providing a good road between them.

The solution was the introduction of tolls so that the users paid for the roads. Private acts set up turnpike trusts, non-profit making bodies which took over existing roads and borrowed money to improve them or build replacements. They were then allowed to charge tolls which paid for the interest on the loans and the cost of maintaining the roads. The very first turnpike act was in 1663 for a portion of the Great North Road but the idea did not make much headway until the second half of the eighteenth century; between 1751 and 1790 no less than 1600 turnpike acts were passed. It can be seen that the turnpike era was contemporary with the period of enclosure and represents another thread in the modernisation of the countryside.

The turnpike system certainly improved the road network. By 1784 it was possible for a national network of mail coaches to be introduced. The full potential of the system was still to come in that the roads were still mainly of earth and the trusts were too often very local and amateurish.

15.10. Macadam and the gravel road

The next stage in the development of the main road network took place after the Napoleonic wars when there was a further expansion of trade. In 1815 work commenced on rebuilding the London to Holyhead road. Ireland had joined the United Kingdom in 1801 and this road was the vital link between London and Dublin. During the 1820s and 30s it was provided throughout with a roadway of stone designed by Thomas Telford, a Scots stonemason turned engineer. A similar road from London to Edinburgh was also proposed but was never built due to the coming of the railways.

The Telford system was far too expensive for any but the most important routes. Fortunately, a cheaper method was developed by Macadam, another Scot and a gentleman amateur roadbuilder who spent many years and a great deal of his own money in experiments. His system of layers of stone of different sizes, which still bears his name today, allowed smooth and durable roads to be built economically and came into widespread use in the 1820s. By the 1830s, fast and reliable stagecoaches had become a reality, often achieving average speeds of more than ten miles per hour.

This exciting age, immortalised by Charles Dickens and celebrated in countless Christmas cards, lasted only for a few years. Steam railways were developed in the

1830s and spread rapidly during the early 1840s. By then, railways linked London with most of the major towns of England in half the time of the fastest coach. As railways spread the coaches were withdrawn and the turnpikes became bankrupt. The last turnpike, on the Holyhead Road in Anglesey, levied its final toll in 1895.

15.11. The building of the country roads

The decline of the main roads in the railway age has given rise to a misconception that this was a period when there was no road development. This is simply not the case; the vast growth in trade and travel brought about by the railways required improvements to local roads as well. Thus the construction of much of the rural road network seems to have been contemporary with the building of the railways.

This was partly achieved by reforms in the method of maintaining and improving roads. In 1835 statute labour was finally done away with and parishes were allowed to raise highway rates and employ professional staff. There were still some 15,000 different parishes and the system remained fragmented and amateurish. In any case, although parishes were required to maintain roads, they had only very limited legal powers to maintain them. It is doubtful, for example, whether they had the power to replace an earth road with one based on the Macadam system.

Further reforms were made by acts of 1862 (5) and 1864 (6). These allowed the formation of highway boards which were a grouping of parishes. A highway board had additional powers of improvement, including the conversion of earth roads to stone. Many country roads were first provided with a stone surface in the Victorian period, allowing all year round use with wheeled vehicles.

This marks an important stage in the development of byways as we now know them. Not all the previous earth roads were made into stone roads, but the improvement was such that most vehicular traffic diverted to those that were. The earth roads declined in importance to become the green lanes of the twentieth century. At the same time, the improvement of roads marked the end of the use of packhorses for carrying goods; packhorse trains were still in widespread use well into the nineteenth century, at least in remote areas.

It seems that the use of saddle horses also declined. The Victorian farmer drove to market in a gig or dogcart whilst his Georgian predecessor would have ridden there. These changes meant that bridleways, although still well-used, ceased to be the vital arteries of transport that they had been in earlier centuries and settled down to a subsidiary role to the new roads. It is interesting to note that this change of role seems to have been reflected in the terminology. During the Victorian era the earlier term *bridle road* seems to have been replaced by *bridleway* or even *bridle path*, perhaps reflecting a view that they were less important than they once had been.

Despite the improvements made by highway boards, they were not established in all areas. At that time there was no elected system of local government in rural areas. Instead a great deal of power vested in the hands of the local Justices of the Peace who met in Quarter Sessions to carry out administrative as well as judicial functions. Importantly, they were responsible for overseeing the work of the parishes in highway matters. The justices had the power to create highway boards, but no obligation to do so. Some parishes jealously guarded their autonomy and were opposed to losing their highway functions. In some cases they were supported in this by local justices who vetoed the formation of a board.

One of the great achievements of the Victorian age was the creation of a democratic local government system. An act of 1888 set up elected county councils who took over the functions of the justices in Quarter Sessions (7). At the same time they became responsible for the former turnpike roads, which were now described as *main roads*. The councils had the same powers as the highway boards, allowing them to improve the roads as well as to maintain them. To these powers was added an important new feature in that the roads were to *vest* in the council. This means that the surface of the road became the property of the council giving it a significant additional control that neither parishes nor highway boards had. As well as allowing it to maintain ownership over materials used on the road, it also meant that there was very much less scope for the owner of the subsoil to argue that improvements to the road were a trespass against him. Parishes were subject to that restriction; for example the courts held that it was unlawful for a parish to erect stone posts to mark where a bridleway ran over a moor as this was outside its powers (8).

This reform was followed by an act of 1894 which divided all country areas into rural districts with elected councils (RDCs) (9). The new councils became responsible for all highways other than main roads, taking over from the highway boards or the parishes where boards had not already been formed. Curiously, the RDCs had the same powers as their predecessors so there was still no power of improvement where a highway board had not been formed. This anomaly remained right up to 1930.

15.12. The end of the private ways

It is possible that the nineteenth century rationalisation of highway law spelt the end of Hale's private way, in the sense of a way required to be maintained by the local community but not being within the normal regime whereby a failure to maintain could be the subject of legal action on behalf of the public. Quite how this change occurred is not certain, but the most plausible explanation is that it arose from the 1835 Highways Act.

This Act imposed legal duties on what were known as *highway parishes*; that is places that traditionally had maintained their own highways. In many cases highway parishes were also the church parishes, but not necessarily. For example, in the large parishes of the North and West where sub-divisions of the parish such as townships had previously maintained the highways, these were regarded as highway parishes.

Within a highway parish the inhabitants had to elect a surveyor who was obliged to levy a rate and use it to maintain those highways that were maintained by the inhabitants at large. It is important to note that for the purposes of the act, the word *highway* was given an extended meaning. In the words of the act, highways "shall be understood to mean all roads, bridges (not being county bridges), carriageways, cartways, horseways, bridleways, footways, causeways, churchways and pavements".

At first sight this seems surprising in that it suggests that all these types of way have become highways, that is, open to all members of the public. The definition is for the purposes of the Act, that is in terms of the maintenance duties of the surveyor. So where a way of any of these descriptions was maintained by the inhabitants at large before the Act, then it appears that it was brought within the maintenance responsibility of the surveyor, even if not a highway in the sense of being open to the public. So in these circumstances any of Hale's private ways that were previously maintained by the parish would be swept within the consolidated responsibilities of the surveyor. This would include any surviving customary ways, and it is noteworthy that the definition specifically includes churchways which normally fall within the definition of customary ways.

It may be argued that in a few rare cases, customary churchways are still recognised today. But it should be noted that a churchway would only be brought within the responsibility of the surveyor if it was maintained by the inhabitants of a highway parish. Where the highway and church parishes coincided then the surveyor would take over. Where the highway parish was, say, a township within a parish then the maintenance of a churchway might still be the responsibility of the parishioners of the whole parish rather than devolved to the surveyors of the individual townships.

It is conceded that this is a novel interpretation of the law, but nobody has suggested a better explanation for where the private ways went to! Whilst it appears to explain how the community maintenance responsibility passed to the parish surveyor and ultimately to the highway authority of today, it does not follow that any ways taken over that were not previously open to the public would automatically have become so. On the other hand, for at least the last century nobody seems to have had any doubt that those routes that were highways for the purposes of the highways acts have carried public rights. The change of attitude may well have taken place in the Victorian era when it was accepted by the courts that where an owner allowed use freely by the local inhabitants then an inference could be drawn that the route had been dedicated to the public as a whole (10). The implication is that even if there were private ways open only to the local inhabitants, they would have become normal public highways through use by the inhabitants.

15.13. *Urban streets*

It is now proposed to look briefly at the development of urban streets during the Victorian period. At first sight it may seem surprising that these should figure in a history of rural paths but the problems of urban areas led to changes in the law relating to highways that still cast their shadows today.

Until the early nineteenth century, even the largest towns were only larger versions of rural market towns. But during the industrial revolution large numbers of people moved from country districts to work in the industrial towns which grew very rapidly. The towns were simply not designed to cope with the new population and there was no effective local government system to do anything about it. Thousands of people were packed into tiny dwellings with no clean water or sanitation and it is hardly surprising that this led to major cholera epidemics killing tens of thousands of people. Public opinion demanded action and this led to major programmes of water supply, sewerage, and the paving and regular cleaning of urban streets.

To achieve these changes it was necessary to introduce new laws relating to highways. Most features only applied within designated urban areas and were included in public health acts rather than highways acts. These were first introduced in 1848 but applied in limited areas which were gradually increased during the

Victorian period. From the Local Government Act of 1896 the urban areas were defined to include all boroughs and cities as well as designated urban districts which, like rural districts, had their own elected councils (UDCs). The distinction thus created, with different highway laws for urban and rural districts, survived until quite recently, only being finally done away with in 1974.

Urban districts were originally parishes that included built-up areas. Although every urban district thus had an urban core, a district could also include rural parts if the original parish happened to be a large one. Thus it was quite possible for rural bridleways to have been in an urban district and to have been subject to different laws from similar bridleways in neighbouring RDC areas. A particular difficulty is that the urban laws relied heavily on the concept of a street; unfortunately it has never been entirely decided by the courts precisely what a *street* means. The definition in the statute includes all highways but in some contexts it has been held only to apply to streets in the normal urban sense. This point will be explored more fully in Chapter 21 with respect to the records held by highway authorities.

15.14. *The coming of the motor vehicle*

It is arguable that the transport system at the start of the twentieth century was better than ever before or was ever to be again if judged on quality rather than speed. A vast network of steam railways provided a level of comfort that has never been surpassed. From the numerous country stations the dusty white roads of the Victorian era provided routes to even the most remote hamlets; routes that were safe for pedestrians, riders and horse drawn vehicles and since the introduction of steam rollers in the 1890s, smooth enough for the latest pneumatic tyred bicycles. These roads were supplemented by an even denser network of footpaths and bridleways linking the most isolated farms to other farms and villages. And in the towns the streets were everywhere paved with granite setts or wooden blocks with pollution-free electric trams along the busiest routes. Yet within a decade these civilised conditions were under threat from the motor vehicle, a problem which a century later we are no closer to solving.

Motor vehicles first made their appearance in the 1890s and grew rapidly in the years up to the 1914-18 war. During the war years the technology was much improved for military purposes. The end of the war saw many surplus vehicles sold for civilian use together with a supply of trained drivers released from the armed forces. All these factors encouraged a rapid growth both of private cars and of commercial enterprises operating road haulage and bus services.

Traffic growth brought about a need for a change in road technology. A defect of the stone roads was that pneumatic tyres tended to pull out the road surface leading to intolerable dust and damage to the road. To prevent this it was necessary to find a new binder to hold the stones together. After much trial and error it was found that materials such as asphalt, tar or bitumen gave the best results and thus was developed the familiar tarmacadam. Although originally intended as a replacement for the stone roads of the countryside, it was found that the new material was strong enough to be used to replace the paved roads in towns.

From the 1920s the stone roads began to be replaced with tarmac, starting with the main roads between towns and gradually spreading to the more minor lanes. Car ownership increased among the more wealthy and there was a rapid development of country bus services. For the first time, mechanical transport was available for most journeys and workaday use of public paths declined. At the same time, though, improved transport and greater leisure allowed people to visit the countryside for pleasure and walking became a popular pastime. This led to the need to preserve paths being recognised and pressure groups began to be formed; the Ramblers' Association, for example, was formed in 1935. Unfortunately, a similar development of riding for leisure did not take place until many years later and the formation of pressure groups to protect bridleways was similarly delayed.

The conversion of stone roads to tarmac was not universal. Until after the 1939-45 war there remained extensive networks of stone and earth roads, particularly in the more remote areas. Although motor traffic tended to use the tarmac roads, horses were still used on many farms. Horse-drawn traffic generally used the shortest routes and the surviving stone and earth roads remained in regular use.

15.15. County roads and trunk roads

Since 1897, both urban and rural district councils had been responsible for the highways in their area, other than the main roads which were the responsibility of the county councils. This was adequate when road maintenance was simple, but as traffic increased and road-making became more sophisticated, many of the smallest districts began to have difficulty in keeping up. This led to changes in road responsibilities which came into effect in 1930 (11). In essence, the effect was that the RDCs lost their highways functions to the county councils, but UDCs continued as before to be responsible for all but the most important roads.

The law made the county councils responsible for all highways in rural districts and gave the councils the same powers for these as they already had in respect of main roads. This meant that a highway vested in the county council even where it had not previously vested in the RDC. It also cleared up the anomaly that RDCs did not have improvement powers where there had not previously been a highway board; now they had the full powers in all cases. All the highways for which the county council was responsible became known as *county roads*; as will be seen in Chapter 21 this terminology has given rise to some confusion.

By the 1930s the development of motor traffic was such that a great deal of long-distance traffic between major towns was travelling by road rather than by rail as before. This led to the same sorts of problems that had been experienced in the turnpike era, in that the cost of providing the roads needed for traffic between towns fell on the rural counties between. The solution this time was for the most important routes between major towns to be designated as *trunk roads*. The Ministry of Transport became the highway authority for these roads, with the same powers that a county council would otherwise have had. This ensured that the cost of these important national roads was met from national funds rather than by the ratepayers of the counties through which they ran.

15.16. The post-war years

The developments of the 1930s were brought to an abrupt end by the outbreak of the 1939-45 war. The need to divert as many resources as possible to the war effort meant reductions in motor traffic as hardly any fuel was available; there was no new road construction and only essential repairs. Horses enjoyed a brief revival, particularly in farming where food production was greatly intensified to reduce imports and the risks to merchant shipping. However, this boom was the grand finale for the working horse. With the end of the war, serious food shortages arose throughout Europe and the need to maintain home food production became paramount. Factories that had produced war materials were switched to tractors. Over only two or three years in the late 1940s the working horse became virtually extinct.

Around the same time riding had reached a low point. The use of horses for workaday purposes had virtually ceased during the 1930s as mechanised transport spread. Riding as a recreation had declined dramatically during the war years due to shortages of fodder and the absence of most young people in the forces. By 1950 and for another twenty years or so, most people regarded the horse as an extinct form of transport, perhaps like a sedan chair or balloon. Few could have predicted the explosion in recreational riding that was to start in the 1970s.

This temporary break in riding came at an unfortunate time. Out of the war came a widespread view that a new and more egalitarian society should be created. One of the results of this was a revival of the idea, first expressed in the 1930s, that public paths should be recorded to assist their preservation for public use. This led in 1949 to the decision that definitive maps of public paths should be produced. The work on this was carried out throughout the 1950s; that is precisely the time that use of horses had reached its lowest ebb. The maps were, of course, supposed to differentiate between footpaths and routes that were available to horses as well, but the accuracy of this depended very much on the skill of the volunteer surveyors. With most people regarding riding as an irrelevance and no organised bridleways lobby, it is perhaps surprising that so many bridleways were actually recorded. Nevertheless, there can be little doubt that thousands of miles of bridleways, in regular use by horses at least up to the 1920s, were recorded on the maps as footpaths.

It has been seen that many of the old stone and earth roads were left behind when the more important roads were tarred in the 1920s and 1930s. They remained in regular use whilst horse-drawn vehicles continued; their rough surfaces posed little problem and it was sensible to go by a short but rough lane rather than a longer tarred road. Arguably, they should have been recorded on the definitive map as Roads Used as Public Paths (RUPPs). However, in many areas they were not recorded, probably because they were still in regular use and thus treated in the same way as tarred road. But their days were numbered.

With the replacement of horses by motor vehicles the position changed. The old roads were often the only access to the more remote farms, but this became regarded as inefficient. So from the mid 1950s the government made available a special fund for the improvement of roads in the country, with particular emphasis on dairying areas to provide efficient routes for the daily milk collection lorries. To save costs, not all the network was upgraded. Generally, priority was given to providing links between farms and the nearest tarred roads; sections linking farms were often left in their original condition. Unfortunately, many of these links seem to have been forgotten by highway authorities which no longer regard them as roads because they are not tarred, nor as public paths because they are not on the definitive map.

Although such routes remain open to all users, they are of particular benefit to non-motorised users because of the virtual absence of motor traffic.

15.17. Local government changes

Finally, it is proposed to bring the story up to date in respect of the changes to the ways in which roads are managed. Despite the great changes in road use since the 1920s, the pattern of organisation introduced in 1930 remained for more than forty years. Counties remained responsible for all highways in rural areas and main roads in urban areas; UDCs had responsibility for the more local highways in their area including public paths. And the government retained responsibility for the key national roads which from the late 1950s included the new motorways.

Change eventually came as part of the re-organisation of local government which took place in 1974. This retained the concept of two levels of local government with counties and districts. However, the new districts were generally much larger than before and the distinction between rural and urban districts was done away with. For highways the rural model was retained with the counties being responsible for all highways other than trunk roads.

Before too long the government had second thoughts as to whether the two-tier system would not be better replaced by single-tier authorities. This had been the situation before 1974 for some of the largest towns that were county boroughs; this meant they had the powers of both a county and a district at once. In 1986 the metropolitan counties (that is those serving the major conurbations) were abolished and the districts given county powers for their areas. In April 1996 the counties in Wales and some parts of England were also abolished. In respect of highways the main change was the transfer of responsibility from counties to districts with in most cases many more smaller highway authorities. Whatever the benefits for other local government services it seems likely to be a retrograde step for highways, which are best organised as a coherent network.

We have seen how the public paths and byways that remain today are really only a vestige of a much greater network that existed in the times when most travel and trade was by horse. It is only relatively recently that public paths have been recognised as an important recreational resource rather than an obsolete relic of the past. This positive attitude to paths in part arises from the fact that county councils have had path networks large enough to employ specialist rights of way staff; it would be a matter of grave concern to rights of way workers if this specialism should be lost as a result of the sub-division of highway authorities.

Legal notes to chapter 15

1. Coke on Littleton 56a.

2. Austin's case (1672) 1 Ventris 189.

3. See Thrower's case (1672) 1 Ventris 208 where Hale ruled that a *common footway* might be a customary way where only the parishioners could bring an action, but that in the particular case the path was a public one. Similarly in Rex v Saintiff (1704) 6 Mod Rep 255 it was held that a *common bridge* in a *common footpath* was a public highway, although the judge commented on the ambiguity of the description in that common could mean common to a group of people less than the public.

4. Rex v Hammond (1717) 10 Mod 382.

5. Highway Act 1862.

6. Highway Act 1864.

7. Local Government Act 1888.

8. See note 8 of the legal notes to Chapter 2 for a summary of Radcliffe v Marsden UDC (1908)

9. Local Government Act 1894.

10. Regina v The Inhabitants of the County of Southampton (1887) QB 590.

11. Local Government Act 1929.

Further reading

(a) *Highway use and control up to 1895.* Douglas Coombs, Rights of Way Law Review (RWLR) 1.1, 1990.

(b) *Highway authorities since 1800.* John Sugden, RWLR 1.1. 1995.

(c) *The making of the English Landscape.* W. G. Hoskins. Hodder & Stoughton, London. 1955.

(d) *The road goes on.* C. W. Scott-Giles. The Epworth Press, London. 1946.

16
PRIVATE ACTS OF PARLIAMENT

16.1. Introduction

Acts of Parliament are of two types: public acts and private acts. Public acts are those with which the public are normally concerned, that is those setting out new laws which everyone must obey. But it is also possible for a private individual or body to secure a private act, normally to specifically allow actions that would otherwise be unlawful. As will be explained in Section 16.3, such acts were once common in association with major works such as canals, railways, docks and reservoirs.

In recent years the need for these acts has been reduced through public acts giving powers for construction projects, subject to orders having been made with the public having a right of objections. For example, powers now exist for new railways to be built through an order under the Transport and Works Act. But private acts are still being made; a recent example was the act authorising the Channel Tunnel Rail Link. It should be noted that this chapter is not intended to assist the rights of way worker in opposing proposals for new private acts, which will generally need the resources of a national rights of way body. Instead, we will be looking at the evidence for the existence of rights of way that can be obtained from a study of private acts and their supporting papers. However, the particularly important topic of the private acts associated with the enclosure movement is not dealt with here because it will be discussed in greater detail in Chapter 19.

Because private acts are scrutinised very closely by committees of Parliament, it is necessary for the promoters to carry out very detailed and precise research into any public or private rights affected by the proposals. The costs of a private act are very high and the proposals may well be rejected if faults are found in the supporting documents. As the supporting papers were a matter of public record they are almost invariably still available, at least for nineteenth and twentieth century proposals.

16.2. What acts are available?

The vogue for private acts for construction projects started in the middle of the eighteenth century. The first act for construction of a canal was for the Bridgewater Canal in 1758. Somewhat surprisingly the first railway act was passed in the same year, for the Middleton Railway in Leeds. However, for the next seventy years or so, most of the private acts were for other canals.

The gradual development of railways eventually led to the opening of the Liverpool and Manchester Railway in 1830, which marks the first true inter-city line. The success of this led to a rapid speculation in railways until by the 1840s it had grown into what was described at the time as a railway mania with applications for private acts covering thousands of miles of railway, many of which were never built. After that the bubble burst and development was more steady but further acts for the construction of new railways continued to be approved up to the 1914-18 war and occasionally right up to the present day.

The Victorian era was also a period of great enthusiasm for public health measures which often included grandiose water schemes. The building of reservoirs required the acquisition of large areas of land and often the diversion of highways that passed through the site. But in addition, the reservoirs often required extensive catchwater drains to collect water and major pipes and aqueducts to carry the water to where it was needed. Even where these were underground, it was still necessary for the water undertaking to obtain an easement from the owner and thus the area affected might extend a long way from the reservoir. In most cases, water undertakings were authorised by private acts of Parliament. Such acts often dealt with works over a wide area, even extending in some cases to the authorisation of individual water mains under streets.

Although canal, railway and reservoir acts are probably the most fruitful sources of information, it is worth remembering that other large works may well have had private acts as well. These might well include docks and harbour works, or some major drainage works such as are found in the Fens.

16.3. Why were private acts required?

At least until the introduction of planning laws in the 1940s, there was little restriction on what private individuals could do on their own land. However, a promoter of a large scheme might very well run into problems in acquiring the necessary land and in making alterations to highways.

If the owners were prepared to sell, a scheme promoter could obtain all the necessary land by negotiation. Indeed, on some early railways, all the land was acquired in this way. The problem was that a single owner could hold the promoter to ransom by holding out for an unreasonable sum. The larger the scheme, and the more other land that had been bought, then the greater was the potential for this. It was thought unreasonable that individuals could profit in this way, particularly where the works being promoted were thought to be of great public utility. A private act normally gave the promoters powers to compulsorily purchase land that was required for the undertaking, at a fair price set by an external arbitrator.

The other major problem was the effect of the works on public highways. Until recent times, a highway could only be extinguished if it was not needed. There was no provision to extinguish a highway that was used but ran across the site of, say, a proposed reservoir. Even a diversion was only allowed if it provided a better route than before. This meant that it was not permissible to make even a small diversion to a road so as to cross over a canal or railway at a more convenient point. Nor could the gradient be steepened to pass over a bridge. Even bridges over highways, or level crossings, were only allowed if specifically authorised by the local magistrates who were often strongly opposed to the new works and reluctant to give permission.

Although some local railways were built within these constraints, it would have been very difficult for the main trunk routes to have come into existence without other powers. These were provided by private acts which allowed changes to highways to be authorised by Parliament and not by local magistrates, even if the effects were to make use of the highway network less convenient.

It will be seen that the main purposes of private acts meant that Parliament needed to consider in particular detail the questions of land ownership together with public and private rights of way. Information on these had to be specifically set out in the supporting documents which will be described in the next section.

16.4. Finding private acts

Most roads and public paths will not, of course, have been affected by private acts of Parliament. However, the number that were affected may well be more than is suspected at first sight. For example, at its greatest extent the railway network of Great Britain extended to more than 30,000 km and included many branches that have long been closed. Most of these would have had private acts. In addition a vast number of bills were presented for railways that were either not approved or were approved but not built. Even so, the supporting documents had to be produced and will have been preserved.

The first stage will be to determine whether the route under consideration ever crossed a railway. This is quite easy to find out from Ordnance Survey maps which show most disused railways as well as remaining lines. Even if the route does not actually cross the railway but comes within about 100 yards of it, then it is still worth checking to see if the site was included in the area within which land could be purchased, and hence for which records should be available.

A similar logic applies to reservoirs. If the path appears to have been diverted around the side of a reservoir, then it is well worth checking whether it was within the limits covered by the act. It is also worth noting that reservoir projects often included many miles of collecting-channels, typically stone-lined drains anything up to 5 metres square in cross section. These were often included in the works specified in supporting documents, presumably to allow the alteration of highways that crossed them. These channels can be found on the Ordnance Survey maps, and if a route being researched crosses one it is worth checking on the papers for the associated reservoir to see if the channel has its own plan and book of reference.

A more difficult problem is to find information about proposals that were never constructed. This is more common for railways where there were often rival bills from competing companies which both wished to construct railways between the same points but with different alignments. In most cases Parliament would only authorise one route but the supporting papers for the failed scheme will still be available. On a similar note, railway companies sometimes found that the authorised route was too difficult to build and changed their mind as to the alignment. If they needed to go outside the limits of deviation their only recourse was to seek another act. So again, there may be more than one set of documents for one line actually built.

Fortunately, railway history appears to have a much greater following than the history of old highways and this means that somebody will have written a history about even the most obscure branch line. From these it will be possible to find out which lines were proposed but never built. Importantly, railway histories normally specify the names of the individual railway bills and the years in which they were submitted. This makes finding the papers much easier.

If the name and year of the bill is known, it is relatively easy to find it. In most cases it was a requirement that copies of the plans and books of reference had to be deposited with the Clerk to the Peace of the County, and these are normally lodged in county records office. Another copy went to the House of Lords Library where a full set is available.

16.5. *Plans, sections and books of reference*

A private act was normally quite short and simply authorised the construction of whatever works were in prospect together with specifying any general conditions that would apply. The real details of what could be done were set out in the supporting documents which had to be submitted for scrutiny by a Parliamentary committee and which, in the event of the act being passed, form a sort of appendix to it. These documents are normally the plans, sections and books of reference.

It was necessary to submit an accurate plan showing the location and extent of the works. From the second half of the nineteenth century these were sometimes on an Ordnance Survey base, but in earlier times these were not available and a new survey had to be carried out. This applied to most railway proposals, and even in the later years railway companies seem to have preferred to carry out their own surveys. A railway plan from the 1840s may well be the first reliable plan available for many areas.

Unlike a modern planning application, it was not necessary for precise details of all proposals to be submitted. For example, a reservoir plan might merely show the area covered by the proposed dam and the area covered by water. A railway plan normally only showed a single centre line. Of much more importance was what were known as the limits of deviation.

The term comes from the canal and railway acts. The principle was to set the limits of deviation, normally as lines on each side and parallel with the centre line. Within these limits the railway promoter was free to build the line, together with any necessary ancillary works such as stations or sidings. Having a reasonably wide corridor gave the potential for the railway to be deviated slightly from the permitted centre line, so long as it remained within the limits of deviation. The corridor between the limits of deviation also provided the area within which the company could compulsorily purchase land, but only for the purposes of building the railway and other necessary works.

Although the limits of deviation were normally set parallel to the centre line, this could be varied. It was not uncommon for limits to divert to miss major buildings that would otherwise have straddled the limits.

In other projects such as reservoirs or docks, limits of deviation were also set around the project. Strictly speaking, the term is a misnomer as a reservoir cannot be deviated, but the practical meaning is the same in that the limits represent the area within which land may be purchased.

Within the limits of deviation, all plots of land were identified and numbered. This includes all public roads and paths. The numbers refer to a schedule known as the book of reference. This provides details for each of the plots in numerical order. It was normal to describe the plot and to specify the owner, lessee and occupier of the land. In the case of public highways it was normal to describe the land as a highway and to specify the highway authority as at least the part occupier of the land. It is these details, together with the plan, which make these documents so important in proving rights of way.

In addition to the plans there were often sections provided showing the gradients along existing roads and any changes if the road was raised or lowered. The need for these sections normally arose from the requirements of the act which often specified the maximum gradients that would be allowed. For example, most railway acts after 1845 include the standard requirements from the Railway Clauses Consolidation Act (1) which specified maximum gradients of 1 in 30 for turnpikes, 1 in 20 for public carriage roads and 1 in 16 for private roads. Where the gradient was already steeper than this, then the carrying out of the authorised works was not to make the situation any worse. It is worth checking the sections against the plan as sometimes additional information is given as to the status of the existing route.

16.6. Interpreting the records

Interpreting these records is not always as simple as it might seem, as individual surveyors seem to have used slightly different conventions and terminology.

This is particularly true of the description of the land parcels where roads and paths were variously described. The strictly correct term of public carriageway is sometimes used, but more often they are described as public roads. The term public highway is also sometimes used. Although the strict legal meaning today includes public footpaths and bridleways, in Victorian times the term was generally restricted to a carriageway and this meaning seems to be used by the surveyors of public works of that era. Where the land was a public bridleway or footpath, this was normally stated specifically.

Very many routes were described as *occupation roads*. This means a vehicular road but one for occupiers of certain land rather than for the public at large. Although altering such roads did not affect public rights, the private property rights of the occupiers were to be respected, although less stringent standards were imposed than for public roads. The maximum gradients from the Railway Clauses

Consolidation Act were described above. There were also standards for height and width of bridges. A private road bridge had to be at least 9' high as against 15' for a public carriageway and 16' for a turnpike. Similarly, there had to be a clear width of 12' for a private road as against 25' for a public carriage road and 35' for a turnpike. No such standards were imposed for public paths. On the other hand, level crossings were acceptable on private roads whilst they could only be provided on public roads and paths with the permission of the magistrates.

This has led to some problems. It is of course possible for an occupation road with private vehicular rights to also include a public footpath or bridleway. The more careful surveyors would record this. However, it seems that more often such routes were merely described as occupation roads, presumably on the basis that the standards that would thus be required were in any case more onerous than if they had been described as public paths. The disadvantage from our point of view is that there is then no evidence of whether public rights on foot or horseback were believed to exist at that time.

It is worth noting that the term *occupation crossing* or *occupation bridge* is still used by railway staff to mean a crossing or a bridge on an occupation road. There is a subtle difference between these and an *accommodation crossing* or bridge. Accommodation works were those provided by a railway as part of a deal to purchase land and typically involved providing a route across a railway between two parts of a parcel of land that had been severed by the line. It was normally agreed that if the same person ceased to own the land on each side then there was no obligation on the part of the railway to continue to provide the link. Over the years many accommodation crossings have been eliminated as land ownership has changed, but occupation crossings cannot be removed in this way.

The owner and occupier of highways are also subject to different conventions. Sometimes the owner of the soil is identified as the owner, sometimes the local surveyor of highways or local board and sometimes both. Where the highway authority is not named as the owner, it will normally be found to be specified as the occupier, sometimes as sole occupier and sometimes jointly with the occupier of adjoining land. This need not even be done consistently within one book of reference; some surveyors seem to have taken the line that the highway authority was the owner or joint owner of carriageways, but only the occupier of public paths. The distinction seems unlikely to be important. If the parish surveyor of highways (or highways board, or local board) is described as either owner or occupier of land described as a road, then it will indicate that it was considered to be a public highway.

This may be important if the description of the plot simply describes it as a road without making it clear whether it was public or not.

16.7. Value of the records as evidence

It has to be recognised that records from private acts are not as strong evidence as records of the highway authority itself. The surveyor of a new railway or reservoir was an independent researcher who provides evidence of the reputed status of the various ways at the time of the survey. Nevertheless, there are very good reasons for believing that the researching of the ways would have been done with considerable care. Consequently, one may reasonably expect that the details recorded will be accurate.

The sorts of projects which required private acts were very big business indeed. The costs of promoting a private bill were themselves immense and would be lost if the bill were to be thrown out because of inaccuracies. Particularly in the case of railways, there were often competing proposals. If a bill were rejected, a rival company might well be given permission instead and the original promoter would lose all. Moreover, having competing proposals meant that inaccuracies were very likely to be found out as companies went through their rival's proposals in meticulous detail in order to find errors that would discredit them. Promoters simply could not afford to make mistakes.

It is not as if descriptions of highways were merely a minor detail of a document intended to describe something else. The plans, sections and books of reference were there to record existing rights and to show how these would be affected by the proposed works. Private rights of ownership, including private rights of way, and public rights over highways were the main rights that were intended to be accurately recorded.

It is also important to note that it was contrary to the financial interests of the promoters to record private and public rights of way. This was particularly true of vehicular rights which often required costly accommodation works. Minimum standards were often set in such matters as bridge widths or maximum gradients of approaches. As standards for public roads were more stringent than for occupation roads, it was contrary to the interests of promoters to record as public what was actually an occupation road.

Courts have generally been more ready to accept as true, statements that were contrary to the interests of the person or body making the statement. Thus the fact that the promoter of, say, a railway admitted the existence of highways that would be costly to accommodate, must be taken as strong evidence that the matters had been closely researched and that the promoter had been reluctantly forced to accept that the highway actually existed. This must remain strong evidence of repute today.

It is also worth noting that many books of reference will be found to be divided into parish sections each endorsed by the local Lord of the Manor. This seems to have been a legal requirement in many cases and again points to the accuracy of the survey having been certified as correct by a local dignitary who might reasonably be expected to know the true position.

In addition it should be noted that Section 9 of the Railway Clauses Consolidation Act required railway companies seeking to provide level crossings over public roads and paths to advertise their proposals in a paper circulating in the county and for these to be approved by the magistrates. If this permission was denied, the company was obliged to provide a bridge. This may provide a further source of evidence, although this will only apply where the line was actually built. It may be that some accommodation roads crossing the line on the level also carried footpath or bridleway rights and that permission had to be sought from the magistrates for level crossings, even where the public rights were not specified on the deposited plans.

16.8. *Private act evidence for deletion of rights of way*

If it is accepted that the recording of highway rights is strong evidence that such rights existed at the time of the survey, does the converse apply? Is the fact that no rights were recorded along a route at the time of the survey evidence that no rights existed at that time? Could information from a private act provide evidence for the deletion or downgrading of a public right of way? This will depend on the particular circumstances of what powers were given to the promoters and what status was recorded for rights of way in the plans, sections and books of reference.

It is arguable that the showing of a highway provides greater evidence for the existence of the highway than the absence of a highway from the plans does for its non-existence. As showing a highway would cost the company more, it would presumably only show the highway if it was convinced that it did exist. On the other hand, it might well try and deny the existence of a disputed route if it could get away with it. It should be noted, though, that in at least one decided case the courts have accepted railway plans which showed no highway in a particular location as evidence that it did not exist (2).

Some private acts had the effect of extinguishing all existing rights of way within the area of the works. This often applied to undertakings such as docks where it was intended, for security reasons, to ringfence the whole site. Clearly, such an act will provide conclusive evidence that no rights existed at the date at which it took effect. Where the works were actually carried out then there is unlikely to be any argument. However, private acts often looked a long way ahead and authorised an undertaking to carry out much more extensive works than were planned in the short term. In many cases these more extensive works were never carried out. This may well mean that there will be land which is within the area covered by the act, but which is not within the ringfenced area of the actual works. Such an area may well include alleged public rights of way.

In cases such as this it is important to check the act to establish the date at which rights of way were to be extinguished. A private act authorises the subsequent purchase of land. Thus, at the earliest, the extinguishment of rights of way will take place at the time of the purchase as otherwise the occupiers would be deprived of access in the interim. It follows that where an undertaking was authorised to buy land and extinguish rights of way, then this will not have occurred if the undertaking never actually bought the land in question.

In other cases an act may allow an undertaking to buy land in advance of future works, but retain it in its existing use until required. Here the power to extinguish rights of way may not necessarily apply on the purchase of the land, but may be a reserve power for the undertaking to use when works are about to commence. In such cases it would be necessary to establish whether the powers were ever actually used.

More usually, however, the act did not specifically extinguish rights of way that were not set out in the supporting documents. In theory, therefore, any public rights of way would remain and any new works obstructing them would constitute an illegal obstruction. If it could be shown from other evidence that a highway existed prior to the construction of the works, then it will remain even though obstructed by the works carried out. However, in the absence of any prior evidence of this sort, the non-recording of a right of way and its subsequent obstruction must be very strong evidence that no right of way existed at the time of the act.

In practice, however, problems normally arise where routes are not physically obstructed and have been used since the construction of the works. For example, public rights may be alleged to exist over routes that were originally accommodation works or occupation roads. Or higher rights may be alleged to exist over routes identified in the supporting documents as footpaths or bridleways. Do the supporting documents prove that no such rights existed at the time of the act?

Accommodation works, such as accommodation bridges or level crossings over railways, were not specified on the plans or books of reference. This is because there were no pre-existing rights to be recorded. Accommodation works exist as part of the purchase agreement for the land, usually to provide a link between two parts of land that was severed. The location of the accommodation works may be anywhere that the owner and the undertaking found convenient and there is normally a right for the undertaking to remove the works if one part of the land comes into a different ownership from that of the other. Although it will often be found that the public regularly use accommodation bridges and so on, it is difficult to avoid the conclusion that any public rights will have come into existence subsequent to the building of the works. It would have been far too risky for the promoter of the undertaking to have tried to cover up the existence of known public rights by not recording them on the plan and book of reference.

For many years it was held that a new highway could not be presumed to be dedicated across a railway by an accommodation route. This was because such a dedication would prevent the railway company from removing the crossing if it became redundant, and it was argued that in making the dedication the company would have acted contrary to its legal purpose. In the early 1950s the then British Transport Commission objected to the inclusion on the definitive map of many alleged rights of way which crossed railways using accommodation works.

However, this ruling was reversed in 1955 and it is now accepted law that a highway can be presumed to have been dedicated over an accommodation route (3). So that even if the deposited plans and documents were taken as proving that no right of way existed at the date of the private act, it would still be necessary to show that no highway could have come into existence subsequently in order to show that one does not exist today.

A different situation applies where a route is recorded as an occupation road. This means that the route is a private right of way for the occupiers of certain areas of land, which they may use on foot, on horseback or with vehicles. Although such routes were intended to be used by vehicles, the specifications for such matters as width of bridges, maximum gradients and so on, were less stringent than for a public road. In view of the importance of this distinction, it seems likely that promoters of private acts would have been careful to ensure that the correct classification applied. It would appear, therefore, that the showing of a route as an occupation road does indicate that no public vehicular rights existed at the time of the act. There is, of course, no reason why public vehicular rights should not subsequently have come into existence through presumption of dedication.

It is, however, common for many private vehicular roads to also carry public rights on foot or horseback. In general the requirements for such users were less stringent than for private vehicular travel and it may be that it was not thought important to record the public rights. Consequently the recording of an occupation road should not be taken as evidence that public rights on foot or horseback did not exist.

A possible exception to this may be where an occupation road crossed a railway at a level crossing. If it can be shown that the railway was built but no application was ever made to the magistrates for permission for a level crossing, then this might well be regarded as evidence that public rights on foot or horseback did not exist at the date of construction of the line.

A similar logic might well be applied to routes recorded as footpaths. Bridleways would generally have required more expensive bridges and the provision of gates rather than stiles at any level crossings. Thus it seems not unreasonable to argue that the recording of a footpath only does indicate that other rights did not exist at the time. Again, there is no reason why such rights should not subsequently have come into existence through presumed dedication.

Legal notes to chapter 16

1. Railway Clauses Consolidation Act, 1845.

2. Attorney General v Antrobus (1905) 2 Ch 188.

3. British Transport Commission v Westmoreland County Council (1958) AC 126.

Further reading

Railway and canal deposited plans. Bill Riley, RWLR 9.3. 1990.

17
TITHE SURVEYS

17.1. Introduction

Tithe surveys provide an important source of information in the researching of public rights of way. These surveys cover the greater part of the country, in most cases a generation or so before the first Ordnance Survey maps. They are official documents, prepared as part of a public process and as such are good evidence for the purposes for which they were prepared. However, they were not prepared for the purpose of recording highways and as such their interpretation requires special care.

This chapter looks at the background of tithes, including a digression into the structure of parishes which is also important in a number of other areas of research based on documentary evidence. The reasons for the tithe surveys is set out together with the implications for establishing from them the evidence to prove the existence of public highways at the time of the surveys.

17.2. Background to tithes

The concept of tithes originated more than a thousand years ago when the Christian religion was first introduced to Britain. A tithe was a form of local tax to pay for the upkeep of the local church and to maintain the priest. A *tithe* meant a tenth and this reflected the fact that the tax was at a rate of 10% of the annual produce of land that was liable. In addition the church had allocations of *glebe* land whose entire output was devoted to church purposes and which was not tithed.

Over the centuries the concept became rather more blurred. The original idea was that tithes were paid directly to the local priest or rector. But in many cases the rights to tithes were granted to some other religious organisation such as a monastery, college or even a bishop who thus became an absentee rector. Out of the tithes, the rector had to meet the expenses of the local church including the stipend of a priest, in this case known as a vicar who substituted for the rector. With improvements in agriculture the tithes often brought in considerably more than the cost of providing a church and vicar and the religious organisations that owned the tithes were able to make considerable profits from them.

The commercial success of the monasteries led to their downfall. King Henry VIII, with the flimsiest of justification, dissolved the monasteries and personally confiscated their assets. These he then sold off for the best price he could get. The assets included the ability to make profits from the tithes and this right was also sold off to private individuals. As in so many areas of life in those times, there were a great variety of different solutions and local arrangements. These complications are outside the scope of this chapter; all that it is necessary to appreciate is that by the nineteenth century there was a complex pattern of local arrangements in which some parcels of land were tithed and others not and that many tithes went not to the church but to private individuals.

The continued development of agriculture meant that the values of the tithes continued to increase, particularly from the mid eighteenth century. Technological development accelerated and during the Napoleonic wars agricultural prices were forced to a high level. It was felt to be unfair that investment in better agriculture meant that higher tithes had to be paid, often to a private individual who obtained a windfall benefit without making any investment. It was also thought to be unfair that more and more of the national income came from industry which paid no tithes. These concerns eventually led in 1836 to the introduction of a new system in which tithes were to be fixed at the prevailing level in each parish so that any further investment gave benefit directly to those making the investment.

17.3. Parishes

It is appropriate at this point to look in a little more detail at the concept of a parish and its boundaries. A study of this at a local level is often necessary to understand other types of historical documents, but as the concept is linked to the tithe system it will be considered here.

The basic building block of local government is the township (also sometimes described as a vill). Broadly speaking, the original settlements of the pre-Norman periods became the manors of the feudal system and these later became the townships. However, this can only be a generalisation and many local variations will be found to exist.

Very many churches were provided by lords of the manor during the feudal period with the tithes from their land being allocated to the church. A parish then became a block of land whose tithes were paid for church purposes within the block. There were two different ways of doing this. Where the population within a township was sufficient to support a church, then the township became a parish. However, in more thinly-populated areas a parish would be formed out of a group of townships which originally shared a single church. The latter pattern is general in Northeast Wales, and north of a line of counties stretching across England from Shropshire to the North Riding. To the south and west, parishes are mainly a single township.

The tithe system had the effect of fixing parish boundaries. Although land ownership boundaries could alter as land was bought and sold, the parish boundaries were fixed because no tithe owner would agree to the loss of tithes from transferring land to another parish. This also had important implications for the parishes with several townships.

As population grew, it became increasingly unsatisfactory for the outlying townships to rely on a central church. To divide the parish would have split the tithe income to the loss of the tithe owner, so instead, subsidiary churches were provided with all tithes continuing to go the parish church. The owner of the tithes could then pay curates to run the subsidiary churches and pocket the profit. Not all townships would get their own church; sometimes a group of townships known as a *chapelry* would share a subsidiary church or *chapel of ease*. Some parishes were immense; the parish of Whalley in Lancashire, for example, contained 105,000 acres and no less than 47 different townships.

In the middle ages, such local government as existed was based on the manor or township. During the Tudor period, however, local government was strengthened with an emphasis on the parish. Parishes were made responsible for highway maintenance from 1555 and from 1601 for supporting the poor of the parish through the new concept of a poor rate. However, in 1662 Parliament allowed parishes to be divided for the purposes of the poor law. This was not always done simply by levying the rate on a township basis; in some cases although the parish was divided, a number of townships would be grouped for poor law purposes. Chapelry boundaries were sometimes used for this, but not invariably.

In a similar way, parishes were also divided for highway maintenance purposes. Townships might maintain their own highways, or even sometimes sub-divisions of a township known as a *hamlet*. On the other hand, townships might be grouped. To make the matter more complicated, townships were sometimes grouped in a different way for highways than for the poor law.

The reforms of local government in the Victorian period set up parish councils, which were responsible for the area known as a *civil parish*. These were defined as the units for poor law purposes. This meant that in the single township parishes the ecclesiastical parish, the civil parish and the township were all the same. However, in the larger multi-township parishes the civil parish was a sub-division of the ecclesiastical parish and might consist of a single township or a group of townships where they had maintained their own poor. These civil parishes became the building blocks of local government, and their boundaries are those shown on the Ordnance Survey maps.

The complication of different groupings of townships for highway purposes was overcome in 1895 by transferring maintenance responsibilities to the new urban and rural district councils (1). Another curious anomaly was cleared up with the abolition of *extra-parochial places* which were in no parish at all. However, there remained some places where parishes overlapped with areas common to more than one parish; a handful still survive today.

Records associated with tithes correspond to the traditional church parishes and not to the civil parishes coming into existence in 1896. It should also be noted that modern church parishes are often different from the traditional ones as they have been modified to meet current requirements. This means that before starting any research on tithe records it is necessary to establish the parish structure during the early nineteenth century for the area to be studied.

17.4. Tithe commutation

In 1836 Parliament decided that all tithes should be converted into a fixed rent charge to be based on the existing tithe return from each parcel of land. Tithe Commissioners were appointed to oversee the process which was carried out on a parish by parish basis. The process was carried out quite quickly and most tithe apportionment documents date from the end of the 1830s.

The first stage was to ensure an accurate map of all the land on which tithe was paid. This was not necessarily the whole parish. Land which was barren and produced no output was not subject to tithes; this often meant that mountain or moorland in the parish was not tithed and hence was not surveyed. In addition there might be cultivated land which for historical reasons was not subject to tithes; for example glebe land. There were also parcels of untithed land arising from the enclosures when it was often the practice to allocate some freehold land to the church in lieu of the tithes on all the rest of the new enclosures. Again, such land would not need to be surveyed.

In most areas the valuations were carried out before the first large-scale Ordnance Survey maps and often provide the earliest reliable mapping of the parish. At the time the surveys were graded as first or second class, depending on the accuracy. However, the distinction concerned the accuracy of the measurements where an error of a few percent in measured areas meant an important amount of money to those involved. The distinction is not important to us; all tithe survey maps should be adequate for our purposes in showing the various land parcels.

It is important to note that the tithe survey is essentially about parcels of land and is effectively a survey of boundaries such as hedges, fences, walls and so on. It was not intended as a survey of highways as such. Where a highway was bounded by hedges, then it will certainly appear as a long field. An unfenced highway such as a gated field road or a cross-field path may or may not appear on the survey, depending on the attitude of the surveyor.

Each tithed parcel of land was given a number on the map. The map was accompanied by an apportionment which is a list of the parcels numbered on the map. The owner of each parcel was given, together with its area and annual return, and in addition the name of each field was given. The names often reflect a folk memory of events or landscape features of which there is no other record.

When the tithe survey and apportionment had been completed to the satisfaction of the Tithe Commissioners, it was approved and became conclusive of the tithe values. The documents became public documents. The official versions are held at the Public Records Office but local versions for almost all parishes are also held at county record offices. Some researchers have reported significant differences between the official version and the certified copies held locally.

17.5. Tithe records as evidence

There can be no doubt that tithe records are very strong evidence in respect of those matters that they were intended to deal with. Like the definitive maps today, they were legally conclusive of the tithes that were liable to be paid. But this no longer matters to anyone; the question today is the extent to which they provide evidence of the status of highways.

In such matters the tithe records were not intended to be definitive. But they are still very important in highway matters because we can take as a starting point the fact that the tithes were correct and we can often infer other matters from these with confidence. This was summed up by Lord Denning as follows:

On the question of whether there was a road at the specific place the tithe map was of much importance. . . . It is of great value. It was prepared under statutory authority by the Tithe Commissioners, with great care and accuracy, to show all cultivated land, arable and pasture, because tithe was payable on land which produced crops. It also had to show waste land and definite roads which did not produce crops, because tithe was not payable on these. If a road passed over a man's land he would naturally require it to be shown, so as not to pay tithe on it. (2)

It is worth noting that the reverse applies. If an area of land was incorrectly excluded from tithes then the tithe owner would lose financially. One may be sure that both sides would be ever vigilant to ensure that no mistakes were made.

In practice, however, the interpretation of the records is often difficult. It is necessary to understand that land might not be subject to tithes for two different reasons; firstly for some legal reason that excluded the land from tithes and or secondly because it was *barren*, that is producing no crops. For example, glebe land was not tithed because all the profit was intended to go to the church. By the time of the survey there were many parcels of land which for historical reasons were free of tithes, although producing crops. On the other hand, land might be titheable but barren, for example because the soil was unsuitable for growing anything on.

This distinction also has an implications for highways. In the nineteenth century, documents often describe some highways as being owned either by the parish or the parish surveyor of highways. The parish was not liable to pay tithes and so a highway that was regarded as being owned by the parish would not be titheable, even where it was not barren. It should be noted that it was not at all uncommon in that era for the wide grass verges of roads to be rented out for grazing with the rents being used to defray the costs of road maintenance. Even so, tithes would not be paid on the rents. On the other hand, a road owned by a private individual would be tithed if it had a grass surface from which a return could be obtained, but not if it had a stone surface which made it barren.

The different reasons for a road being tithed or not can interact in various complex ways, and it is proposed to try and simplify the matter by considering separately what the surveyor could have done depending on whether he considered a road to belong to the parish or not.

17.6. Roads belonging to the parish

The question of which highways belonged to the parish is an obscure one. At the time of the tithe surveys the concept of the vesting of the surface in the highway authority had not been introduced and the question of whether the public had any property rights in highways seems to have exercised the minds of lawyers. Nevertheless, it does seem clear from contemporary sources (for example, railway acts of Parliament) that at least some highways were regarded as belonging to the parish or to the parish surveyor of highways.

Not all public highways were regarded as being owned by the parish; for example, footpaths or bridleways through fields were regarded as belonging to the owner of the fields. It is not clear what the distinction was between those highways that belonged to the parish and those that did not. One possibility is that carriageways were regarded as belonging to the parish whilst footpaths and bridleways did not. Or it may be that highways on which the parish actually did maintenance work were regarded as belonging to them. Or again, those roads which were fenced off from neighbouring fields and linked to the main highway network might have been regarded as belonging to the parish and not the adjoining owner. Probably the most likely explanation is that there was no general rule and, like so much else of life at that time, it was the subject of immemorial custom. Perhaps an arbitrary network of highways was regarded as belonging to the parish based on a combination of historic acts of ownership such as maintenance or sale of herbage to offset highway rates.

Tithe maps differ in the ways in which they depict land which is not subject to tithes. In some cases these areas are simply not shown on the survey, in the same way as if they were outside the parish. In other cases the survey records the parcels of land and gives them numbers, but the schedule indicates that they are not titheable. Both methods may apply to public highways. The latter system is obviously more helpful to us in that the parcel of land occupied by the highway will be numbered and recorded as a public highway owned by the parish or the parish surveyor and with no titheable value.

On many tithe maps a network of roads is shown running between titheable fields but without numbers or a reference on the apportionment. Sometimes these roads will be coloured, but this is not invariably the case. This may be indicated by a key, but even where this is not present it is often possible to infer what is meant by the fact that roads known to be public roads at the time are shown in the same way.

It should not be assumed that all roads owned by the parish were shown. Where there are significant areas that are not subject to tithes in any case, for example barren mountain or moorland areas, then there was no need for the surveyor to record roads as being separately excluded from tithes. Sometimes public roads will be shown across such areas, presumably to give a frame of reference. However, it is not unusual for tithe maps to completely exclude such areas and thus provide no details of public roads across them.

Where a tithe map excludes land because it is a public road, then this must provide good evidence that there was a public highway at the time. What is not entirely clear is the status of the highway. In most cases, those roads owned by the parish seem to be vehicular routes. However, it is not clear whether this will invariably be the case and it may be that some roads were considered to be owned by the parish for other reasons and had merely bridleway or pedestrian rights.

17.7. Roads not belonging to the parish

Let us first consider the situation where the surveyor found a route which he considered did not belong to the parish but ran over land that was subject to tithes. Such a route might be a private occupation road for the benefit of the owner, or it might be a minor public highway. Often the two would coincide with, say, a bridleway running over the private road to a farm.

Where a road ran through fields without being fenced off from them, then it was not usual to regard the road as being a separate parcel to be shown numbered on the apportionment. In many cases the surveyor will have found that the road was capable of producing a return, for example where a grass road ran through pasture land. In this case the area of the road would be titheable like the rest of the field and there was no reason to make any special mention of the road. It seems likely that such routes would not be recorded on the tithe map.

Where the road physically existed and could not be cropped, then it would not be tithed. But even so it need not necessarily have been recorded as such. The surveyor would have had to allow for the part of the field that was barren in working out the value of the total land parcel but would not necessarily have had to make this explicit in the apportionment. He might indicate the edge of the road by a pecked line on the map, but on the other hand he might not. It seems to have been a matter of personal preference. There are many examples where such roads are shown in one parish but the same road is not shown where it crosses the boundary into the next parish.

Where a road was a separate fenced-off lane, then there is a better chance of a record being made. The lane is likely to have its own number and details given in the apportionment. The name of the parcel is often instructive where it describes it as a road or lane, sometimes saying where it goes to and from. If the road was described as barren, or not tithed, then there was clearly a physical road there at the time. However, this does not prove any public rights over it as it may equally have been a private occupation road. On the other hand, a description of a route as a *private road* should not be taken to indicate that no public rights existed. In the context of tithe records the term seems merely to indicate that the route was regarded as being privately owned and not one of the class of highways regarded as belonging to the parish.

It should be noted that a road being fenced-off does not always mean that there will be a separate record. Some surveyors included lanes in with adjoining fields in the same ownership to give a bigger parcel. The position then becomes similar to a field road where there may not be any details recorded and any barren part being allowed for in the calculation of the value of the whole.

We also need to consider the case where a road not owned by the parish ran over land that was not tithed in any case. Here there was no need for the surveyor to pay any attention to whether the road was barren or not as either way there would be no tithes payable. Again it seems to have been a matter of personal preference as to whether such a road would be recorded on the tithe map.

It will be appreciated from the above that only limited information can be obtained from tithe surveys where the alleged highway runs over land that is recorded as titheable. Firstly, the absence of any record does not mean that no road existed as there are a variety of reasons why it should not be shown. Where a road is shown then that should be taken as very good evidence that a physical route existed. However, this is not necessarily a public highway as it could alternatively be a private occupation road. On the other hand, a description of a route as a private road should not necessarily be taken as meaning that no public rights exist.

17.8. Summary

Tithe surveys can provide useful evidence towards proving public rights of way, but will generally be most useful in supporting other evidence; rarely will they be able to provide a conclusive case on their own. In the most favourable situations the recording of a public highway will provide very strong evidence that a highway of some sort existed, but there will remain at least some doubt as to precisely what rights exist. In other cases a tithe map will provide evidence that a physical track existed at the time of the survey. This may well be important in proving the precise location of a route for which other evidence is available to show the legal status.

Legal notes to chapter 17

1. Local Government Act 1894. See Chapter 21 for more details on local government changes.

2. Kent County Council v Loughlin (1975) Sol Jo 528. See also Attorney-General v Antrobus (1905) 2 Ch 188 and Giffard v Williams (1869) 38 LJ (Ch) 597.

Further reading

(a) *Discovering Parish Boundaries*. Angus Winchester, Shire Publications Ltd. 1990.

(b) *Tithe map case studies*. John Andrews, RWLR 9.3. 1994.

18
HISTORIC MAPS

18.1. Introduction

This chapter deals with historic maps and the use that can be made of them in proving the existence of rights of way. All historic maps will be considered, but inevitably the greatest attention must be given to the Ordnance Survey maps, as representing the official maps of the nation. Modern Ordnance Survey maps were considered in Chapter 4 in the context of surveying routes as they exist at the moment; this chapter looks in more detail at the older maps with particular attention to the larger scale maps.

18.2. Development of cartography

Land survey, measurement and map-making have a long history going back to Egyptian times. Most early maps were essentially sketches rather than based on proper measurements and it was not until the seventeenth century that more scientific approaches allowed accurate surveys to be made. To do this required the use of new measuring instruments such as the theodolite and level. It would have been almost impossibly tedious to have carried out the necessary calculations before the invention of logarithms by John Napier in 1614. For some three centuries there was then little change in the technology until the very recent introduction of radio distance measuring, lasers and air photography with all the calculations carried out by computers.

The traditional methods of land survey effectively involved setting up a system of imaginary triangles with the corners at salient points, and then measuring angles and distances to determine the shape and size of the triangles which could then be plotted at a reduced scale onto a map. To produce an accurate map over a large area requires the measuring of some very large triangles which allow a framework within which successively smaller triangles can be added to pick up finer and finer detail. The techniques existed from the seventeenth century to produce an accurate and detailed map of a whole county; but in the absence of any government initiative, no such project was carried out for another two centuries.

There was, however, a market for surveyors in preparing estate plans. The owners of large country estates found it useful to have maps of their holdings showing the individual fields and their names and areas. There are some such surveys in existence from the seventeenth century, but the main vogue appears to have been in the eighteenth century and associated with the new craze for agricultural improvement which also led to the enclosure movement.

These surveys were of varying accuracy, presumably on the principle that you got what you paid for. A very accurate survey such as was later carried out by the Ordnance Survey would probably have been far too expensive for the average owner and those who wanted a particularly cheap job tended to finish up with a fairly poor standard of accuracy. Inevitably, estate surveys were based on a local system of triangulation without any reference to a framework of larger triangles. This means that even where neighbouring estates were both surveyed it is quite possible that the surveys will not properly join up due to slight distortions of the survey.

In addition to the business of surveying estates, there was also a commercial market for county maps. There are examples from as early as Tudor times, but again the greatest enthusiasm seems to have been from the middle of the eighteenth century contemporary with the vogue for agricultural improvement. The early maps are often available as reproductions and although of artistic merit are of little value to rights of way work in that they do not show roads or paths. From the eighteenth century improved roads began to be of sufficient interest to map purchasers for them to be included.

Modern small-scale maps are based on a simplification of the information that has been collected as part of large-scale surveys covering the whole country. This was a luxury unavailable to the producers of eighteenth century maps when many local areas had not been surveyed at all. These maps were based on coarse triangulation between a few salient points such as mountains or church towers with much of the detail sketched in. It follows that the accuracy of some county maps is usually inferior to that being achieved during the same period by estate plans which were being prepared using the same methods later employed by the Ordnance Survey.

It should be noted that in many counties there are bibliographies of published estate and county maps. Public libraries should be able to assist in identifying available maps and their locations.

18.3. Estate maps

From the eighteenth century there was an increasing enthusiasm among the landed gentry for the improvement of their estates. Often this was achieved through schemes of enclosure which required their own mapping. The topic of enclosure documents is an important one which will be dealt with separately in Chapter 19. But even where there was no enclosure, owners found it useful to have a survey of their land as a basis for considering ways in which the estate could be improved.

These surveys were internal documents for the estate and were not available to the public at large. In most cases they were not printed and only one or two hand-drawn plans were produced. Fortunately, a large number have survived in records offices, libraries or private collections. It should be noted, though, that where a private owner such as an estate has deposited a plan for safe keeping in a records office, that owner is entitled to restrict those who may see it. If a disputed right of way runs over land in the ownership of the depositor of the map, then that person may legitimately prevent access to the map if potentially it could prove matters that were contrary to his interests.

Given that these maps were for internal estate use, the surveyor would show the information that his client required. The most important aspect was usually the boundaries of fields, woods and so on which are normally depicted with a solid line. Often the name of each field is recorded, with sometimes the measured area. The surveyors also normally recorded the various buildings on the estate farms.

It is often assumed that estates of that era were continuous over huge areas. But although the lord of the manor usually owned most of the area, there were often some farms owned by other freeholders, including yeoman farmers who owned their farms. These would not usually be surveyed, presumably because the estate owner did not wish to pay for a survey of land which he did not own. Sometimes these gaps are marked as belonging to another owner, but this is not always the case and there may well be blank sections of map, which can easily be mistaken for unenclosed areas.

The depiction of roads and tracks varied, presumably depending on the requirements of the client. In view of the need to depict field boundaries, lanes with a hedge or wall on each side will normally be recorded although it will not necessarily be possible to tell whether a lane or a thin field is indicated. Unfenced roads may or may not be indicated, but if they are, then the edge of the road or track will normally be shown by a dashed line, which seems to have been universally used as the appropriate symbol. It should always be remembered that maps of this sort are primarily concerned with the use being made of land rather than rights which may exist over it. Consequently, unfenced roads are most likely to be shown if they physically occupied an area which could not be used for agriculture, for example if a bare earth or stone roadway was there. It may well be that surveyors did not indicate other rights of way if they did not occupy any space. It is possible, for example, that where paths ran across grassland which was still able to be used for grazing, such paths were not recorded by the surveyors.

In some cases roads have writing alongside to indicate the status, for example a public highway from one place to another or a private road for the use of certain people. Such information can be very valuable. As the map was normally being produced for the landowner, it seems unlikely that he would have accepted a map showing roads or paths with a status which he did not accept. If the owner accepted the status at the time then it would be very difficult for a modern owner to argue that the status was incorrect. Unfortunately, however, indications of the status of a route are relatively rare in estate plans and the most that can normally be shown from them is that a route physically existed at the date of the survey. This can sometimes be useful in association with other evidence to show that a particular route has been in existence for at least two centuries or so.

18.4. County maps

At the same time as many maps were being produced for private estates there was also a vogue for small-scale maps, normally produced for a county. Unlike the estate maps which were for a private owner, the county maps were prepared on a commercial basis for sale to the public, albeit a rather limited part of the public who could afford them.

The earliest maps are of little interest to us in that they did not indicate highways and restricted themselves to showing physical features of the counties such as mountains and rivers together with the location of towns and villages. But as travel became less difficult for the wealthy at least, a demand arose for information about which way to go.

The earliest information was in the form of strip maps. In these only the route to be followed is shown and this is slightly distorted so as to go in more or less a straight line up the middle of the page, albeit showing any bends or turnings at junctions. Features along the road such as side roads, villages, rivers, bridges and so on are shown alongside and there is often a written description giving additional information, sometimes more in the style of a guide for tourists.

The format was probably invented by John Ogilby who published his *Britannia* in 1675. The format proved popular and his work was not only reprinted many times up to 1764 but was also widely copied by other makers of strip maps, for example those published by Cary and Paterson right into the nineteenth century. The concept has even been revived by the AA and RAC to supply computer generated strip maps for any journey requested.

It is worth noting that although Ogilby was a commercial map-maker, he did have some official status in that he was given a royal warrant from Charles II who appreciated the importance to commerce of people being able to travel around. The royal warrant authorised Ogilby to have free access to local public records and there seems little doubt that he only included routes that were established as public routes at least for travellers on horseback. The routes had all been checked by surveyors who rode the routes accompanied by labourers who measured the distance using a calibrated wheel; the frontispiece to the publication includes a delightful little picture of the process being carried out. Indeed it was Ogilby's publication with its accurate measurements which finally established a standard statute mile in place of the various slightly differing standards that had applied in different locations.

Ogilby also introduced a terminology of road classification which survived for more than two centuries. In those days the Royal Mail worked by carrying letters from London to post towns throughout Britain. Letters that were not to or from London were always routed via London. There were no postal services on routes such as Liverpool to York; a letter sent from Liverpool to York would be treated as a Liverpool to London letter, sorted and then sent on as a London to York letter. Consequently, in that era a special significance was attached to the roads that ran radially between London and the provincial post towns. Ogilby described these as *direct roads* and the roads that ran between them as *cross roads*.

This terminology continued to be used by later map-makers who often divided roads into two classes: firstly the direct or post roads and secondly the cross roads. The original concept became blurred with the introduction in 1720 of cross-road posts on routes such as Exeter to Chester, using roads which whilst not direct in Ogilby's sense had now become post roads. Moreover, the introduction of turnpike roads led to most people regarding roads as either turnpike or local and the old concept of direct roads became of little relevance. However, the term *cross road* seems to have continued in use to mean firstly a public road other than a post road and latterly a public road other than a turnpike. With this meaning the term survived until the early twentieth century, leaving yet another puzzle for the researcher of old documents.

With information now being available as to the main roads at least, eighteenth century county maps began to include road information to allow their purchasers to find the way. Map scales also became larger with many counties eventually being mapped at a scale of one inch to the mile, although with nothing like the degree of detail that we are used to on the later Ordnance Survey one inch maps. As the map scales increased it became possible to show far more local roads than were recorded on the earlier strip maps and road books.

The later maps are generally at a sufficiently large scale and show enough other detail to correlate the roads shown with roads and paths shown on modern Ordnance Survey maps. It should be noted that turnpike roads are usually distinguished from the more local roads (normally still described as *cross roads*) by showing them wider or by heavier lines. Solid lines normally indicate a road that it is fenced on each side; a dashed line means an unfenced road and not, as is sometimes supposed, a road proposed or under construction. In the days before enclosure, unfenced roads across commons or open fields were not at all unusual.

County maps were prepared on a commercial basis to show purchasers how to travel around the country. There would have been no value in showing routes that were not available to the public. The maps were intended for the wealthy people who travelled in carriages and would generally only show carriage roads; occasionally bridle roads were specifically marked, presumably to indicate to the map users that they could not go that way by carriage. Thus although the maps had no official status they must be taken as indicating where the surveyor believed the public had a right to go. Having said that, the publishers would not have had unlimited resources to check the accuracy of the information that they were supplying and it does seem that some errors crept in. It also appears that publishers were not above copying the products of their competitors and sometimes errors on one map were copied onto others. So it is not safe to jump to the conclusion that having several different maps show the same feature proves conclusively that it must have existed.

In most cases, of course, the roads shown on county maps will be found to be still in use. Occasionally, however, it will be found that what was recognised as a public road in the eighteenth century is now recorded only as a public path or even not recognised at all. In such cases a county map may provide useful evidence.

18.5. The ordnance survey

As the name suggests, the Ordnance Survey had a military origin. For many centuries the defence of Britain was in the hands of the Royal Navy and the possibility of large-scale military operations on British soil was never seriously considered. So the lack of accurate survey information was not thought to be a real problem. But the near-success of Bonnie Prince Charlie's rebellion of 1745 caused the government to think again. Between 1747 and 1755 a military survey of Scotland was carried out under the direction of William Roy and from 1789 extensive military surveys of southern England were carried out, doubtless with an eye to the possible threat from France which led to war being declared in 1793. In 1795 the Ordnance Survey was formed to produce a full topographical, as distinct from military, survey of the whole of the United Kingdom.

During the first half of the nineteenth century the Ordnance Survey published maps at a variety of scales as no decision had been made as to which were the most useful scales. Most of these maps covered the southern part of England. However, in 1801 Ireland joined the United Kingdom. It was thought important for military reasons to have a good survey, because many Irish people were opposed to the links with Britain and supported the republican elements in France and the United States. Between 1825 and 1842 the whole of Ireland was surveyed at a scale of 6 inches to the mile (ie 1:10,560). The success of this survey was such that it was decided to carry out a survey at this scale of all of Great Britain and this was completed over the next twenty years or so. The first edition six-inch maps from the middle of the nineteenth century are a vital tool in the researching of rights of way.

Although the whole of Britain was covered, in practice each county was treated as a separate survey with its own projection and grid. Hence these maps are often described as the *county series*.

18.6. The county series of maps

For the researching of old roads and paths, a thorough knowledge of the nature of the Ordnance Survey county series maps is essential. Covering the whole country with regular updates from the middle of the nineteenth century, these maps are exceptionally accurate and detailed. Errors are virtually unknown and, being official government records, are extremely strong evidence of what physically existed on the ground at the time of the survey. We will consider in 18.9 the extent to which other matters such as rights of way may be inferred from the map evidence.

The county series of maps covers the whole of England and Wales at a scale of six inches to the mile, but also includes larger scales in some areas. It seems that in the early days a decision was taken county by county as to whether the surveyed scale would be six inches to the mile or 1:2,500 (that is roughly 25 inches to the mile). Where the larger scale was chosen then the whole county was surveyed at that scale, but six-inch maps were then drawn using the information from the larger scale. In some urban areas where there was a need to record a lot of detail, the base scale was even larger but again this would be used to produce a 1:2,500 map as well so that the whole county was covered.

At first the 1:2,500 maps were only produced for counties where there was a significant amount of development, for example around coalfields or major urban areas. Over the years the large scale mapping was found to be very useful and was gradually extended to the more rural counties. However, it was not always extended to the whole county; sometimes areas of moorland or mountain were excluded and remained at the original six-inch scale. Indeed, this is still the case although the six-inch scale has been replaced by 1:10,000.

Up to about 1880, where a county was mapped at both 6-inch and 1:2,500 scales the plans were drawn quite separately. With the development of photographic methods it became possible to draw the base maps at the 1:2,500 scale and produce the 6-inch maps from them.

The 1:2,500 mapping is obviously more useful when it is available. It is not always realised that it is possible to tell from a six-inch sheet which areas were also available at a larger scale. This is found from the way in which boundaries are depicted.

When the surveys were carried out the Ordnance Survey was charged with collecting more than mere topographical information. For example, the surveyors were charged with finding out from the local inhabitants what were the correct names of each place and how it should be spelt. They even employed scholars to advise on the correct spellings, particularly of Welsh and Gaelic names. In many cases the modern spelling of place names first took a definitive form from the first editions of the county series maps. Similarly, the surveyors were charged to establish the precise location of the various boundaries between parishes, townships, hamlets and so on. This was done with the aid of local people and the information was collected in meticulous detail. For example, where the boundary ran along a hedge the surveyors found out which area the hedge was considered to be in and thus how far in front or behind the roots of the hedge the boundary line actually lay.

Even the largest scale maps could not show this information to scale and so the information is written alongside the boundary using standard abbreviations which appear rather obscure to the uninitiated. For example, CR means Centre of Road; 3'9" RH means 3'9" in front of the Roots of a Hedge. This information is rarely of any value to us except to know that it is only found on the largest scale published. So if the six inch sheet has this sort of information written along the boundaries, it means that there will not be any larger scale maps available.

18.7. The county grid

The county series maps do not have any grid lines marked on them which gives the impression that prior to the national grid the concept of a grid was unknown. However, the surveyors did use a grid but it was not marked on the map as users were thought not to be interested.

Each county had its own grid which was based on a landmark in the centre of the county. Obviously, this meant that the grid lines in adjoining counties would not correspond. Less obviously, they would not even be parallel. This is because the process of warping the spherical surface of the earth to fit on a flat map results in distortions such that a north-south grid line only points precisely north at the centre of the projection. With separate projections for each county the grid lines at the edge of the two projections will be distorted in different directions and not fit together.

The county grid was based on imperial measure and had half-mile squares in place of the modern kilometre squares. Each six-inch sheet covers an area six miles from east to west and four miles from north to south; in other words the map is twelve squares across by eight squares deep.

The maps cover the county in a regular grid; there are no overlaps and the maps form into regular rows and columns. A six-inch map exists if any of the county lies on the sheet. In practice this means that some sheets show only a tiny corner of the county. Obviously, where none of the county falls within a rectangle of the grid then no sheet exists. This means that there is not the same number of sheets in each row or column.

The sheets are numbered consecutively starting at the left-hand end of the top row and moving to the right, then starting on the second row and so on. Because there are different numbers of sheets on each row, there is no logical method of working out what the number of the sheet above or below a particular sheet will be. However, the number of the adjoining sheet will be found in the centre of each edge of the sheet. On some earlier editions normal numbers are used, but in most cases the six-inch sheet numbers are given in Roman numbers.

Where the survey was carried out at 1:2,500 scale, the sheets again form a regular pattern. Each six-inch sheet is divided up into sixteen 1:2,500 sheets, in four rows and four columns. This means that each sheet covers three grid squares across by two down, that is an area of a mile and a half by a mile. The numbering is done the same way as the six-inch sheets, the top row being numbered from left to right 1 to 4, the next row 5 to 8 and so on down to 16 at the bottom right hand. Each sheet has a unique number in the county which is formed from the Roman six-inch sheet number followed by the number of the 1:2,500 sheet from 1 to 16, for example VII-7.

18.8. Information shown on county series maps

At first sight it may be thought that all Ordnance Survey maps will be true to scale. But if this were so, then at the smaller scales some features would be too small to see. For example, on modern 1:50,000 maps the narrowest farm roads are shown by parallel lines about 0.5mm apart; if this were true to scale it would mean a road 25m wide, that is about twice the width of many A class roads in the countryside. To produce maps that people can read it is often necessary to exaggerate the size of some features such as roads and paths, albeit that the centre line should be shown in the correct geographical position.

The 1:2,500 maps are completely true to scale. This gives the important advantage that it is possible to scale off the true width of any road or path. The width shown is that of the actual surface of the path, that is the area made up or if an earth path then the area devoid of vegetation. The edges of the road or path are shown by dashed lines. Where the route follows a hedge or fence on one or both sides then the edge may be shown in one of two ways. The edge may be the solid line of the fence in which case it means that the worn or made-up surface goes right up to the fence. Or both the solid line of the fence and the dashed path edge may be shown. This means that there is some area of verge between the worn or made-up section of the route and the fence itself.

The six-inch maps are also largely true to scale. The first editions were drawn with fine lines and showing a great deal of detail almost like a miniature 1:2,500 map. However, later editions tend to be more diagrammatic. In general, roads and paths of around 20' width or narrower seem to be shown with conventional parallel lines which scale to around 20' width. Roads more than this width are shown true to scale although the depiction of a made-up road within fence boundaries is rarely used, being reserved for exceptionally wide verges which can be shown to scale. It follows that it is not usually possible to scale the precise width of a path from the six-inch maps.

The use of solid lines for hedges, walls and fences extends to gates. Thus if a road or path is gated then the line of the fence will extend across the route. There is no distinction made on the map as to whether there is a gate or a continuous fence with stile.

Some information is given about the surface of routes. On six-inch and 1:2,500 maps from 1884 to 1907, many roads are shown with the line on one side thicker than the other. This is known as shading and is supposed to give the impression that the road is slightly raised from the map. The map key gives no indication what this symbol means. Researchers of OS records have found instructions that there were supposed to be three categories of shaded roads with successively thinner shadings:

(a) Turnpike and main roads (the latter being the former turnpike roads maintained from 1889 by the new county councils - see Chapter 21).

(b) Metalled public roads for wheeled traffic kept in good repair by the highway authority.

(c) Metalled private carriage roads.

Unfortunately, it does not seem possible to identify the different types of shading on the published maps. The implication of shading is thus that the surveyor found a metalled road, that is to say one provided with a stone as distinct from an earth surface.

In addition, both 1:2,500 and six-inch maps show initials alongside some tracks to indicate the use. The initials used are FP (for footpath) and BR (for bridle road). More research is needed as to the basis for these initials. At the very least the initials must indicate a route capable of being used in the appropriate way; a bridle road must have been capable of being used on horseback and presumably was being so used at the time of the survey. It is less clear as to whether the legal status of the route was investigated. As will be discussed in the next section, the disclaimer published by the OS is rather misleading and it is possible that the symbols do indicate what the surveyor thought the legal status to be even though the maps were not conclusive.

Where a track is shown without either symbol it means that it is used by vehicular traffic, albeit that in many cases this will not be for the public but will be for private access or farm use. No information is available as to whether there might be public rights on foot or horseback on private vehicular routes.

Some insight may be gained from spot heights. The process of measuring heights was a laborious one based on the use of a level which determines the difference in elevation of two points a short distance apart. A whole series of levels had to be taken to run lines of levels from the datum point at Liverpool to points all over Great Britain. As it is easier to take levels on hard surfaces, the lines of levels were normally run along roads. On the finished maps, spot heights are shown at intervals along public roads.

It is sometimes argued that spot heights alongside roads must be evidence that these were public roads. It certainly suggests that the surveyors went that way, but they did not invariably follow public roads. The surveyors had a power to enter onto private property for the purposes of the survey and although they preferred hard roads, it is clear that lines of levels were run along bridleways and footpaths, private roads or even across country as found convenient. Although spot heights were shown along public roads on the maps, they were shown at other points as well. So a line of spot heights along a road probably indicates nothing more than that the road physically existed as a clear route at the time. But we know that anyway from the fact that any such route will be shown on the map.

The Ordnance Survey recorded additional information which was not included on the maps but retained in their own records to assist in maintaining consistency in future revisions. These records, where they survive, are now in the hands of the Public Records Office although it should be noted that the OS lost many important records when its premises in Southampton were bombed in the 1939-45 war. More research is needed as to the potential value of the surviving records.

Ordnance Survey maps contain a huge number of names of areas, buildings, streams, roads and so on. The Ordnance Survey was charged with establishing the local name for these and did this by asking those local people most likely to know the answer. For example, if the question was the name of a house or farm then the best person to ask was the owner. As well as recording on the map what was found, the OS also kept detailed records of how the name had been found out.

Our interest lies in roads, tracks or bridges that were given a name. These are recorded in a series of *Object Name Books* that are preserved at the Public Records Office. For each road or track the owner is given and if a public road then the record is signed by the appropriate surveyor. Similarly, for bridges the record indicates who is responsible for maintenance.

Further research is needed into this and similar aspects of the work of the OS. It is clear that the OS did not merely record what physically existed but also looked at abstractions like names and boundaries. In this context it seems entirely plausible that it also recorded the legal status of highways, but with the careful proviso that the record should not be regarded as conclusive.

18.9. *Interpretation of ordnance survey maps*

For many years Ordnance Survey maps have carried a disclaimer that the representation of a road, track or footpath was no evidence of a right of way. Many people take this at its face value and assume that this means that OS maps have no evidential value. Fortunately, this is far from being the case.

What the Ordnance Survey really means is that, despite its maps being the official Government maps, they are not conclusive evidence of the status of routes in the way that, say, the definitive map of public paths is. But this is quite different from saying that the maps have no evidential value, and the disclaimer is somewhat misleading. The OS has always justifiably prided itself on the accuracy of its maps and the care with which they are prepared means that they must be very strong evidence indeed of the existence of what they show.

This would still be of value if the Ordnance Survey made no attempt to indicate the status of any routes. But this is clearly not the case. Modern OS maps show motorways, trunk roads and classified A and B roads. Such roads by definition can only be public rights of way, yet the OS disclaimer still covers them. On the face of it we are told that whilst the M25 certainly exists as a physical entity, there is considerable doubt as to whether it is lawful to drive along it. What would a researcher in two hundred years time make of all this?

The correct interpretation would be, of course, that although an OS map showing the M25 is not conclusive evidence that at the date of the map there was a right for the public to drive along it, nevertheless the map must be very strong evidence that this was indeed so. The surveyors must be assumed to have checked very carefully not only that a dual-carriageway road actually existed but also that it was generally believed to be open to the public. Moreover, it seems reasonable to have assumed as a public body that the OS would have checked with the appropriate highway authority, in this case the Highways Agency.

Although the M25 case is an extreme example, many Ordnance Survey maps do give similar information about vehicular roads. For example, the various versions of one-inch and 1:50,000 maps have always showed a variety of types of roads.

It appears that around 1885 the OS decided to improve the depiction of roads on the one-inch maps. From 1886 these indicated roads as being of one of three types: main or turnpike roads, ordinary metalled roads and minor roads including carriage drives and cart roads. From 1897 four types of road were shown. OS instructions indicate that the classifications were based on returns from rural district surveyors who supplied coloured maps of the roads in their areas which they had verified by signing. Unfortunately, none of these key documents has survived but it is clear that the information shown on the OS maps must have corresponded to the surveyors' own records.

It will be shown in Chapter 21 that very few highway authority records survive from this period, so this is important information. The disclaimer covers the possibility that the highway authority was mistaken as to the status of the road, but in the absence of other information it must be very strong evidence that the roads shown did indeed carry public vehicular rights.

Probably the greatest variety was on the popular edition maps of the twenties which showed no less than eleven different types of road with nine different types being shown coloured. These ranged from "main roads fit for fast traffic" to "indifferent or winding roads under 14' wide". The key adds a note that private roads are uncoloured. It is clear that the maps are intended to indicate that all the coloured roads are open to the public and that the colouring is intended to assist motorists, even though the normal disclaimer applies. Not all the coloured roads of the twenties have become tarred motor roads and some now meet the criteria for byways. Their depiction on OS maps as available to the public must be important evidence of their status despite the disclaimer.

For many routes the Ordnance Survey gives no clue as to what the legal status was believed to be. But the information provided by the Ordnance Survey large-scale maps may well be valuable when taken together with other evidence. The maps can provide positive evidence of the physical existence of a route at the date of the map. The larger-scale maps also provide information as to the width of the route and whether metalled or not, which will give a strong indication of the use being made. A route which is 10' or more in width is likely to have been used by vehicles, particularly if the letters BR or FP are not shown alongside. Where BR is shown then the route was found to be in use by horses and where FP then it was used by pedestrians.

Obviously, this would not be sufficient to show use by the public as of right. But it may be very valuable information if used in association with other evidence. If it is sought to prove the existence of a highway then it is necessary to be able to show precisely where it ran. Many documentary sources provide evidence of status but fail to indicate the precise route. For example, quarter sessions records may indicate that a particular parish was ordered to put into repair the cartway from A to B. This provided strong evidence that at that date a public cartway did indeed exist from A to B. But this will be of no value unless it can be shown precisely where the highway ran. But if contemporary OS maps show that a single cartway physically existed from A to B then it seems reasonable to infer that this was the one that was referred to in the court records and that it must, therefore, have been a highway at that time.

Finally, it is important to note that, despite the disclaimer, in the period before the definitive maps most people seem to have accepted that routes shown on the Ordnance Survey as bridle roads or footpaths did have the equivalent legal status. This may mean that owners would at the time have accepted that the rights existed and have acted accordingly. In particular the existence of such public rights would have given a good case for a reduction in the assessment for the 1910 Finance Act valuation and in many cases the owner would have claimed it. The Finance Act records are a large subject in their own right and are dealt with separately in Chapter 22. However, it is worth noting that the valuations were based on the contemporary OS maps and thus the showing of a route as a metalled road, a bridleway or a footpath was often the trigger for a claim. Hence those routes recorded on the OS maps but not included on the definitive maps should be taken as a priority for investigation through Finance Act and other records.

Further reading

(a) *What is a Cross Road.* Susan Taylor, South Pennines Packhorse Trails Trust. 1997.

(b) *The evaluation of older maps.* Yolande Hobson, RWLR 9.3. 1991.

(c) *Ordnance Survey Maps: a concise guide for historians.* Richard Oliver, The Charles Close Society. 1993.

(d) *Ordnance Survey Maps: a descriptive manual.* J.B.Harley, Ordnance Survey. 1975.

(e) *Roads on OS 1:2500 plans 1884-1912.* Yolande Hobson, RWLR 9.3. 1999.

19
ENCLOSURE AWARDS

19.1. The objectives of Enclosure

The background to the enclosure era was explained in Chapter 15. Here we will look in more detail at the process of enclosure under parliamentary powers and the relevance of the records associated with this.

The process of enclosure was carried out in a very dispersed way with different parcels of land being enclosed at different times, in most cases between 1750 and 1850. Each enclosure was a separate process and the approach differed from one to another. Consequently, it is not possible to set out precise rules as to what might be expected in every enclosure; it is only possible to set out basic principles which should assist in understanding the documents.

Enclosure was essentially a redistribution of property rights among the existing owners. In the enclosure of open fields the owners of the strips were allocated a new block of land in exchange. Where common land was being enclosed the owners of common rights were given blocks of land in exchange, with the owner of the soil of the common (usually the Lord of the Manor) retaining the remainder free of any common rights of others. The objective was that after the enclosure the owners should have land whose value was proportional to the value of the land, or common rights, that they had before the enclosure.

Thus the real business of enclosure was essentially a private one between the various owners. However, it was often not possible to have a redistribution without altering the public roads and so an enclosure also had a public side. It was not part of the enclosure process to provide the public with a better highway network at the expense of the owners; the essential requirement was that the new system should be a reasonable exchange for what was lost. In general, the enclosure process does not seem to have created new highways except where they replaced ones that had been closed; in many cases existing highways were merely retained or diverted a little.

19.2. The process of Enclosure

The first stage was to obtain authority for the enclosure to be carried out. Originally this required an Act of Parliament and each one set out different rules for the particular enclosure. By 1760 a more or less standard set of conditions was in use, but these had to be stated separately in each act. To save time and expense an act of 1801 provided a set of standard clauses that were automatically to be included in individual acts unless the contrary was stated (1). From 1845 a further general act removed the need for further individual acts by allowing authority to be given by a national body known as the Inclosure Commissioners (2).

The individual enclosure act defined the area where the enclosure could be carried out and authorised local commissioners (or valuers after 1845) to carry out the enclosure. Although the rules that the commissioners had to follow were largely standardised there were often subtle differences between different acts; this creates many of the difficulties today in understanding what was going on.

The commissioners first had to establish the existing position including the precise boundaries of the area to be enclosed, the authenticity and value of any property rights and the existing public rights over the area. They must then have worked out a possible redistribution and identified where public highways would need to be altered. The proposed highways were then marked out on the ground (or *set out* in surveyors' jargon) and notice given to the public who had a right of objection and some mechanism for arbitration in case of disputes. Only when the road network had been fixed was a final redistribution of land made.

The commissioners gave notice of the new allocations and fixed a day for the ownership to change. At this stage the commissioners prepared the award, a document which recorded all the decisions that had been made. The award was specifically intended to provide a permanent record and was enrolled as a public document. This was particularly important in that the title deeds of the new owners consisted of a copy of the award which was intended to provide conclusive evidence of the position after the enclosure.

It is very important to be aware of the difference between the original act and the award. The act merely authorised the enclosure and does not in itself provide evidence that it took place. The award, by contrast, was the end of the process and was intended to provide a permanent and conclusive record of the position at the end of the enclosure.

19.3. Enclosure awards

It will be appreciated that the enclosure award is the key document in proving the existence of highways. The first problem is to find it. The starting point will be the County Records Office; later acts provided that a copy should be enrolled with the

Clerk to the Peace of the county and these should now be in records offices. It was also very common for a copy to be held by the parish and kept with other key documents in a parish chest. Many such records have now been removed for safe keeping in official records offices, either at the county or sometimes in the keeping of the church authorities. Even where county records offices do not themselves have a copy of the award, they often have lists showing where copies are to be found.

The award is generally in two parts: the award proper and an accompanying plan. In most cases a special land survey was carried out covering the area to be enclosed because existing surveys were not available. However, some later enclosures did instead make use of existing surveys, particularly after the completion of the first Ordnance Survey large-scale mapping. Where a special survey was carried out, the plans were hand-drawn rather than printed. As the few copies produced were the only large-scale plans of the area available they must have provided rather a temptation to those who needed a map. Consequently, many seem to have disappeared. If it is found that the copy of the award which is consulted does not have the attached plan, it is worth checking on any other copies known to exist to see if they do retain the plan. Otherwise, records offices may have information of an available copy; for example some enclosure maps may have found their way into library or museum collections.

The award proper is normally a hand-written document prepared on sheets of vellum. As the documents are long and the interpretation may hang on individual words, it is desirable to obtain a photocopy of the full document which can then be deciphered at leisure. Sometimes a records office will have a transcript which will save a lot of time; it is always worth checking. Otherwise the document needs to be read to see if it indicates any evidence of highways. If so, it generally saves time in the long run to prepare a typewritten transcript so that it is easy to refer back on obscure points. Ideally, a transcript should cover the whole document, but failing that it should cover at least the sections on public and private roads.

An enclosure award usually includes sections which describe the public and private roads set out. The arrangement of sections varies between awards and it may be necessary to read the whole document to find the relevant sections. It should be noted that the various sections are not always placed together; there may be other matters between, for example, the section on public roads and that on private roads. Again, it may be necessary to read the whole award to find all the details.

Each section is normally in the form of a series of paragraphs each concerned with a particular road. Again, there is no universal form but a typical example might read as follows:

"We appoint one private carriage and public bridle and foot road of the width of 20' called the Blackstone and Whitestone Road, starting at a place known as White Cross and leading eastwards to a junction with the road known as the Greenstone Road at the point known as Black Moor, and as the said road is set out and delineated on the said map or plan. And we appoint the said road to be for the use of the owners and occupiers of the new enclosures in the parish of Whitestone and we order that the said road shall for ever be maintained at the expense of the said owners and occupiers."

This example gives all the necessary information as follows:

- The name of the road

- The width of the road

- A description of the route of the road

- Whether public or private or in this case both

- If private those who have a right to use the road

- Those who have a duty to maintain the road

Unfortunately, not all awards are as clear as this and necessary information is often missing. Section 19.5 will consider what presumptions ought to be made when some information is missing.

Having recorded the details of the roads set out, the next stage is to identify them on the map. Enclosure maps, like the awards, are not always the easiest documents to follow. They are often to peculiar scales, are orientated in whatever direction the surveyor found convenient and relate to features of the landscape that no longer exist. The important thing to remember is that the surveys are usually accurate and always include a scale and north point. If a photocopy can be obtained it will be possible to use a variable reduction photocopier to bring the map to a conventional scale, say 1:25,000. It can then be rotated to bring the north point to the top and compared with a modern map. Alternatively, it may be better to reduce to 1:10,560 and make the comparison with a first edition 6" map if one is available. For example, an enclosure map for a common will show the boundaries of the common which in most cases would remain as field boundaries after the enclosure. Relatively few boundaries would have changed by the time of the first edition OS sheets and thus the shape of the common will probably be able to be seen. Subsequent hedge removal often means that modern fields straddle the old common land boundary which may no longer be so obvious.

If the enclosure map is compared with OS maps in this way it will usually be possible to identify the roads described in the award as modern features or at least features that existed at the time of the first OS map. It is also worth noting that early large-scale maps often show the names of lanes and seem to have taken these from the enclosure awards. Thus the name used in the award will often be found alongside a route that physically existed at that time and thus provides a link between the enclosure and OS maps.

It is obviously more difficult if the enclosure map is missing. However, many roads described in awards can be identified on early OS maps where there is a reasonable description in the award and especially where the OS map gives the name of the road. Although this would seem to give reasonable grounds for assuming that the two roads are the same, nevertheless it will always be easier to prove if a copy of the enclosure map can be located.

Let us assume that a road has been described in an award as having public rights and that it can be shown where the route described actually is but public rights are not yet recorded on the definitive map. Surely this must represent a cast-iron case for a definitive map order? Unfortunately, this is not the case as there are still potential arguments as to what the award means, whether the commissioners had the power to make the award and whether the route ever came into use. These points will be dealt with in sections 19.4 to 19.8.

19.4. Types of road set out

To be able to interpret properly the meaning of the roads described in an award, it is necessary to look more closely at the way in which the commissioners worked and what they were trying to achieve.

The commissioners had to devise a new pattern of roads and paths that provided to the public a fair exchange for the network that existed before the enclosure. At the same time, their task of providing the owners with a fair replacement for their old lands meant that it was necessary to provide each holding with a vehicular

272

access. These requirements were met by setting out both public and private roads. In addition, the arrangements for maintenance had to be specified in the award and again would be expected not to burden the public with a more onerous task than before the enclosure.

Public highways were set out to allow movements across the area being enclosed in exchange for routes that existed before. The new routes might be carriageways, bridleways or footpaths which would normally correspond with the highways that were being replaced. The standard clauses of the 1801 act required public carriageways to be maintained by the inhabitants of the parish, as would be the case for any other roads coming into existence. The same approach was also applied in most earlier enclosures.

In addition to the public roads, commissioners also set out a bewildering variety of different types of private road. Unfortunately, as indicated in Chapter 15, we do not know precisely what was meant by a private road in the enclosure era and commissioners do not always specify precisely what they mean, presumably because it would have been obvious to the professionals of the day who possessed knowledge that has since been lost.

Where commissioners specified who had the right to use the private roads these usually fall into three main groups. Firstly, there are private roads for the use of the owners and occupiers of the new enclosures adjoining them; this creates what we would today regard as an easement. Secondly, there are many awards that treat the entire network of private roads as a whole and grant rights over them to all the owners and occupiers of any of the new enclosures. Thirdly, the principle is often extended so that the entire network of private roads is available to all the owners and occupiers of land in the parish, that is including the ancient enclosures as well as the new enclosures made by the award. However, it is by no means unusual for commissioners not to state who the roads are for the use of, leaving us with the riddle of whether they meant one of the above three types or for them to be open to the public as a whole.

Enclosure awards also specify who had the obligation to repair the private roads. In general, the obligation was laid on those who were given a right of way. Thus where a road was available to the adjoining owners they would normally be required to maintain the road. Where all the roads were for the use of all the owners and occupiers of the enclosed lands, it was common for a special rate to be levied on the new enclosures to pay for the road network. Where all local inhabitants had a right of way, commissioners usually required the roads to be maintained by the inhabitants in the same way that public highways were to be maintained.

However, the standard clauses of the 1801 Act specified that the cost of repairing the private roads had to be met by the owners and occupiers of the new enclosures; it was no longer possible to require the other people in the parish to contribute. Nineteenth century acts rarely require private roads to be maintained in the same way as public highways, nor specifically state that they may only be used by the inhabitants. Unfortunately, sometimes they give no indication at all as to who has the private rights, which obviously leads to confusion today.

Commissioners' frequently set out what were described as private carriage and public bridle (or sometimes foot) roads. This almost certainly means that the road is both a private vehicular route for a limited group of people (who are not always specified), together with a public highway on horseback or foot. (3) Such a combination is common enough today; many rural bridleways and footpaths run along private farm accesses that are private rights of way for all types of traffic.

19.5. What did the commissioners mean?

Enclosure awards were the culmination of a long and hugely expensive process, and were intended precisely to record for future generations the new ownership and rights of way. A copy of the award formed the title deeds for the new owners and so it was essential to them that it was drawn up accurately. It seems surprising, therefore, that today we cannot always understand what the documents mean. In the circumstances, we should reject the idea that this arises from faulty drafting of the award; the documents must have been completely clear to professionals of the time and the problem is that we have lost the key to some jargon or conventions of drafting of that era.

The greatest difficulty arises from the meaning of *private roads*. Commissioners often described roads as private but without saying whom they were private to. In addition, some modern readers seem to have difficulty in accepting that there could be private roads open to all the inhabitants of a district, even where the commissioners clearly said so.

There should really be no problem in the latter case. We know that some customary ways existed in the enclosure era and that these were open to local people and were required to be maintained by them (4). Given that such routes existed, it does not seem at all surprising that commissioners should have set out such routes in their awards, possibly along the lines of existing customary ways. The only mystery is what subsequently happened to them.

What conclusions should we reach when commissioners specify a private road without saying whom it is private to? If we accept that this was clear to contemporary readers there appear to be two possible explanations. Either the term private road had a precise meaning in the jargon of the enclosures or else there was some other convention by which its meaning became obvious from another part of the award.

There has been a great deal of ingenious speculation as to whether a private road might have meant some more minor road open to the public. As indicated in Chapter 15, we know that many of our modern minor country roads were once regarded as private in the sense that although they were maintained by the inhabitants, any failure to do so was regarded as a private matter between the inhabitants. It is certainly possible that at least some private roads were regarded as being open to the public at large.

However, it seems unlikely that a private road automatically meant one open to the public. We know that at least some private roads were customary ways open only to the inhabitants. And we also know that commissioners very frequently set out private roads that were available only to specified people. So even if some private roads were open to all the public, this was not invariably the case and it seems unlikely that commissioners would have used the word in such an ambiguous way. Moreover, there is the frequent description of roads as having both private vehicular rights and public rights on foot or horseback. If private roads were available to the public in vehicles, then the greater rights would have automatically included the lesser. Certainly, the courts have been unwilling to accept the proposition that a private road meant anything else than what it says: one having rights for a group less than the public at large (3).

In the author's view, a more likely explanation lies in the convention that a private road was to be maintained by the individuals who had the use of it. In almost all awards those required to maintain each road were specified. It is suggested that if a private road is specified as being maintained by a group of people, but the rights over it are not defined, then the correct assumption is that those who maintain it are those who have a right of way. Thus where the owners of the new enclosures are required to maintain the road then they are the people who have the right of way. Where a private road is required to be maintained by the inhabitants in the same way as public roads, then the proper interpretation is that the commissioners intended a right of way for all the inhabitants, effectively creating a statutory form of customary way.

If this approach is adopted then we can understand whom roads were intended for in almost every case. It is very rare for those responsible for the maintenance of private roads not to be specified. For later awards subject to the 1801 Act, there was a standard requirement that private roads were to be maintained by the owners and occupiers of the new enclosures and so this can be presumed even in the relatively rare cases where no maintenance responsibility is specified. However, this in only one interpretation and it is an area where further research is required to establish what the commissioners really meant.

19.6. What happened to the private ways?

The doubt as to what the commissioners meant by private roads should not obscure the more important question: what later happened to the private ways? After all, we don't really care what were the rights of villagers in 1800; we want to know what rights exist today. We will look at two types of private roads: those where all inhabitants of an area had a right of way and duty to maintain, and those where all the owners and occupiers of the enclosed lands had similar rights and responsibilities in respect of a whole network of private roads.

Considering first the roads for all inhabitants, the key aspect to examine is what has happened to the obligation to maintain. The parish surveyor was required to maintain in perpetuity the private roads in the same way as the public roads. As we know that no new legislation has repealed this, it follows that the parish surveyor has still a duty to maintain the private roads. The duties of the parish surveyor have passed on to the modern highway authorities so it would seem, on the face of it, that these authorities now have a duty to maintain the private roads. However, this duty would be quite separate from the duty to maintain public roads and the private roads would remain only for the use of the local inhabitants.

The only plausible way in which this would not be so is if the original roads had subsequently become public highways. In this case the highway authority would still have to maintain the roads but under normal highways legislation and the roads would, of course, be available to the public at large. Our problem is to establish whether this is likely to have happened.

Parish responsibilities for highway maintenance ceased more than a century ago and since that date the highway authorities have been conducted on professional lines with numerous records. There is simply no evidence that any authorities maintained roads other than under highways powers. The only plausible explanation is that sometime during the nineteenth century the duty of the parish to maintain private roads was subsumed within the wider duty to maintain the public highways.

Further research is needed to establish how and when this occurred. As explained in Chapter 15, there are grounds for thinking that the 1835 Highways Act converted most customary ways into highways but roads set out under enclosure acts were specifically excluded and thus may have survived longer. Even so, the final result can hardly be in doubt. Somebody has to be responsible for maintaining the private roads; does anybody seriously suggest that villagers might still be liable to statute labour on their private roads, or that highways authorities have consistently evaded their private road responsibilities for over a century?

The issue is different where a group of private individuals other than the inhabitants of a parish were required to maintain private roads, perhaps through the payment of a separate rate. Is it possible that the duty to pay such a rate still exists?

To answer this question we need to look at the reforms to the rating system that were carried out from 1925. This led to the final abolition of highway rates, and their consolidation with all other local authority rates into a general rate. The question is whether rates associated with the maintenance of the private roads would have been similarly consolidated.

The basic principle was that all rates were to be consolidated; no other authority or person was to levy a rate. A rate was defined as "a rate the proceeds of which are applicable to local purposes of a public nature..." but excluding "any rate which is assessed under any commission of sewers, or in respect of any drainage, wall, embankment or other work for the benefit of the land..."

It would certainly seem that a case could be made for regarding expenditure on a local road network as being a local purpose of a public nature, particularly if over the years the network had come to be used by the local public rather than merely those people whose land had been newly enclosed a century or so before. Although there is an exception for private rates concerned with works for the benefit of the land, it is noteworthy that roads are not specifically specified. It seems at least possible that they would not be regarded as being merely for the benefit of the land if they were being used more widely by at least the public of the locality. This appears to indicate that at least in some cases, rates for private roads might properly have been consolidated into the general rate.

Importantly, the process of preparing the valuation provides us with valuable information as to whether a private roads rate survived the consolidation. The valuation started with an estimate of the gross value of each hereditament and then various reductions were made to produce a net value. Any separate rates that were for the benefit of the land were to be deducted at this stage. Thus a record should survive of any private road rates which still continued after the 1925 valuation. It seems logical to argue that if a parcel of land was originally liable for the payment of private road rates under an enclosure award, but such a rate was not recorded in 1925, then it should be assumed that one of two things must have occurred: either the need for the rate had already been abolished or the rate was accepted as fitting the criteria for consolidation into the general rate.

The duty to levy the rate and pay for the maintenance of the roads had been established by statute and could not have simply lapsed. The only really feasible situation in which the rate could have been abolished pre-1925 would be if the roads had become maintainable by the public and hence the purpose of the rate had ceased to exist.

If, on the other hand, the rate for the private rate had been consolidated into the general rate, then the roads would have been funded in the same way as highways. The very fact of such a consolidation would point to the roads having become public through use, albeit previously maintained through the private rate. So all the possible explanations lead to a single conclusion: where a road was originally maintainable by a private rate under an enclosure award but no such rate is recorded in the 1925 valuation, then the correct conclusion is that it must now have become a highway maintainable at public expense.

Thus in many cases we probably have no need to establish precisely to whom commissioners intended a private road to be private to. The key point may well be to establish who was required to maintain the private road; in very many cases this duty would appear to have devolved to the modern highway authority and the route today to be a public road, irrespective of what its original status was. Unfortunately, however, the courts have still to accept this logic and the whole business of proving rights from enclosure awards is still far too often bogged down by arcane arguments about what a private road meant in the eighteenth century, and precisely what individual commissioners intended their awards to mean.

Even where a road was clearly intended to be private and was to be maintained by those served by it, it is still possible that it will by now have become a public highway by use leading to a presumption of dedication, although this will of course have to be proved in individual cases (5).

19.7. Powers of the commissioners

It seems quite clear that the original intention of Parliament was that proper provisions were made for challenging the legality of commissioners' actions during the carrying out of the enclosure and that the award document was intended to be conclusive. For two centuries or so, nobody ever seems to have had any doubt that this was the case. Unfortunately, in modern times it was held in what is known as the Andrews case (6) that the award is not conclusive where the commissioners purported to do things which they were not authorised to do. This creates a great deal of complexity in trying to establish which rights of way exist.

It is not always easy to discover precisely what powers the commissioners had in individual cases. As the powers were included in the enabling act they differ from enclosure to enclosure. Even with the standardised enclosures after 1801, the individual acts can add extra powers or specify that some of the standard powers should not apply. This means that to check the matter fully it is necessary to obtain a copy of the individual act. It is also necessary to understand what it means; this is not always easy as some eighteenth century acts are drafted in a fairly obscure way.

A further problem is in establishing what the commissioners had actually done. The award tells us what the commissioners believed the end state to be; it does not record precisely how they got there. For example, the commissioners may well say that at the date of the award a particular route was a public carriage road; this will not tell us whether the route was there before and lands allocated around it or whether they created it as a new road. One may be authorised and the other not; the award does not enable us to say whether the commissioners acted within their powers or not.

First let us look at what commissioners actually awarded and then what powers they had to do so. Most awards made under the 1801 Act set out public carriage roads, almost invariably thirty feet wide or more. They also set out private carriage roads, generally less than thirty feet wide. Some are simply for private use, but in very many cases are specified as private carriage and public bridle or foot roads; we must assume here that the commissioners intended a public path to exist along the same line as a private vehicular route, a common enough concept both then and now. Finally, in many awards the commissioners set out bridle roads or footpaths along routes with no vehicular routes either public or private.

So what powers did the commissioners have to do this? In the Andrews case it was held that the standard powers under the 1801 Act allowed the commissioners to close or divert existing public carriage roads, and to create new ones so long as they were at least thirty feet wide. They also had a power to create private roads of any width which had to be maintained by the owners and occupiers of the ground that had been enclosed. But they did not have a power to create new public bridleways or footpaths, nor to divert or close existing paths except in a very limited way to fit in with the new carriage roads. Existing bridleways and footpaths would, therefore, continue to exist after the enclosure.

It is important to note that the commissioners in any particular award would also have any additional powers that were specifically allowed by the individual act. In some enclosures, such as that considered in the Andrews case, there were no additional powers in respect of public paths. But in very many acts, the commissioners were given powers to divert public paths and occasionally they had powers to create new ones as well. That these clauses were included in private acts does support the idea that during the period of the enclosures there was an acceptance that the standard powers of the 1801 Act did not allow changes to be made to public paths.

If an award sets out a public carriageway, this means that the commissioners ordered that at the end of the process a public carriageway should exist along the line shown; we have no way of telling whether it was there before or whether it was created as part of the enclosure. Either way the highway must have existed at the end of the process in that if a public carriageway was not already there then the commissioners had full powers to create one. The only complication is whether it was finally completed or not, as discussed in 19.8 below.

So what conclusions should be reached if the commissioners set out in the award a public bridleway or footpath, despite having no powers to do so in the individual act? If it is accepted that existing paths could not be altered then it would have been perfectly logical for them to have been allowed for in the new layout of land. As the commissioners clearly had the power to establish the pattern of land-holding there would be no reason why they should not, for example, set out a long thin field along the line of an existing bridleway and describe this in the award. Where a path is described in an award it seem reasonable to assume that this is what was meant, rather than that the commissioners were ignoring their powers and attempting to create a new path. This must mean that the award is good evidence that the commissioners believed that a public path must already exist along the line of the route set out. However, there must remain a possibility that the commissioners were wrong in this. As they did not have a power to create a new path, it must follow that the setting out of a footpath or bridleway in an award cannot have the same conclusive nature as the setting out of a carriage road.

The situation is quite different where the private act gave additional powers to create or divert footpaths or bridleways. The difference between the power to create or merely to divert is not of much concern to us now; either way there was a power to create new paths. In enclosures where the commissioners had powers to divert existing paths but not to create new ones, it is submitted that the correct conclusion to be drawn from the setting out of a public path is either that there was one there already or that the commissioners created a new path as a diversion of an old one. There seems no logical reason why a modern tribunal should jump to the conclusion that the commissioners were acting outside their powers in trying to create a new route without extinguishing an old one. The implication is that in enclosures where the commissioners were given powers to divert paths, then the setting out of a path should be regarded as conclusive in the same way as the setting out of a carriage road.

19.8. Construction of public roads

A further difficulty arises where public carriage roads were set out. As far as the owners and occupiers of land were concerned, the execution of the award was the culmination of the whole process. At that time all existing rights ceased and the owners took possession of their new allotments. All routes that were not required were closed and the new routes thrown open for use. The execution of the award is conclusive evidence that all the stages described had actually been carried out. However, although the legal work of re-distributing the land was now complete, the practical tasks were just starting. These included building walls and fences round the new holdings and constructing any new roads. These stages could not commence until after the re-distribution of land because of the potential effect on farming operations within the old holdings.

The 1801 act introduced a novel feature that has been an abiding aspect of highway law ever since; this is the concept of adoption. At common law, any new highway that came into existence was required to be maintained by the local inhabitants. The 1801 act specified that this would not apply to new public carriage roads until they had been properly "formed and completed" at the expense of the enclosure. Where carriage roads already existed then the inhabitants had to continue maintaining them but only to the original standard. These also were to be "put into complete repair" at the expense of the enclosure. When this work had been completed then the magistrates at their special highways session could certify that the work had been done and the roads could be adopted as normal roads maintainable at public expense.

To carry out these works the commissioners appointed a surveyor and paid over to him the cost of the improvement works. This was to be done before the execution of the award; it follows that the award is conclusive evidence that the surveyor had been appointed and that the money necessary to carry out the works had been paid. However, as the actual work lay in the future, there is at least a possibility that the work was never carried out.

In the Victorian era there was a court ruling on this aspect (7). In this case a public road had been set out and described in the award, but due to changing circumstances the road had been found to be of little use. It was established as fact that the road had never been used by the public nor had it been formed by the surveyor. The court decided that it had not become a public highway. The logic was that where a new road is created by statute then it does not actually become a public highway until all the required stages have been completed. Thus an enclosure road will only become a public highway through statute following the certification by the magistrates.

The fact that there had been no public use was regarded as crucial and the judge expressed the view that the decision would have been different if it had been used. This is an important point which probably has wider implications than for the carriage roads. The logic appears to be that the commissioners in setting out a road dedicate it to the public on behalf of the owners. Section 35 of the 1801 Act describes the effect of the award:

"...and all other matters and things therein mentioned and contained shall, to all intents and purposes, be binding and conclusive, except where some provision to the contrary is herein or shall be by any Act contained, unto and upon the said proprietors, and all parties and persons concerned or interested in the same, or in any of the lands, grounds, or premises aforesaid..."

The point here is that the new owners are required to be bound by the matters described in the award and in the case of new roads this represents an express dedication at common law. So once the public then start to use the road it becomes a public highway without there being a statutory creation. At common law, of course, a highway can only come into existence if there is both dedication and acceptance by the public.

Although the matter has not yet been considered by the courts, it seems possible that the same will apply where public paths are set out in an enclosure for which there are no powers to create or divert paths. Although the award cannot represent a statutory creation, it is arguable that the existence of the path is binding on the new owners and that even if the path did not exist before the award then there would have been an express dedication at common law which the owners have no power to rescind. Given that there was any evidence of use, even in modern times, then the path would have become a public highway.

The problem today is that it is not always known whether the road set out in the award was actually formed and adopted. It is important to appreciate that stone construction of local roads in the countryside was not usual until well after the enclosure period. So the requirement to form the road simply meant to remove vegetation and level out an earth road. It follows that it is not easy to tell today simply by looking at the site whether the road was actually formed.

The first stage is to check whether a certificate can be found in court records. Many do survive, often simply certifying that all the roads set out in a particular enclosure have been adopted. If a certificate is found then this in association with the relevant award, is conclusive evidence that a public carriage road existed at the date of the certificate.

What if the certificate cannot be found? There is a legal presumption that where the law specifically requires something to be done then it will be presumed that it has been done unless there is evidence to the contrary. Whilst the commissioners were not obliged to set out any roads at all, once they had done so and the award had been enrolled then the owners of the allotted land, through the surveyor, had a legal duty to form the roads. This means that it should be presumed that the roads were formed and certified unless the contrary can be shown. In particular, where it can be shown that the road was actually formed but no certificate survives, then in the light of this presumption it seems reasonable to infer that it was certified but the certificate was subsequently lost.

The most obvious way of showing that the road was formed is the evidence from early OS plans. In most areas the first editions are from the middle of the nineteenth century and thus shortly after the enclosure era. Ordnance Survey maps of that era did not record legal status but they are very strong evidence as to what physically existed. If a road set out in an award is recorded as physically existing a few years after the award then it seems reasonable to infer either that it existed before the enclosure or, if a new road, that it had been formed as part of the enclosure.

Even if the road was never certified, if it was constructed and used by the public it would have become a public highway at common law. The OS plans are also useful to establish this. Many routes were shown as bridle roads or footpaths. Whilst this will generally be inadequate to establish that the routes were used sufficiently to presume dedication, this is not necessary for enclosure routes. For example, a path recorded on an OS map as a bridle road must mean that the route was physically available and in use by people on horseback; given that the award is conclusive proof that the route had been dedicated to the public it seems reasonable to infer that there was sufficient public use to establish acceptance and hence that the route can be presumed to have public rights at least to bridleway status.

There may be very unusual cases where a road never was formed and certified, as in the Victorian case referred to above. It should be noted that such roads are dedicated to the public as a condition of the owners enclosing the land; such a dedication cannot lapse and is still valid today. Owners have no legal right to prevent the public from exercising their rights even if they have to remove obstructions to do so. Once the public do so the route must become a public highway, even though two centuries or so may have elapsed since the original dedication. At least, this would appear to be the logical answer from a legal standpoint, although it must be admitted that it never seems to have happened so far!

It is worth noting differences in the law following the 1845 act. From that time the valuer was required to complete the roads before the execution of the award. It follows that an award prepared under the 1845 act is conclusive evidence not only that the roads were thrown open to the public, but also that they had already been constructed and thus must have been public highways at the date of the award.

19.9. Boundary problems

Each enclosure award deals with land within a clearly defined boundary which is recorded on the map. It will often be found that public and private roads are set out ending right on the boundary. What conclusions can be drawn in such cases?

It is important to remember the remit of the commissioners. They had a duty to balance the rights of the respective owners as against those of the public. Their job was to establish a new pattern of roads that was a fair replacement for what had been lost; they were not in the position of a modern road planner who looks to maximise the public benefit and thus may propose roads that will only be needed at some stage in the future.

If the new roads were to provide a fair replacement for those that existed before it was necessary for the new roads to reach the boundaries of the area being enclosed at the points at which the public previously entered. It follows that the award gives useful information on the contemporary status of the roads extending beyond the boundary of the enclosure. If, for example, a public carriage road is set out across a common to the edge of the previously enclosed area, then it must follow that the commissioners believed that there was a continuation with the same status. Although this is not conclusive in the same way as for the area actually being enclosed, nevertheless it must provide extremely strong evidence of the status at the time. Firstly, the commissioners had a clear duty to inquire into rights of way that existed and had a power to examine witnesses under oath. Moreover, the proposals of the commissioners had to be advertised and the owners of the time had a right of objection. The fact that they obviously accepted the position at the time must give additional weight to the argument that the commissioners assessed the existing rights correctly.

The greatest problem today is in establishing where the route went to after it crossed the boundary of the enclosure. Fortunately, the awards themselves often provide the answer. For example, a road might be set out as "leading eastwards to an ancient lane to Barchester" or indeed the name given to the new road may well indicate its destination. Often an examination of the earliest OS maps of the area will indicate a lane in the corresponding place. Obviously the extent to which the rights can be worked out will differ from place to place, but as a general rule it can be expected that many awards will provide information for routes over a wider area than the boundaries of the enclosure.

It should be noted that although one would not expect a highway to be set out leading to a dead-end at the boundary of the enclosure, the reverse does not apply and there may well be cases where previous highways through existing enclosures were truncated. For example, consider a village where several lanes ran out to a common and travellers might use any of them to reach the common and pass over it to another village. The commissioners had a duty to provide a fair replacement, but this might reasonably have been a single road across the common linked to just one of the previous lanes. The other lanes could have been retained as field accesses but stopped off where they met the common. Many villages do have dead-end lanes which probably arose in such a way.

19.10. Ownership of enclosure roads

Finally, it is necessary to consider the ownership of the soil under the roads set out in an enclosure. This may be of importance in that the making of a definitive map order requires the owners to be notified. It may also be useful in cases of presumed dedication where it is necessary to refute an owner's evidence of no intention to dedicate; this is effectively done if it can be shown that the alleged owner has, in fact, no valid title to the land.

Title deeds often do not indicate a title to land under an adjoining road. Normally there is a presumption that the owners of land on each side of a road also own the land under the road up to the centre line. However, this is based on the assumption that the land ownership pre-dates the highway which came into existence through the owners dedicating a way over their land. It is then assumed that any later sales of the land on each side implicitly included the land under the road, even where this was not specified in the conveyance.

The above is presumed to be true if there is no other information. However, it will not apply if it is known that other circumstances apply, for example that both the road and the land ownership came into existence at the same time. To take a modern example, housing developers often buy a field, lay out roads and house plots and then convey the individual plots to the new owners. In this case the developer retains the ownership of the land under the road.

A similar argument applies to allotments made under an enclosure. The allotments came into existence at the same time as the roads and thus unless the allotment specifically included the road, then the ownership of the road remained in the hands of the original owner of the common, normally the Lord of the Manor. There are exceptions to this rule, however. Sometimes roads are described as running over an allotment and will thus form part of that holding. Occasionally the Lord of the Manor is specifically granted an allotment in lieu of the roads and thus has no claim to them; here it has been argued that the ownership to the centre line principle is implicit even where the award does not actually say so.

286

In most parishes the enclosures effectively ended any real role for the owner of manorial rights; in some cases the rights have been sold to outsiders who would like some sort of feudal title. It is not impossible that the only person with any legal right to dispute the use of an enclosure road may live many miles away, possibly even in another continent!

It is worth noting here that the statutory origin of enclosure roads also means that they cannot be assumed to have been dedicated subject to limitations and conditions not set out in the award. For example, a common law right to plough is assumed to have arisen because the owner originally dedicated the route whilst reserving a right to plough it. If a path has been regularly ploughed as long as anybody can remember then it will normally be presumed that such a dedication took place. But the origin of an enclosure road is known and cannot have been subject to such a condition. However long an enclosure road has been ploughed, it cannot be presumed there is a common law right to plough it. Similarly, if an award specified a road without gates and fences on each side, then however long a gate has existed it cannot be assumed that the right to have a gate was a condition of the original dedication.

Legal notes to chapter 19

1. Inclosure (Consolidation) Act 1801.

2. Inclosure Act 1845.

3. In a recent unreported case concerning a "public bridle and drift road and footpath and private carriage road..." Mr Justice Sedley ruled that the meaning was that there was a public bridleway co-existing with a private vehicular route and specifically rejected the argument that it meant a public road for private carriages. See Dunlop v Secretary of State for the Environment and Cambridgeshire County Council (1995).

4. *Halsbury's Laws of England* on customary rights of way. Volume 12 paras 436-9.

5. Regina v Bradfield Inhabitants (1874) LR 9 QB 552.

6. Regina v Secretary of State for the Environment ex parte Andrews (1993) unreported.

7. Cubitt v Maxse (1873) LR 8 CP 704.

Further reading

(a) *Inclosure awards: public rights of way*. Christine Willmore, RWLR 9.3. 1990.

(b) *Inclosure commissioners at work*. John Sugden, RWLR 9.3. 1992.

(c) *Ex parte Andrews: case note*. Christine Willmore, RWLR 9.3. 1993.

(d) *Inclosure awards*. Tim Hart, RWLR 9.3. 1994.

(e) *What is a "private carriage road"?*. Christine Willmore, RWLR 9.3. 1995.

(f) *The enclosure and redistribution of our land*. W.H.Curtler, Oxford University Press. 1920.

(g) *Domesday of English enclosure acts and awards*. W.E.Tate and M.Turner, University of Reading. 1978.

20
COURT RECORDS

20.1. Introduction

This chapter examines the records of highways that arise from the activities of courts of law. It looks at the important role of the justices of the peace in Quarter Sessions who for centuries exercised a vital role in the administration of highways, including a direct executive responsibility for the more important bridges. It also examines the role of the justices in the closure and diversion of highways, and the information that can be obtained from the various orders made.

20.2. Why the courts are involved

At first sight it might seem surprising that the records of courts of law should be so important in the proving of rights of way. To understand this it is necessary to look back at the historical development of our local government system, and to see the way in which the English approach of evolution rather than revolution has meant that administrative systems often reflect a shadow of what went before.

As far as can be established, before the Norman conquest in 1066 there was little in the way of a national system of government and each manor governed itself according to immemorial traditions. These included local manorial courts which dealt with both criminal offences and the determination of disputes between neighbours.

After the Norman invasion a simple solution was adopted; the village headman was replaced by a Norman Lord of the Manor. His responsibilities included the running of the manorial courts in the same way as they had been done before. Because these were subject to immemorial tradition there was a good deal of local variation with different manors subject to different rules.

Eventually, however, kings began to realise that this system was not only inconsistent but gave local barons far too strong a power base. Gradually a national system of courts was introduced and the powers of the manorial courts whittled away. Today only a tiny handful of manorial courts still exists with very limited powers over such matters as grazing rights on commons.

It is worth noting that in many areas the manorial courts operated in parallel with the national system for centuries, and the records of a surprisingly large number have survived. Occasionally they include references to highways, even in one or two cases going back as far as the thirteenth century. Even where there are references to highways they may well be described by names that have long been forgotten and thus the routes cannot be traced. The chances of finding a useful reference in manorial records are slim and if we had to research them from scratch it would probably not be worth doing. Fortunately, however, these records have long been of great interest to local antiquarians and in many areas it will be possible to find transcripts of the records, local history books that describe them and even friendly enthusiasts who will be only too pleased to say whether there are any references to highways.

The barons' loss of power would probably never have been accomplished had they not been given something in return. The new national courts were very much dependent on local justices of the peace, or magistrates as they were also known. The powers of the manorial courts were largely transferred to the magistrates who were appointed by the King. In most cases the local lords of the manor were appointed to be the magistrates and thus little appeared to have changed. The subtle difference was that the power base depended on the patronage of the King; any lord of the manor who stepped out of line could be disciplined by being removed from the ranks of the justices.

This approach has stood the test of time; even today magistrates are still appointed by the Queen. However, in our democratic times the selection favours those citizens who have already made a contribution to public life, perhaps as elected councillors, major employers, trades unionists or those with a distinguished record in the voluntary service. This was not always the case. Until well into this century the ranks of the justices were largely filled by the landed gentry, and even today such individuals may be over-represented on the bench. It is within this context that we need now to look at the role of the magistrates in highway matters.

20.3. Highways duties of the magistrates

The duties of the magistrates were at both a local and a county level. At a local level there were courts known as the Petty Sessions. There a bench of one or more magistrates could dispense justice in minor criminal matters. Petty Sessions had some limited powers in civil matters. The main one that concerns us is that the magistrates could (and still can) authorise the extinguishment of highways.

The magistrates also operated through the Quarter Sessions. This was a court which dealt with matters for the whole of a county and, as the name suggests, it met quarterly at the county town. As a criminal court, a bench of magistrates from all over the county could deal with more serious offences. In addition the magistrates in Quarter Sessions had an important adminstrative role in that they effectively comprised the only form of local government at county level and thus formed the link between the national government and local government at the parish level.

Most of these duties were taken over by the county councils following their formation in 1889 as part of the Victorian move to democratic institutions (1). Before that, the magistrates in special sessions acted in a similar role to councillors today, with the important difference that they were not accountable to the public. The role of the magistrates included taking an executive role in the administration of the highway system, particularly at a strategic county level.

In the period when highways came under Quarter Sessions, the basic responsibility for maintenance still rested with the individual parishes. Each parish elected an amateur surveyor who was responsible for levying a highway rate and arranging to have the maintenance carried out. In carrying out these duties the surveyor was accountable to Quarter Sessions and where the roads were not up to standard he could be summoned to appear before the court. Indeed, for many years before the changes in the 1835 Highways Act, such actions were almost routine in that the parishes were restricted in the amount of money they could raise. If Quarter Sessions found that the roads were out of repair then they could authorise additional rates or could fine the parish. As the fines had to be used to repair the roads, such fines were not so much a punishment as a back-door method of funding maintenance where it became essential.

The responsibility of the parishes extended to the smaller bridges by which highways crossed streams and small rivers. It would have been impossible for local communities to have maintained the bridges which crossed the wider rivers. So it became established that some bridges were *county bridges* and thus maintained by means of a rate on the whole county. County rates also paid for items such as county jails and asylums. To administer the construction and maintenance of county bridges many counties appointed a county surveyor, sometimes also known as the bridgemaster. The earliest recorded county surveyor was one Richard Porter who was appointed by the Essex Quarter Sessions in 1704. Thus it will be seen that county employees and county rates preceded by some centuries the formation of democratic county councils.

20.4. Quarter sessions records before 1889

In carrying out their highways functions, it was normal for Quarter Sessions to keep minutes of their deliberations in the same way as councils of today keep minute books. In most counties these records are preserved going back in some cases for more than two centuries; there are some Quarter Sessions records from as early as 1650.

Although these records can be very useful, it is important to be aware of the drawbacks. The records are, of course, hand written and often of great length. The information is a chronological record of the decisions of the justices and not normally referenced geographically. Thus whilst it is easy to find what decisions the justices took on a certain date, it will be much more difficult to find all the decisions over two centuries that refer to a particular section of road or bridge. Fortunately, in some counties the records have been summarised and even indexed so that useful information may be gleaned.

Quarter Sessions records give particularly good information on the county bridges as these were the direct responsibility of the court. More research is needed, however, into the criteria that were applied in deciding which particular bridges were to be paid for by the county rather than the parish. County bridges seem to have generally been on the more important routes, usually on roads linking market towns. As these roads mainly became the classified road network of today, many of the county bridges recorded in the Quarter Sessions records will be found to be either still in use or replaced by later bridges on modern roads.

However, the network of main roads was not completely stable and, particularly in the turnpike era, the main roads between market towns were subject to alteration so as to give improved routes with less severe gradients. So it is sometimes possible to find records of county bridges that are no longer on main roads, or even on any recognised highway at all. Frequently the records specify the market towns between which the road ran and thus give evidence of a route not only over the bridge but at least some distance on each side towards the market towns. Such roads would certainly have been of at least bridleway status and most likely carriageways. Where the records do not specify the type of traffic using the bridge it is usually possible to tell by the width. For example, it is unlikely the county would have been prepared to pay for a bridge wider than the five feet or so needed for pack-horses unless there was a public vehicular right. It should be noted, though, that the existence of a pack-horse bridge does not necessarily mean that the road was not a public carriageway as it was not at all unusual for bridges for horse and pedestrian traffic to be provided with a parallel ford for vehicles.

Similar information can be obtained from the records relating to roads that parishes failed to maintain properly. Where a parish was charged with failing to carry out its duty, then there will be a record of the event. As it was necessary to show that the road was a public highway, it is often described as running between two market towns. This not only shows that the section of road in question was a highway, but may also indicate the status of other sections of road between that out of repair and the market towns specified.

Useful information can sometimes be obtained from more general instructions to the parish surveyors. For example, in the early eighteenth century there appears to have been a power for the justices to require signposts to be erected. In many counties there are records of the Quarter Sessions giving such instructions. These often simply require signposts to be erected at all road junctions. Sometimes, however, the instructions specify precisely where the posts were to be erected.

There are a few cases where the signposts still exist, particularly in hill-country areas where stone guide posts seem to have been used. The combination of the actual location and the instructions as to where they were to be erected may be of value. For example, Quarter Sessions often required posts to be erected at junctions along roads between market towns with the appropriate towns shown. So if a post survives from that period with market towns on it, that must be good evidence that the point was on the main route between the two towns. Like the county bridges, this may well provide important information further along the route.

Perhaps the most important type of information to be obtained from Quarter Sessions records relates to the diversion and closure of highways. However, this part of the work of Quarter Sessions was not transferred to county councils in 1889 and many useful records can be found from later years.

20.5. Records relating to closures and diversions

Justices of the Peace have had an involvement in the closure and diversion of highways for very many years, and still do today. For many years there was a general power for highways to be diverted or closed by means of an order signed by two magistrates (2). As today, a highway could only be closed if it was unnecessary or diverted if the replacement route was shorter or more commodious.

Powers were also included in most enclosure acts to allow magistrates to close sections of highway through existing enclosures that did not fit in with the new arrangements in adjoining enclosed land. Similarly, the many private acts associated with the construction of turnpike roads often allowed changes to the surrounding roads. To protect the revenue of turnpike roads it was often necessary to close routes that bypassed toll gates. Where a new road alignment was provided, new links were often needed to ensure that other roads and paths linked up properly with the new alignment and did not come to a dead end on old roads that were being extinguished.

Because public highways were regarded as belonging to the parish in which they were situated, a proposal to close or divert a highway could only go forward to the magistrates if the inhabitants of the parish "in vestry assembled" had given their approval. This aspect still survives today in that an application to the magistrates' court to close a highway still cannot proceed without the approval of the parish council, where one exists.

If the inhabitants agreed, an order including a plan of the road to be closed and any new route to be substituted, went before two magistrates who could accept or reject it. If they proposed to accept it then the proposal was advertised to the public.

If nobody objected, then the order did not become final until it had been confirmed at a sitting of the justices in Quarter Sessions. Once confirmed, the order and plan was passed to the Clerk to the Peace of the county to be included in the official records.

However, if anyone objected then the matter had to be considered by Quarter Sessions. The case was heard before a jury and if they accepted the proposal then the order would be recorded as before. The same system applies to this day, although the appeal is now to the Crown Court, which has taken over the functions of Quarter Sessions.

There seems little doubt that the country gentry blatantly abused this system. Owners of country estates regularly applied to have inconvenient paths or even roads closed or diverted, and the fact that most local people were their tenants no doubt meant that they had little formal opposition from the inhabitants in vestry assembled. Their friends on the bench would helpfully agree, even where the correct criteria did not apply.

By the nineteenth century, however, a more democratic spirit applied and the arbitrary way in which routes were closed was felt to be unacceptable. It may be of interest to learn that one of the agitators on this was the poet Wordsworth. He was one of the earliest and most uninhibited rights of way activists who thought nothing of demolishing stone walls that he alleged had been built over rights of way! Concern increased during the nineteenth century and was one of the main reasons that led to the loss of powers of the magistrates to the elected county councils, and ultimately to the transfer of most responsibility for closures and diversions to the highway authorities.

The magistrates' courts retained their pre-eminent role in the closure and diversion of highways until after the 1939-45 war. It was only in 1949 that highway authorities were themselves given powers to make orders closing or diverting public paths and so all changes to the path network before then were subject to the magistrates' court procedure (3). Also in the late 1940s, town and country planning legislation allowed highways to be altered to allow developments that themselves had planning approval. So, although the magistrates still have a role in changes to the network, they are involved today in a relatively small proportion of changes compared with the former position.

Unfortunately, it is not always possible to locate the individual orders, from earlier periods. It should be noted that in some counties the orders are held by the County Surveyor rather than in records offices. This is because they are still effectively working documents. Some of the more organised counties have indexed the orders so that those for a particular area can be located. However, this is by no means true of all counties and many of the individual orders seem to have been lost.

20.6. Interpreting closure and diversion orders

At first sight it might seem strange that an order which closed a public highway at some stage in the past should be of value in proving the continued existence of a highway today. There are a number of reasons why this should be so.

Firstly, it was possible for a highway to be closed for some types of traffic while retain other public rights. Thus a carriageway might be stopped up but retain bridleway or footpath rights. An order of this sort must be very good evidence that a bridleway or footpath existed at the date of the order.

Secondly, the highway to be closed must link with other highways and the orders often provide useful information about these. In many cases the order maps survive to show the location of the highways to be closed and these can provide invaluable information about other parts of the network. For example, in almost all cases a highway will meet other highways at each end. An order map may thus provide good evidence of these highways at the date of the order.

A diversion order may also provide evidence of routes that join the highways being diverted. In many diversions the old and new routes run parallel. Thus a path that meets the old highway may need either to be truncated or extended, depending on whether the new highway is on the same or opposite side as the path. The order will have to allow for this, and will be good evidence of the existence of the intersecting path. It will often be found that there were a surprisingly large number of road improvements in the eighteenth and nineteenth centuries, not least those in connection with the construction of the network of turnpike roads.

Legal notes to chapter 20

1. Local Government Act, 1888.

2. Powers for the magistrates to approve alterations to the highway network have existed for many years and the modern version is in section 116 of the Highways Act, 1980. See Chapter 10 for more details.

3. Powers for highway authorities to make orders to alter public paths were first introduced by the National Parks and Access to the Countryside Act, 1949. The equivalent legislation is now in sections 118 and 119 of the Highways Act, 1980. See Chapter 10 for more details.

21
HIGHWAY AUTHORITY RECORDS

21.1. Introduction

This chapter looks at the records that may be maintained by a highway authority in addition to the definitive map. These records arise mainly from the responsibility of the authority to maintain the highways.

Highway authorities have, of course, a legal duty to maintain those highways that are maintainable at public expense; unlike many other areas of local authority control there is no discretion not to maintain if the authority feels other priorities are more important. On the other hand, local authorities are bound by legal requirements that prohibit them from spending money on things which Parliament has not specifically authorised them to spend money on. So it would be illegal for an authority to spend money mending a road that was not a highway maintainable at public expense, except where the road is associated with something on which the authority is separately allowed to spend money, like a private road to a school. With an authority caught between these two separate controls, it is essential that it keeps careful records of which highways are maintainable at public expense.

In addition, all highways maintainable at public expense are said to *vest* in the authority. This means that the surface of the highway is the property of the authority, including any road materials. This concept started when paved streets were being introduced during the Victorian period, presumably to prevent the owner of the soil being able to take away the paving for his own use. The concept of vesting was gradually extended and now applies to all highways. Thus highways are the property of the highway authority and one might reasonably expect that they would have a record of their property. As will be seen, however, authorities tend to take a rather cavalier attitude to these records which creates a great deal of difficulty for us in understanding them.

Highway authorities are, of course, public bodies and thus have to be accountable to the public. This generally means that a record has to be kept of the decisions that have been made. Such records are normally described as the minutes of the council and are public documents. Minute books are usually available for local authorities from the Victorian period and may well give additional information that is not recorded in the records of the authority as to which highways are maintainable at public expense. The greatest potential will be where local authorities were formed early on; for example, some local boards were responsible for highways from the 1850s although there was no legal requirement to record highways until the 1920s and between these dates discrepancies might well have crept in.

A further advantage of the public status of highway authorities is that meetings have always had to be open to the public and thus are reported by the press. In our own age of sound-bites, newspaper reports will only cover particularly notable issues, but this was not always the case. In earlier times, local newspapers often reported council debates word for word and the records of the discussion often give much more information than the minutes which recorded only the decisions reached. Many public libraries have microfilm files of local newspapers going back well into the Victorian era and these may well be a source of useful information. The task of the researcher is assisted by the fact that local council reports were often a regular feature appearing at the same place in the paper at regular intervals.

21.2. The structure of local government

To understand highway authority records it is necessary to have some knowledge of the structure of local government at the time the original records were produced. The current structure of local government was described in Chapter 6, but this reflects the system after the major changes of 1974. This section, therefore, examines the structure of local government that existed from the formation of county councils in 1889 which represents the first stage in the creation of the modern system of local government over the whole country. Prior to that date the system was very variable with some areas having their highways under the control of elected boards whilst others retained the traditional system of parish control. The parishes rarely kept any records, but the minutes of the various boards can also be very useful in the areas in which they existed.

An Act of 1888 created elected County Councils. These replaced control by the justices in Quarter Sessions (1). The new councils came into effect on 1st April 1889. The councils controlled what were known as *administrative counties*. These were based on the historical counties but excluding the largest towns (that is those with a population of at least 50,000). These towns became *county boroughs* which meant that they combined the powers of a county council with those of a borough council.

Under a further act of 1894, the whole country was divided up into districts with elected councils which came into effect on 1st April 1895 (2). These districts were known as rural districts, urban districts, boroughs or cities. The last three were for most purposes the same as each other, the titles of borough or city being a relic of earlier systems with the title retained mainly for ceremonial purposes. For simplicity, all three will be referred to as urban districts in the rest of this chapter.

Administrative counties were sub-divided into rural and urban districts. There were thus two levels of local government. In rural districts there was actually a third level as parishes were also given their own elected councils. However, in the county boroughs there was only one level in that the council combined the powers of the administrative county with those of an urban district. Such towns had at least borough status or in the case of the very largest were designated as cities like Manchester or Birmingham.

This system remained unchanged right through to 1974. However, it should be noted that the boundaries of the areas were subject to change. For example, as the major towns and cities spread, their boundaries were often enlarged. Also, there were substantial changes in the early 1930s when many of the very small authorities were merged for greater efficiency. This sometimes led to urban areas becoming rural or rural areas urban, which may make it difficult to trace the various records.

21.3. Urban districts

During the Victorian era great strides were made in public health measures such as the provision of sewerage and clean water to combat epidemics like the catastrophic cholera outbreaks of the 1830s. Power for existing local authorities to carry out such works were first granted in the Public Health Act 1848, which allowed local boards of health (later urban sanitary authorities) to be formed. The problem was that there was no requirement for the powers to be adopted and so local boards existed only in some areas. Where they did exist, their records may well provide evidence concerning highways going back as far as the 1850s. Urban district councils were created in 1895, and given the powers of the boards of health which also applied in boroughs, county boroughs and cities.

The urban districts were highway authorities and had inherited the duties of the parishes in respect of maintenance. They were subject to the same rule that all roads from before the 1835 Highways Act were to be maintained by the authority, but that later roads would only become the responsibility of the authority if they had been adopted. Before roads could be adopted they had to be both constructed "in a substantial manner" and certified as being of use to the public.

But in addition to this basis of highway legislation, the urban districts had other important responsibilities laid down in the public health acts (3). Importantly, these included powers and duties in respect of streets. The authority had to pave all streets that were highways maintained by the public. Where there were other streets, then the authority could have them paved at the expense of the owners fronting onto the street and then adopt the street as maintainable by the authority. And where a new street was proposed then the authority could compel the developer to build it as a paved street and then adopt the street as maintainable by the authority.

It is worth noting that the rules for adoption of new streets under the public health approach were different from the alternative highways approach. On the one hand, the public health acts were more particular about the standard of construction. New streets were to be paved, which meant a proper urban construction of stone or wooden blocks. By contrast the Highways Act only required roads to be constructed in a substantial manner. As even gravel roads were not introduced in country districts until the latter part of the nineteenth century, it seems that properly made earth roads could well have been adopted in the early years. On the other hand, the public health approach did not require the new streets to be of public utility; this was quite deliberate in that it was thought to be in the interests of public health for the public to have control over dead-end courts and alleys which had posed some of the greatest health problems.

To enable the authority to exercise greater control, the public health legislation first introduced the principle that streets that were maintained by the authority should be vested in the authority. This meant that the actual surface of the street belonged to the authority rather than to the owner of the sub-soil. This made it clear that the expensive road materials then coming into use, such as granite setts or wooden block paving, remained the property of the authority. It also seems that the vesting reduced the potential of the owner of the soil to regard works by the authority as a trespass.

However, the effect of the public health acts is complicated by doubt over the meaning of the word *street*. At common law a street means a thoroughfare with buildings alongside; a street has the same meaning as in everyday speech. But in the public health acts a wider definition is given which includes any highway as well as various urban spaces which need not be thoroughfares. This allowed the acts to apply to courts and alleys that were not highways as well as to streets in the common law sense that were also highways. However, a literal interpretation of the definition would also imply that highways that were not built up were also streets, including footpaths and bridleways. Although there have been a number of legal judgments on this matter, the only clear conclusion appears to be that the term *street* can have different meanings depending on the context; for our purposes it is sufficient to note that it is unclear whether the term *street* does or does not include roads and paths that are not built up. This means, for example, that it is unclear whether rural bridleways in urban districts vested in the highway authority under the public health legislation; this matter was not cleared up until 1959 when the various highways and public health powers were brought together in a new Highways Act.

21.4. Lists of streets

An implication of the public health acts was that the question of whether a street was a highway maintainable by the public could have great financial consequences for the frontagers. If the street was not properly made up and was not maintainable by the public then the frontagers might well be required to meet the substantial cost of having the street made up and adopted. Once it had been adopted, of course, the frontagers would have no further costs in that future maintenance would have to be paid for by the public. So inevitably, there tended to be arguments as to whether particular streets had been adopted or not.

To reduce the scope for arguments, the Public Health Act of 1925 required that urban districts should maintain a list of those streets that were maintainable by the public (4). This list often took the form of a plan showing the streets as arguments quite often arose as to how much of a street was maintained; for example, whether verges were part of the street or not. The list of streets was a public document and was available for public inspection. However, unlike the later definitive maps, there was no mechanism for members of the public to challenge the accuracy of the lists.

The difficulty in interpreting the lists is that there seems to have been confusion among those who prepared them as to what should be shown. Municipal engineers almost invariably referred to them as the records of "adopted streets" and seemed to feel that only streets that had been adopted could be included. This, of course, is incorrect in that streets that existed prior to the 1835 Highways Act were maintainable by the public, even though they had never been adopted. Moreover, the requirement of the Public Health Acts that a street could only be adopted if it had been paved led to a belief that all adopted streets must be paved; this is also incorrect in that an earth road constructed in "a substantial manner" could also have been adopted. Finally, there was the understandable confusion as to whether rural highways were streets in any case.

This means that it is not now possible to tell what the person producing the list believed he was trying to record. In practice the lists are generally found to be comprehensive in recording highways that have been paved, either because they have been paved at private expense and formally adopted, or improved to adoptable standard by the highway authority. These streets are not restricted to vehicular routes in that paved footpaths are often included; in principle it seems quite possible that a paved bridleway might well be included in a list of streets. Lists of streets only rarely include routes that have not been provided with a paved surface, even where they were clearly known to the authority to be highways maintainable by the public. It is not clear whether these omissions were because such routes were not believed to be streets, or whether it was believed that only paved streets could be included.

The implication is that the recording of a route on an urban district list of streets must be very strong evidence that a highway of some sort existed, but the status of the route is still open to argument. The fact that an unmade route is not shown should not be regarded as evidence that no highway existed, but clearly it will be necessary to seek other sources of evidence.

21.5. Rural areas and the county road

Until 1895 roads other than main roads were the responsibility either of individual parishes or highway boards that had existed since the mid-nineteenth century. The latter had a more professional approach and minute books setting out their decisions often survive. Parish records rarely seem to be available from before the formation of elected parish councils in 1895.

The rural districts came into existence in 1895 and acquired the same responsibilities and powers as the parishes or highway boards that had previously existed in their area. As with the previous bodies, the highways were not vested in the district. As parishes had more limited powers of improvement than a highway board, the districts similarly had limited powers in parishes that had never been in a highway board area.

The main roads continued to be maintained by the county councils as they had been since 1889. The county had the improvement powers of the former highway boards, but in addition the main roads vested in the council. From the 1890s the county councils were actively involved in improving the main roads to meet the new demands of pneumatic tyred bicycles and later motor vehicles, with stone roads being increasingly tarred from the 1920s.

As traffic increased and new road making techniques were introduced, the small rural districts had increasing difficulty in maintaining the roads adequately. So in 1930 there were major changes with the county council becoming responsible for all highways in rural districts (5). In urban districts the two-tier approach continued right through to 1974 with the county council being the highway authority for the more important roads and the urban district for the local roads and paths.

At this time the concept of a *county road* was introduced. A county road was simply any highway for which the county council was the highway authority. As the county had taken over all highways within rural districts, it follows that rural footpaths and bridleways became county roads. Within urban districts, however, county roads were only the major routes. Thus although the legal definition is the same, the practical meaning of a county road was quite different in rural and urban districts.

The county council was given the same powers in respect of county roads as those it already had for main roads. This meant that for the first time, all highways in rural areas vested in the highway authority and there were powers to improve all highways whether or not they had previously been in highway board areas.

However, although the legal definition makes it clear that a county road included all highways, it seems clear that the term was not used in that way by the county surveyors and their staff who were responsible for maintaining the highways. The invariable usage was that a *road* had its normal meaning of a route for vehicles. Thus although all vehicular routes were regarded as county roads, even if they were only of earth construction, footpaths and bridleways were not considered to be county roads.

21.6. Handover maps

Up to the changes of 1930, county councils were responsible for relatively limited networks of important roads and there can have been little doubt as to where they all were. But overnight they became responsible for thousands of miles of minor highways, including green lanes, bridleways and footpaths. It would obviously have been impossible for the counties to have known where all their highways were without information being provided by the rural districts as part of the handover.

There was no legal requirement for handover records to be prepared and no government instruction or advice has been located. However, it seems to have been the almost invariable practice for a handover map to be prepared by the county council based on information provided by the district councils. The amount of information varied with some counties preparing a map of all highways including public paths. In most cases, however, the handover map seems to have only included roads with vehicular rights. Unlike the municipal engineers' concept of a street, however, the rural surveyors seem not to have hesitated to include roads that were not tarred. In the early thirties, of course, many of the local roads in the countryside were still of stone or earth but in general use by horse-drawn vehicles.

In most counties the handover maps continued to be updated and used as the record of roads to be maintained. They were later generally described as the *county roads maps*. They showed, of course, what the county surveyors considered to be county roads, that is highways with vehicular rights. Only very rarely did the county roads maps depict footpaths and bridleways and thus include all county roads in the correct legal sense.

21.7. *Interpretation of county roads maps*

Our problem today is interpreting the county roads maps and evaluating their importance as evidence. There are two main difficulties; their legal status and understanding what those who prepared them meant to record.

The county roads maps were prepared as internal documents. Unlike the street records in urban areas, there was no legal requirement to have a record. Consequently, the public had no way of knowing that it existed and no legal right to inspect it. In practice, some counties adopted a positive approach, printed a coloured version of the map and put it on sale to the public. Unfortunately, other counties appear to have regarded the map as a well-kept secret! Either way there was no formal way in which members of the public could challenge the accuracy of the map.

It is sometimes suggested that the internal status of the map makes it of limited value as evidence. As the maps are internal documents they are clearly not definitive. Nevertheless, they do represent important evidence as to what the council as highway authority believed to be the roads for which it was responsible. Although the council had no duty to have a record map, it did have a legal duty to maintain public highways and was prohibited from spending money on other routes. Given the scale of the network, there is an implicit requirement to have accurate records as otherwise the legal responsibilities could not be carried out. The highway authority should, after all, have the best idea of which highways it had to maintain. Thus the internal record maps should be regarded as very likely to be correct unless information to the contrary can be found.

Given that the map is accepted as evidence, what does it actually prove? It is sometimes suggested that as the legal definition of a county road includes all footpaths and bridleways, then the recording of a county road can only be evidence of the existence of some sort of highway but without any information as to its status. However, this approach ignores the way in which the term *county road* was actually interpreted by county surveyors, and the fact that the map was an internal document. As indicated above, county roads were normally considered to be vehicular routes only. So if a county surveyor produced a record of county roads for his own use, the definition of a county road would be that which was used in his department, rather than the strict legal definition. In other words, where a map was produced recording county roads, what was intended to be included were only those highways with vehicular rights.

This can normally be seen from a comparison of the definitive map produced in the early 1950s with the county roads maps of the same date. In almost all cases, the footpaths and bridleways recorded on the definitive map are additional to the routes shown on the county roads map. If the county roads maps had been intended to show all public highways then the public paths on the definitive map should already have been shown on the county roads map. If the county roads map already included public paths then why were they not added to the definitive map? And where did all the additional public paths come from?

The simple fact is that all the evidence indicates that those who prepared the county roads map intended to record only vehicular routes. There may well have been some errors but the maps must represent good evidence that a highway existed at the time of the map with rights on foot, on horseback and for vehicles.

It should be noted that the county roads maps were only intended to show the roads that were maintained by the council. There may well be other roads that were maintained by private individuals under some very ancient arrangements. Although these are not county roads, some county roads records helpfully identify the privately maintained roads using a different colour.

21.8. Consolidation of the records

In 1974 local government was re-organised and the distinction between urban and rural districts was abolished. The boundaries of both counties and districts were altered, with far fewer districts being formed by groupings of the old districts. The two-tier system of highway authorities was finally abolished with the counties being given responsibility for all highways in their areas with the exception of trunk roads.

The requirement for lists of streets to be prepared for urban districts was meaningless under the new arrangements. So Parliament adopted a very simple solution; the requirement to have lists of streets was extended to the former rural areas. As urban districts had covered a relatively small part of the total area of England and Wales, it follows that counties were suddenly required to produce lists of streets for much greater areas than had previously been recorded.

In most counties, an equally simple solution was adopted; the existing list of streets for urban areas was combined with the county roads map for rural areas to produce a new record for the whole area. This means that the county roads map is no longer an internal document and the councils are obliged to make it available for inspection by the general public; this point still seems to have not got through to a few of those councils who regarded the county roads map as a secret document!

The problem with the consolidation of the two maps is that they were originally produced under quite different assumptions as to what should be included in urban and rural areas respectively. Thus maps for areas that were formerly urban districts often exclude unsurfaced carriage roads but include surfaced public paths. Maps from former rural areas are generally restricted to vehicular roads but include unsurfaced earth or stone roads. This distinction can easily be lost as the knowledge of the boundaries of the old districts fades.

Where rights of way workers need to make use of highway authority records, therefore, it is strongly recommended that old maps are consulted to see whether the area being studied was in an urban or a rural district at the time the records were prepared. The records can then be interpreted appropriately taking into account the different assumptions which appear to have been made by those who prepared the records.

It is also worth noting that the various record maps are normally produced by adding the detail to a base map by hand and thus only one copy may be available. When the map is worn out or needs extensive update, then a copy is made by hand. This is a process liable to error and it is often the case that the various editions do not exactly correspond. Thus it is always worth trying to find the earliest maps available, for example the handover maps for rural areas or lists of streets from the 1920s for urban areas. If a route is recorded on an old map but not on the latest edition then it is worth asking why. Where a route has been properly extinguished it should have disappeared from the map, but otherwise all routes shown on the earliest maps should have been copied onto the later maps and remain as part of the present record.

Legal notes to chapter 21

1. Local Government Act 1888.

2. Local Government Act 1894.

3. Powers concerning streets were first introduced in the Public Health Act 1848 but these originally applied only to a few large towns. They were applied to all urban areas by the Public Health Act 1875.

4. Public Health Act 1925. The requirement for a list of streets to be maintained is now contained in section 36 of the Highways Act 1980.

5. Local Government Act 1929

Further reading

Highway Authority Records. John Sugden, RWLR 9.1. 1995.

22
1910 FINANCE ACT RECORDS

22.1. Introduction

This section deals with perhaps the most obscure form of public record that is likely to be found in the researching of rights of way. However, although difficult to deal with, these records are proving to be of immense value and could potentially be used much more widely if steps were taken to make them more easily available.

22.2. Background to the records

To understand the point of these records it is necessary to look briefly at British politics as they were before the 1914-18 War. Before the rise of the Labour Party in the twenties there was not the polarisation of politics based largely on wealth that has remained to this day. Instead the political divide was between the old money of the land owning and farming society and the new money of the manufacturing classes who had gained prominence during the Victorian era. The Conservative Party was associated with the former group whilst the Liberal Party represented the latter.

At that time, the traditional land-owning families still owned vast areas and earned substantial amounts from their various tenants. This did not just mean agricultural tenants; many industrial sites were not owned by the manufacturers who had to pay rents to the owners of the land. They found it particularly galling that the owners could reap the benefits of increases in the value of the land arising from commercial activity that the owners had played no part in, or arising from public investment in roads, water supply, sewerage and so on. The opponents of the landed classes found a powerful ally in the Liberal politician David Lloyd-George.

In 1908 a new Liberal Government came to office, led by Yorkshireman Herbert Asquith. His new cabinet included two promising young ministers: the Chancellor of the Exchequer, Lloyd-George and the First Lord of the Admiralty, Winston Churchill, who became two of the greatest premiers of the twentieth century leading the country to victory in the first and second world wars respectively.

Lloyd-George set about his task with an almost revolutionary zeal, laying what was eventually to be come the basis of the welfare state. In his 1908 budget he introduced old age pensions and followed this up in 1909 with proposals for national insurance. To meet the huge cost of this he turned to his old adversaries the landowners and proposed new taxes on unused land and on any unearned increase in the value of land. Not surprisingly, this was very controversial and led to a constitutional crisis when the House of Lords refused to ratify the proposals which had been agreed by the House of Commons. Asquith called a general election in 1910 with the electorate asked to ratify both the budget and his proposals for reform of the House of Lords. When the Liberals were returned to power, thus giving Asquith his mandate, the Lords had to accept defeat. The 1910 Finance Act became law and the powers of the Lords were altered so that they no longer had a power of veto on budget matters.

The 1910 Finance Act included a new tax known as increment value duty. The intention was to tax increases on the site value of land, excluding anything built or growing on it, on the sale of the land or the death of the owner. Suppose, for example, a parcel of land was worth £1000 in 1909. If in 1914 it was sold for £1400, then the person selling the land would have to pay tax on the increment value of £400.

There was also a tax known as undeveloped land duty. This was a tax on the amount by which the value of land exceeded its value for agriculture. Thus no tax was payable on land that had no value except for agriculture. Where land was in use for agriculture but had a higher value because of other potential uses, then the duty was payable.

To apply the taxes it was necessary to commence a huge valuation of all land as it was on 30th April 1909. This was carried out through local valuation offices of the Inland Revenue. It is the records of this valuation that provide the vital information on rights of way.

The tax, incidentally, was a flop and the Government never received anything like enough to pay for the cost of the survey. It was scrapped by the 1920 Finance Act.

22.3. Why the records are useful

In working out the value of land it was necessary for the valuers to take account of public highways. It seems that vehicular roads were treated differently from public paths.

Roads were regarded as being owned by the highway authority and thus increment value duty was not payable on them by adjoining owners. The survey records consequently show roads as not being part of the land parcels that are being valued.

This may often be valuable in proving that a particular route was regarded by the Inland Revenue as a public road in 1909. Bearing in mind that few highway authority records exist from before the 1920s, this is obviously a very important source of information.

Public paths were treated as being within the parcel of land but were a significant factor in reducing the value of the land. There was a rule that an owner could not claim a reduction in the future value of land due to a right of way if no claim had been made for a reduction on the original valuation. As the effect of rights of way tend to be proportionately greater when land is developed, it follows that the owner would be liable to less future tax if he was able to claim a reduction in the 1909 value on account of rights of way. The records include details of where reduction of value have been claimed and allowed in respect of the existence of rights of way.

22.4. How the valuation was carried out

The valuers took as their starting point the existing records of rateable values which were in use as the basis for charging local authority general and highway rates. From these was prepared what is known as a *valuation book* which lists all properties on which rates were payable, the owner, tenant, land use and rateable value. There is an entry for each of what is known as an *hereditament*. This was a unit of land in separate occupation. For example, where an owner had a large estate with many different tenant farmers, each separately tenanted farm became a separate hereditament. Each unit was given a sequential number, known as the hereditament or assessment number.

The information from the valuation book was then supplied to each owner who had an opportunity of claiming reductions in value, including the presence of rights of way. When the claims had been made, the valuers visited each property to check the details, including aspects such as rights of way on which deduction had been claimed. The valuers entered all the details into what was known as a *field book* which gives for each hereditament the calculations of the value of the property, including any deductions for rights of way. These were prepared on a provisional basis and sent to the landowner who had a right of appeal. If the owner did not appeal, then the details in the field book became the basis of the assessment.

As the tax was only to be paid at some time in the future when the land changed hands, it was obviously necessary for good records to be kept. The core record was the set of field books which during the period that the tax was in force were kept up to date as land changed hands, tax was paid and a new starting value applied. In order that the items in the field book could be found, the Valuation Offices prepared a series of record plans. These were based on the largest Ordnance Survey plans available (normally the 1:2500 county series plans or 1:1250 where these were published in urban areas). On these were marked the boundaries of each hereditament and the assessment number which allowed each area to be found in the appropriate field book. Public roads that were not valued could be identified by the fact that the boundaries of the adjoining hereditament excluded the roads and that the strips of land occupied by the roads did not have an assessment number.

Valuation Offices had two sets of record plans. There was a working copy which was prepared as the work was carried out and was subject to changes as errors and so on were found and corrected. When all this had been done a final copy was prepared and this was intended to be the official record for future use.

22.5. *Location of the records*

At the time of the survey the records, like all other tax records, were regarded as confidential and were not available to the public. On the abolition of the tax, the various records were maintained in the private archives of the Inland Revenue. Eventually, however, it was recognised that whilst they were of no value for taxation purposes, the records had great value for historical research and were offered to records offices for reference by the public. The valuation books were offered to local records offices, where most of them now are. The field books and the final record plans were sent to the Public Records Office at Kew. Where the working copies of the record plans still survived, they were offered to local records offices. However, by no means all these records had survived and where local records offices were not interested then even the surviving plans were destroyed.

In practice, this means that the records that will be of most value to rights of way workers are those located at Kew. The valuation books are of little value without the record plans as without them there is no way of telling which hereditament is which. In any case, the field books include details of the value deductions made for rights of way following claims made by owners and are therefore more useful than the valuation books. The location of the records obviously makes it difficult for researchers who are based away from the South-East. The Public Records Office will supply copies of specified records, but these are costly. If real progress is ever to be made towards properly recording rights of way, there is a need for a better system to be devised; some suggestions are made in 22.8.

22.6. *Interpreting the records - public roads*

The starting point of any research will be to examine the record plans for the area under consideration. It will be found that the network of public roads will be indicated by the fact that they will not be included in the hereditament boundaries on each side and that they will not have an assessment number. Most of the roads will, of course, be known roads today but it will often be found that there will be additional tracks recorded in the same way which may nowadays be only green lanes. What conclusions can be drawn from this?

Obviously the valuers regarded these roads as belonging to the highway authority rather than part of the surrounding land. Strictly speaking, this was not legally accurate in that at that time only urban streets and main roads actually vested in the highway authority; the surface of most rural roads belonged to the owner of the subsoil. However, the logic of the valuers was clearly that as the owner could not use or develop the land, it was unnecessary to include it in the valuation.

It might be argued, of course, that although the valuers intended to indicate a public highway, they were expressing no opinion as to its status. However, examination of the records for any area will show that the strips that were not valued included what are known to have been public carriageways at the time. On the other hand, the valuers clearly recognized the existence of public paths over the parcels of land that were valued and did not exclude the strips occupied by the paths from the valuation. This raises the obvious question of the basis for the different approaches.

At first sight it might seem possible that the valuers were taking a similar line to their predecessors who carried out the valuation for the tithe surveys. There the valuers appear to have recorded roads not so much on the basis of legal status as whether they were barren, that is capable of being used for crops. So on a tithe survey a private stone road would be excluded from the valuation whilst a green lane might be included.

But there is an important difference between the two surveys. The tithe annuities were to be paid on the basis of the value of the land at a fixed date. If a road had a stone surface then it meant that it had no agricultural value at the date of the survey and this affected the tithe annuity; whether it was public or not had no real bearing on the question. But the valuation for the 1910 act was intended to deal with future changes in land use and aimed to establish the site value exclusive of what was on it. So that the land occupied by a private stone road would have to be valued as it could have been later used for other developments. The only logical reason for excluding a road from the valuation was on the basis of its public status which effectively prevented it being developed. It must be presumed that the valuers assumed that carriageways were more permanent than public paths and that the latter, albeit reducing the value of the site, did not totally prevent it from being used in other ways.

Thus the only plausible explanation for the way in which valuers discriminated between the different types of highway is that they intended to treat public vehicular roads differently from public paths and that where the valuers excluded a road from the valuation, this was because they believed it to have public vehicular rights.

If it is accepted that the valuers believed the roads shown to be public carriageways, we still have to ask ourselves how they would know. The key point is that the question of whether an alleged road should be excluded from the valuation is central to the matters being considered by the valuers. It follows that they would have had a clear duty to investigate the matter closely and only to exclude a road if they were fully satisfied that it did indeed have that status. Their obvious method of finding out would be to check with the appropriate highway authorities.

By this time the parish administration of roads had been done away with and for more than a decade all roads had been controlled by district or county councils. These were professionally run and it seems reasonable to assume that their staff would have had a good knowledge of the status of the various roads, although few local authority records survive giving this information. But the valuers of the Inland Revenue doubtless consulted the officers of the local highway authority in deciding which areas to exclude from the tax and so it seems likely that the record plans depict the authorities' view as to which were public roads. This is particularly valuable, given that few highway authority records of public roads survive from before the 1920s.

Of course, the highway authority may have got it wrong. But as the official body responsible, it was the most likely organisation to have a correct set of records. In the absence of other evidence to the contrary, the fact that a road was excluded from the valuation must represent strong evidence that it was a public carriageway in 1909.

22.7. Interpreting the records - public paths

Public paths were treated quite differently from public roads. Where footpaths or bridleways ran across land, the strips occupied by the paths were included in the hereditament which was first valued on the basis that no rights of way existed. Then an adjustment was made for the reduction in value caused by the presence of the path.

Fortunately for us, a record of this adjustment has been preserved. There was a reason for this. If an owner failed to claim any reductions for paths in 1909 and then claimed a reduction when the land was developed, then the increase in value of the site would have been minimised, together with tax liability. To avoid this there was a rule that no reduction for rights of way could be made in later years if there had been no reduction at the start. This meant that there had to be records of any reductions for rights of way as well as the valuation after allowing for these. The record is in the field book.

A record in the field book must be very strong evidence that public paths existed across the hereditament in 1909. In most cases the paths recorded are those claimed by the owners at the time. It was a criminal offence to make a false claim and punishable by up to six months in prison with hard labour. It would also have been the clear duty of the valuation officer to check that the paths did exist and that the claim was valid. So that it would be very difficult now for the present owner to allege that the claims were false.

On the other hand, it is often not clear which path was involved. A hereditament was a parcel of land with a single occupier. In the countryside this effectively means that the hereditament consists of the farm and all associated fields used by either a freehold farmer or, more often, a single tenant of a large estate. Having said that, it must be remembered that farms were smaller in that era and many farms then would today be regarded as little more than smallholdings.

Our problem is that the valuers did not map the rights of way which were recorded. They merely identified for each hereditament the fact that there were rights of way. How are we to find where they were?

The key is provided by the large scale Ordnance Survey maps on which the valuation was recorded. These maps show all the routes that physically existed as vehicular roads, bridle roads or footpaths. The latter two had initials BR or FP alongside so that they could be identified.

Although the OS for many years have issued a disclaimer to the effect that the depiction of a path is no evidence of a right of way, nevertheless in the pre-definitive map era paths shown on the OS plans were regarded by most people as representing an official record of public paths. An owner would have been on fairly safe ground in claiming a reduction based on paths shown on the Ordnance Survey but would probably have had great difficulty in persuading the valuers of the existence of paths not shown. So it seems a very good starting point to assume that the reductions in value recorded are keyed to the paths shown on the contemporary OS maps.

Where there is only a single path recorded across an hereditament then it seems reasonable to accept that this corresponds to a reduction in value. If there are several paths then the matter is more difficult. Sometimes it is possible to track the same path through several hereditaments with reduced values and conclude that they all refer to the same path. However, there are endless variations which mean that sometimes the matter is quite clear whilst in other cases it remains just as obscure as before. It is worth noting that Finance Act records are more likely to be useful in areas where no paths at all have been recorded on the definitive map. If a good network of paths has already been recorded, then these are likely to cloud the issue of whether there were still more in existence in 1909.

For similar reasons the relative scarcity of bridleways may make it easier to find evidence for them. Many valuers seem to have recorded reductions for bridleways separately from those for footpaths. It is not now clear whether this was invariably the case, or whether the valuers who recorded footpaths only were using the word in a shorthand sense to mean public paths. Certainly, where reductions are recorded for bridleways it is more often possible to correlate this with the bridle roads recorded across an hereditament than would be the case for footpaths and there is less likelihood of the truth being obscured by bridleways already on the definitive map.

22.8. The way ahead

It should by now be clear that the Finance Act records are potentially among the most valuable to us. The main problem in using them so far has been the difficulty of accessing the records at Kew. It is proposed to digress slightly to look at ways in which this situation could change in the future and to suggest a way forward.

We are living through what has been described as the "Information Revolution". New computer systems offer vast increases in the amount of information that an individual can access. These changes have been driven by increases in the amount of information that can be stored in computers and the development of the internet.

One of the uses computer power is being put to is in what is known as document image processing. Instead of information being stored on paper, it can be scanned and stored as a computer image. It can then be displayed on a screen or printed out again if a paper copy is required. This technology will replace micro-filming of documents offering record offices a way of storing their documents in a way that is safer, occupies far less space and avoids the documents becoming worn out through constant handling.

The internet is a system by which all the computers in the world can communicate and share information. A private individual can buy a suitable computer and link to the internet by plugging into a telephone socket. In addition cable TV companies are now offering the internet through a normal television set. With a link to the internet it is possible to obtain in seconds any of the information stored on any internet server anywhere in the world. Most of the information is useless to most people but that is the real power of the internet: anyone can have immediate access to the most obscure information that can be imagined. It doesn't come much more obscure than the valuations of individual plots of land for a tax that was itself abolished nearly eighty years ago!

However, that is precisely what the internet could offer us. Document image processing offers the most efficient storage system for the various field books and record plans in any case. If they were stored on a server linked to the internet, then internet users could inspect any of the documents from their own homes. This offers the potential for a vast increase in the efficiency of use of this and other similar archives. With such developments, real inroads could be made by volunteers on what is at present a task so large that it would be expected to take decades before any progress could be made.

Further reading

Rights of Way and the 1910 Finance Act. Zara Bowles, RWLR 9.3. 1990.

Valuation office records created under the 1910 Finance Act (information sheet 68) 1987, Public Record Office.

23
NEGOTIATING SKILLS

23.1. Introduction

It will have become clear from earlier chapters that much of the work of a rights of way volunteer might well be described as defensive. We have, in theory at least, a superb network of rights of way but we spend huge amounts of time trying to protect it from those who would destroy it. Outside the stockade, so to speak, are those who attack through legal means such as promoting orders to stop up paths or remove them from the definitive map. Even worse are those to resort to unlawful means such as by obstructing paths or even physically assaulting those who try to use them. Organisations that are supposed to be helping us seem impotent, or incompetent or even downright corrupt. It is hardly surprising that rights of way workers become hard-bitten and cynical of the whole process!

There has been an unfortunate side-effect to all this. Many rights of way workers appear to have developed a belief that everyone else is an enemy to be attacked. This can lead to a feeling that there is no value in talking to anyone outside their particular organisation, even including those who might well be expected to be allies. Any idea of negotiation is seen as a weakness; a backsliding from a resolute defence of our existing position.

The purpose of this chapter is to challenge this view. It will be argued that nobody should be seen as an enemy; rather that they are people pursuing different objectives. Negotiation can be a process that lead to gains for both sides, and hints will be given as to how this can best be achieved. Like many inter-personal skills, the art of diplomacy and getting the best out of any negotiations cannot be learned overnight but it is hoped that the reader will at least be convinced that it is a skill worth striving for.

23.2. Why negotiation is helpful

Many rights of way volunteers start with the assumption that those who oppose us are implacably opposed both to us as individuals and to the organisations which we represent, and that in consequence there will be no basis for a useful dialogue. On the face of it, this is unlikely to be true, although it must be said that some individuals (and even organisations) go out of their way to be unpleasant.

317

In practice, it is much more probable that our opponents will be driven not by personal animosity, but by the hope of achieving some objective of their own. For example, landowners will probably be trying to increase the value of their property. As rights of way tend to decrease property values, they will want to avoid any new rights of way coming into existence and, if possible, to reduce the effect of existing paths. Councillors, on the other hand, will want to be returned at the next election and will want to give the impression to the public that they are responsive to public needs. Similarly, all the other various parties that we become involved with will all be pursuing their own individual objectives, just as we are.

If the objectives were such that they were completely incompatible then negotiations would serve no useful purpose. At first sight this may often appear to be the case; for example, our objective of improving the rights of way network would seem to be diametrically opposed to a landowner's objectives if he wished to eliminate rights of way over his land. However, it is important to remember that the aspirations of any party can only be achieved within the rules.

No matter how much an owner wishes to eliminate rights of way over his land, he is going to have great difficulty in achieving this if rights of way workers adopt the techniques set out in earlier chapters of this book. With any luck, the owner should quickly realise that the best he is likely to achieve is a modified network which may have less adverse effects on the value of his land. We, on our part, are pursuing an objective of improving the network, not of opposing all changes. There may well be an alternative arrangement of paths on the land that will both provide a better network for us as well as reducing the effect on the owner. Here a negotiated deal might well benefit both sides.

This simple example brings out two important points in the art of negotiating. Firstly, the parties should be in a trading situation with the aim of agreeing a deal where both benefit. If this principle is kept firmly in mind then there should be no suggestion that in negotiating we are in any way backing away from a resolute persual of our objectives. This brings us to the second point: it is important to be able to negotiate from a position of strength, which may well mean ensuring that the other side are potentially threatened in some way. There is no getting away from the fact that many negotiations are conducted against a background that might well be described as a genteel form of blackmail!

23.3. Negotiating from strength

It follows that it makes no sense to go into negotiations without having first worked out a plan of campaign. Basically, we have to consider what we are prepared to offer the other side, and what we would expect them to give to us in exchange.

We might be prepared to genuinely give something up in exchange for something else. For example, if changes are proposed to a network of paths, we might be prepared to accept the extinguishment of a path which duplicated another path, or was in a situation where it was of little value, if we obtained in exchange a new path that formed a particularly useful link.

In many other cases, however, whilst we may expect to have to provide something that the other side values, it need not necessarily cost us anything. A council, for example, may be prepared to assist us merely in exchange for our goodwill. The objective of councillors is to be re-elected and this depends on the public at large thinking they are doing a good job. It will, of course, be much more helpful to them if in exchange for whatever they provide, we on our part publicise how good a job we think they are doing.

Then we have to consider the matter of genteel blackmail. Here what we are giving is an undertaking not to carry out some potential threat. An example was given in 14.11 where we considered the "time capsule" concept in collecting evidence. In this case what we offer is an undertaking not to submit a formal claim for a path to be added to the definitive map, in exchange for the owner allowing the public to use the path without prejudice to its status.

Of course, we can only give undertakings of this sort if we have some sort of threat that we can carry out if we do not get our way. In order to bargain from a position of strength, it is useful to go to some effort both to work out as many potential threats as possible and to make them as potent as possible. For example, it is of no use offering not to make a claim to add a path to the definitive map unless the evidence is such that there is a reasonable chance that the application would succeed. It may well be that when the plan of campaign is worked out, it becomes clear that other action need to be taken to make the threat more potent, in this case by finding further evidence of the status of the route.

23.4. The other angle

In working out what we can offer we need to consider what the other side will think is of any value. And we also need to try and work out what they may be prepared to give up, both so that we can suggest it to them and so that we can prepare ourselves by working out what we feel is a reasonable deal.

This points to an important requirement: we need to be able to put ourselves in the shoes of those on the other side. Although this seems obvious, in practice many rights of way workers get so personally involved in the cause that they find difficulty in imagining how those on the other side must feel. All that is needed is a little imagination, and it is probably true to say that those lacking in such imagination will have great difficulty in becoming effective negotiators.

The starting point must be to try and work out what the objectives of the other side are. As indicated above, it is unlikely that their objective is related to any personal animosity; it is much more likely to depend on much more tangible things such as potential loss of money or votes. It is also worth noting that not all those on the other side of the negotiating table will necessarily share the same objectives. For example, a council may want to be popular with the electorate and so be re-elected. But in any negotiations the council will almost certainly be represented by an officer. Although no officer will admit to pursuing personal objectives which differ from those of the council, it is quite clear that this is often the case. An officer, for example, will have a vested interest in expanding his work area which might well be in conflict with the desire of the council to cut costs to keep council taxes down. In a similar way, a solicitor or land agent employed by an owner might well be more interested in generating work and professional fees than in the strict interests of his employer.

It is always possible that when the whole position has been worked out, there is no basis for any negotiations at all. There will be cases where the objectives of the parties are so diametrically opposed that no deal is possible. For example, suppose an owner simply seeks to apply to have a right of way extinguished because it is inconvenient to him and a rights of way organisation determines to oppose him. The owner is going for full closure and is not interested in any compromise. Any rights of way organisation will oppose this and will not be prepared to accept any half measures. Nor will they have any potential threats other than an intention to object which the owner presumably expects anyway. In such a case nobody can really expect that the parties will be able to come to any sort of deal, and negotiations will be simply a waste of time. It is important to reject the optimistic view that if reasonable people sit down to negotiate, then there is always going to be a potential solution. In all too many situations, this is simply not the case.

It must, of course, be accepted that people often act in irrational ways and that, in any case, the rights of way worker is unlikely to be in possession of all the necessary facts to be able to predict in every case what the reaction of the other side is going to be. Nevertheless, exercising imagination and with the benefit of experience, it is often possible to make a reasonable guess at what is going to happen. Although negotiators have always to be prepared for the unexpected, nevertheless their position is always strengthened if they have at least some idea of what might happen.

23.5. Establishing diplomatic relations

It will not be possible for any negotiations to take place unless there is some forum for discussion. It would be possible for a meeting to be convened to discuss some specific point, but it will always be easier if the various parties already know each other. This is the reason why in international politics most countries try and maintain diplomatic relations with other countries. The breaking off of diplomatic relations always makes it more difficult for international negotiations to take place, and may well lead to wars. We should note the lesson from this and try to establish and maintain diplomatic relations with the relevant parties.

This, of course, begs the question of who are the relevant parties. In looking at this, it may be useful to consider these in three groups: our allies, neutral bodies and those who are likely to be opposed to us.

23.6. Our allies

One would have thought it fairly obvious that in developing a power base, it is likely to be useful to form alliances with other bodies with similar aims. Unfortunately, for far too many rights of way workers, it appears that this is not obvious at all. Perhaps because of the confrontational nature of much of the work, many volunteers appear to develop a confrontational approach to everything. Look under the surface of any organisation involved in rights of way and the chances are you will find a body riven with internal disputes and schisms!

If volunteers will not even speak to people within their own organisation, it is perhaps not altogether surprising that they fail to communicate with other similar bodies. There is an unfortunate tendency to look at other groups in respect of potential differences, rather than in terms of common areas for working together.

An example might be useful here. In recent years a growth in interest in the use of four-wheel-drive vehicles on green lanes has led to some groups carrying out extensive research into the legal status of many tracks that are either not recorded on the definitive map at all, or recorded only as public paths. Many walkers have taken a very aggressive stance to this sort of work and have often opposed claims to add to the definitive map routes where vehicular status has been very clearly shown to exist. In taking such a line, walkers are concentrating on the negative aspects, namely that some very limited vehicular use might take place along routes that they regard as footpaths. But they are allowing their views about motor traffic to blind them to the areas of common interest. Researching the status of ancient routes may often lead to the addition of green lanes that were not shown on the definitive map and which have been closed to walkers as well as to vehicles.

A more subtle point is that arguing that vehicular rights that exist in law should not be recorded because they are inconvenient to walkers must undermine the whole basis of rights for walkers themselves. There are huge networks of footpaths in deep rural areas that are rarely used and whose value to walkers is greatly outbalanced by their inconvenience to farming. But rights of way organisations rightly campaign for their retention on the basis that, however inconvenient they may be to others, the public have a legal right to use them. By rubbishing the claims of vehicular users to have their legal rights, walkers inevitably undermine the whole basis of their own rights.

This is not to say that all user groups need to agree a common stance on all aspects. What they vitally need to do is to meet and to discuss their differences and common interests. This should lead to agreement on where the groups can co-operate and hence where some work might be usefully shared to save effort. On matters where there remain differences, it is always useful to have these out in the open and to know precisely what they are. It often proves that the differences are by no means as large as was first suspected and that the groups can agree to cooperate whilst continuing to recognise that they do not agree on all points. Make no mistake about it, any disagreement between those groups that ought to be allies will the ruthlessly exploited by those whose aims are very different from our own. The situation described above provides a useful example; land owners who are opposed to any people using green lanes over their land are quite clearly exploiting the current differences between the motorised users and walkers.

23.7. Neutral parties

Let us now consider relations with those bodies that are actively involved in the process, but which might be expected to maintain a relatively neutral stance. This includes national bodies concerned with the countryside such as the Countryside Agency, English Nature and the Sports Council as well as local authorities. The latter are included as neutral parties as this is how they usually represent themselves. Strictly speaking, this is not quite accurate in that although as surveying authorities they have to adopt a very objective approach in deciding which rights should be recorded on the definitive map, nevertheless they have a legal duty to defend the rights of the public to the use of highways that are known to exist and should thus be anything but neutral when it comes to dealing with obstructions.

It is vitally important to maintain a good working relationship with the highway authority. As pointed out in Chapter 6, this means finding out who actually controls rights of way matters in the council and then working closely with them. It should always be remembered that even though a council may not place much priority on rights of way work, nevertheless the person actually carrying out the work is likely to be an enthusiast and much more amenable than the official face of the council leads one to expect. Even though the officer will not be able to go against the formal policy of the council, it will usually be possible to achieve positive results if a constructive attitude is adopted.

Many councils now operate rights of way consultative meetings to which all groups representing users and owners are invited. Although these are intended to provide a channel of communications between the council and the various groups, there is a further advantage in bringing together groups that would normally only meet after a confrontational situation had already occurred. For example, it may be an ideal opportunity for user groups to meet the landowning and farming groups and allow other meetings to be set up to negotiate matters of conflict or concern.

23.8. The other side

This brings us the third group with which we need to establish diplomatic relations, that is those who we are most likely to be on the other side. It is sometimes suggested that rights of way workers should maintain a dialogue with all the owners and farmers in their area. Although nice in theory, there is no possible way in which this could be achieved. With the present number of volunteers available it is necessary for groups to look after large areas with hundreds or even thousands of owners. Even if it were known who they all are, it would be impossible to talk to them all. But in any case, there is no way of knowing who owns or occupies land so even if volunteers had the time to talk to all these people, it would not be possible to find out who they were.

In practice, we are left with the organisations that represent owners and occupiers, that is principally the Country Landowners Association (CLA) and the National Farmers Union (NFU). The officials of these organisations are usually approachable and happy to discuss problems and to negotiate with us.

It is, however, very important to understand the different basis of which the two sides operate. Rights of way organisations normally have charitable status and represent all members of the public who wish to use public paths in the appropriate way. Individual members join to help the organisation, both financially and by taking part in the work but they do not have any right to special treatment in respect of their own rights of way problems. In negotiating changes on behalf of the public as a whole, there is nothing to prevent the organisation agreeing to a loss of a path in one place in exchange for paths elsewhere.

On the other hand, organisations such as the CLA and NFU exist primarily to provide services to their members. This will include specialist advice on such matters as rights of way. It follows that these organisations are unable to take a broad view but must defend the interests of whichever member calls them in, even if that member is clearly acting in an entirely unreasonable way. It must also be obvious that the CLA or NFU is in no position to broker any sort of agreements that involves a loss to one owner or farmer with a corresponding gain to another. So although these organisations are fond of arguing that there is considerable scope for changes to rights of way networks that are to the benefit of all, in practice their own constraints make it virtually impossible for them to deliver the changes. This does not mean that the CLA and NFU are not worth talking to, but it must always be understood that their room for negotiating is extremely limited.

23.9. The professional approach

Finally, we come to the way in which the actual negotiations themselves should be conducted. To a large extent, skill in this area will only come with experience but it is possible to set out a few broad principles that should be followed. The golden rules are:

- Be professional
- Never make empty threats
- Always allow other parties to retreat with dignity

What is meant by being professional? The essence of this is that the professional plays to win, but at the same time does not get personal about it. Consider, for example the way that barristers act in court. There is no question that they are out to win; after all they are effectively paid on piece-work and solicitors will not give them briefs unless they have a good track record. At the same time, they have no personal animosity towards the barrister representing the other side. It is customary for them to describe each other as "my friend" and this is not empty courtesy; it is often literally true. Barristers often specialise on cases of a particular type and are on friendly terms with the others who work in the same area.

This is a concept which many in the rights of way voluntary sector find hard to grasp. On the one hand, there are some who seem to feel that it is not really playing the game to be absolutely determined to win. In particular, it is sometimes suggested that we ought to take a sympathetic line with the problems that owners and farmers may have. This is the wrong approach. As indicated in 23.4, it is important to put oneself in the shoes of other people so that we have some idea what line they will want to take in the negotiations. To that extent, this means understanding the problems of other people. That does not mean that we should depart from our objective of getting the best possible deal for the public. We should see ourselves as trustees for the public and on this basis we have a moral duty to get the best deal for them, even if at a personal level we sympathise with the problems of individuals.

It may be worth saying, although it should be obvious, that this equally applies to members of the organisation. It would be quite indefensible for an organisation that had charitable status on the basis of protecting public rights, to take a softer attitude to a problem that happened to be on the land of one of its members.

Unfortunately, a resolute pursuit of the objectives often seems to be confused with being unpleasant or aggressive, even to those who should be our allies. Playing to win requires keeping a calm head and avoiding getting worked up. Otherwise, it will be very difficult to think clearly and produce the clear and logical arguments that will be needed in any successful negotiations.

Playing to win sometimes requires the making of threats. Obviously, this should be done in a friendly manner albeit making it quite clear that you are serious. In all this there is a golden rule: never threaten to do what you cannot or will not do. There is no guarantee that the planned negotiations will be successful and the other side may call your bluff and dare you to carry out the threat. In that case there is no option but to carry out the threat because otherwise nobody will believe you in the future.

It is important to be careful not to force the other side into a corner. The object of the process is to come to a deal with both sides feeling that they have gained something from the process. Of course, if the ground has been properly prepared then the outcome ought to be that you gain a lot and the other side precious little. This may be the case where you have a potential threat and the other side have to make concessions merely to prevent you carrying it out. The key point is that nobody likes to feel that they have lost completely and will want to be able to feel that they have got at least something out of the process. Even if completely beaten, they will want to retreat with dignity. It is always good tactics to make sure that they have the ability to so. Without this it will be difficult to reach a final agreement. Even if the other side has no option but to concede, if they cannot do so with some semblance of dignity, then it will tend to sour relations and make it difficult to have any useful negotiations with them again.

24
MANAGEMENT OF VOLUNTEERS

24.1. Introduction

In this chapter we look at the ways in which volunteers can be organised so as best to achieve their objectives. This is an area which is often overlooked, but is increasingly important. It is simply a matter of management, and we can learn a great deal from the techniques that are used in all walks of life to manage operations both large and small. The field of management is a huge one which can only be briefly dealt with here, but it is hoped that a brief introduction can at least set rights of way workers in the correct direction and give them leads for further study.

24.2. Why management is important

Rights of way work is perhaps unique in the voluntary field in the extent to which the key roles are occupied by volunteers. The voluntary sector, by definition, relies on volunteers but in most fields the volunteers provide enthusiastic but relatively unskilled support to a core of professional staff. Rights of way work is quite different. The minor importance given to rights of way by those in official circles means that organisations which should be active in protecting rights of way, such as the highway authorities, often appear amateurish and impotent by comparison with the voluntary organisations that specialise in such work. The limited resources available to voluntary bodies usually means that they are able to employ few professional staff relative to the number of volunteers. In many cases those with the greatest knowledge and experience of rights of way matters are volunteers rather than the paid staff. Indeed, this book is designed to encourage precisely this culture of self-dependency among rights of way workers.

All the indications are that the role of the volunteer will increase in importance in future years. The more work we do, the more we realise the huge amount that remains to be done. Fortunately, more and more volunteers are coming forward to carry it out. It must be clear that this voluntary effort will only achieve its objectives if it is properly organised. This calls for good management.

It is important to avoid the trap of assuming that management is something that is only done by sharp-suited "executives". Any sort of endeavour requires management, whether running a household or a multi-national company. Many of those with the greatest management skills are to be found outside the world of business, for example working in charities, churches, trades unions and so on.

It is also important to avoid the fallacy that management is easy, and that all managers do is to issue orders in between expense account meals. To manage successfully is a skill that takes time to acquire, and many never achieve it. Given that management is necessary in all fields of human endeavour, we all know people who never seem to be able to organise anything! Nevertheless, it is a valuable skill and one which is just as important in the voluntary sector as it is in the world of business.

Not only is good management just as important to us as it is in business, but it is also significantly more difficult. This is for two reasons. Firstly, it is rarely possible to select volunteers in the way that is done for a paid job. Anyone managing volunteers has to arrange a system that will work reasonably well even with incompetent workers. Secondly, nobody has to volunteer and they may give up at any moment. It follows that motivation of volunteers is even more important in the voluntary sector than in paid employment. As will be seen, motivation is vitally important in today's business world, but few people will resign in frustration if things go slightly wrong. In the voluntary sector this happens all the time!

24.3. Changes in management techniques

With the emphasis on management science today, one might imagine that management is a new technique. Nothing could be further from the truth; two thousand years ago the Roman Empire was being operated as a single centralised organisation in a way that we could not even contemplate today. The tradition continued in military matters and by the Napoleonic wars of the early nineteenth century both sides were deploying huge armies and navies which would have clearly have involved management on a grand scale.

During the industrial revolution, these management techniques were copied and improved to enable the construction of large engineering projects. For example, most of the main inter-city railway lines were built in the 1830s and 40s almost entirely by manual labour, and at a speed which we cannot match today with all our earth-moving machinery. Similar techniques were used to run the industrial enterprises that followed, including railway companies, steelworks and shipbuilding yards employing thousands of workers. Truly, the Victorian period was a golden age for management.

When it became recognised that there was a need for a strong public sector to deliver such things as new sewerage and water schemes, the same techniques were adopted. A belief in the advantages of a centralised approach continued through the first half of the twentieth century, reaching its height in the 1939-45 war when a centralised management system was applied not only to huge military forces but also to most other aspects of national life which were also centrally organised to assist the war effort. The success of these techniques in winning the war encouraged their continuation in peacetime with key industries being taken into public ownership and managed centrally.

However, this proved to be the turning point. Experience showed a number of problems and increasingly it has been found that less centralised and more devolved systems of organisation can achieve better results. This fundamental change of management technique has important implications for management in the voluntary sector and it is well worth looking in detail at the two styles.

24.4. Centralised management

The centralised system of management that achieved so much in the past is essentially hierarchical. By this is meant that there is a clearly-defined pyramid of control with a single "boss" at the top. The boss, be it a commander in a military sense or a managing director in industry, is fully in control of all aspects of whatever operation is being managed. He gives his orders to a series of subordinates. They in turn pass on the orders to their subordinates and so on right down the tree. It was often reckoned that a span of command should not normally exceed around six people, but if there are enough layers then the number of people at the bottom of the pyramid can be very large.

The role of the intermediate layers of management are primarily supervisory. They are there to pass on the instructions and to make sure that they are carried out. They also act as a conduit for information to pass up the tree to enable the boss to make the correct decisions. It will be seen that such a system depends greatly on the skill of the boss to make the right decisions. On the other hand those lower down do not have to think much as they have little opportunity to make any decisions. It is essential that they act in a very disciplined way so as to make the organisation work perfectly.

Under ideal conditions, a centrally planned and managed organisation can be a perfect machine with all parts operating smoothly together and all contributing to achieving the corporate aim. The fatal flaw is that any imperfection in any part of the organisation will have serious effects on its performance. Decision making as far up the pyramid as possible requires a perfect flow of information to enable the decisions to be correctly made. Any failure in upwards communications is bound to have a serious effect. Even with perfect information, the system requires a very high level of skill in those at the top of the pyramid. As mistakes there will cause serious problems it is necessary for those at the top to have a very good knowledge of the workings of every part of their organisation, something which is increasingly difficult in our age when technology changes so fast that senior management are likely only to have a knowledge of practices that have become obsolete.

There can be similar problems with downwards communications. If staff are not allowed to think for themselves but are required only to carry out instructions, then any failure in communications leaves them not knowing what to do. Of course, the system requires that they actually do carry out their instructions. So any failure on the part of the supervisors either to pass on instructions or to ensure that they are carried out will cause problems.

Finally, the fact that staff are not required to think for themselves does not make for job satisfaction. More importantly, it stifles any innovation. Consequently, the traditional centralised system of organisation is only really suitable for situations of stability where everyone knows what to do and management is about checking that they actually do it. In our times of rapid change this essentially Victorian approach has become outmoded and is everywhere being replaced by a new culture of devolution and empowerment.

24.5. Devolution and empowerment

In recent years a different system of management has come to the fore, based on the concepts of devolution and empowerment. The basic principle is that decision-making is devolved to more junior members of staff who are thus empowered to act in a management rather than a supervisory role.

It is important to appreciate that this is not simply a cop-out by senior management. In many ways, running a devolved organisation is more difficult than the traditional hierarchical structure. Unless senior management understand the new approach the effect is likely to be a form of anarchy with all the different parts of the organisation working in different directions.

It is important to work to a series of objectives. To avoid this senior management has to decide what the objectives of the overall organisation are and then to devise a series of objectives for the individual teams. How the teams achieve this is left up to them, but it is important that the extent to which they achieve the objectives is monitored so that appropriate adjustments can be made.

This approach very much simplifies communications in that it is no longer necessary for detailed commands to be passed down the tree as to precisely how jobs are to be done. The right communications are still very important. Problems generally arise if objectives are set by senior management without reference to staff who are then presented with objectives which they know are unattainable. For a system of empowerment to work properly it is vital that the teams carrying out the work are fully involved in the setting of both the corporate objectives and those that they themselves are to achieve. There should always be agreement by those charged with achieving them that the objectives are indeed attainable.

A devolved system relies much more on the skills of the staff so, management has a much greater role in facilitating their work, particularly in ensuring that they have the necessary training. This is another part of communications in that management needs to keep abreast of the training needs of staff and ensure that training is available. In our fast-changing world this is both important and difficult.

The above has been written in the context of two layers, that is senior management and teams that carry out the work. Obviously the system can be extended to several layers with teams actually achieving their objectives by empowering other teams or individuals. However, it has been found that devolution and empowerment require far less layers than did the hierarchical approach and this has led to what has been termed "de-layering", that is to say dispensing with middle management and supervisory staff. Huge organisations are now run with very little middle management and have a structure which is sometimes described as a "flat pyramid".

Although there have been substantial cost savings, these have been only a small part of the advantages gained from a culture of devolution. The new system harnesses the inherent strengths of the people who are doing the job and who are in the best position to work out the most efficient way of achieving the objectives. It encourages innovation, which becomes more and more important in our changing world. Perhaps most importantly, it gives people much greater job satisfaction. The best work is always done by those who enjoy doing it.

Although the new system harnesses latent skills, it is also less sensitive to small numbers of people who do not perform as well as they might. Firstly, having fewer layers of management and better monitoring of performance means that under-performers can be identified and appropriate action taken. In very many cases the problem can be identified as someone with the wrong skills or aptitude for the job being undertaken, or inter-personal conflicts within a team. Moving staff into other jobs for which they are more suited or providing additional training will often solve the problem.

In any case, a flat pyramid approach is itself less dependent on every member of staff being perfect. For example, imagine an organisation with a large number of empowered teams reporting to a Managing Director. If one of the teams is inefficient that is unfortunate but should not too seriously affect the performance of the organisation as a whole. By contrast, the hierarchical system would have required a number of layers of management to supervise and pass instructions to the staff. Any lack of performance or failings in communications would have had a much more serious effect.

However, it is important to appreciate that empowerment will inevitably lead to an organisation operating in a less consistent way than occurred in the former approach. The very fact that individuals are encouraged to work out the best way of achieving objectives, must lead to them working in different ways. Given a completely free rein, teams might well work against each other. Management will need to anticipate this and set some rules as well as objectives, but these need to be framed so as not to inhibit innovation. Management has always to consider whether consistency matters anyway, so long as the objectives of the organisation are being achieved.

24.6. Devolution and empowerment in the voluntary sector

Running an organisation in the voluntary sector is little different from running a profit-making business and the techniques of devolution and empowerment are at least as useful. In practice, they will be found to be even more valuable in the voluntary sector because they help us to reduce the effects of three special problems which we inevitably encounter:

- Job satisfaction is clearly even more important in the voluntary sector in that those who do not enjoy the work will not merely perform less well; they will simply not make their time available to the organisation.

- Communications are always more difficult in the voluntary sector. Volunteers are spread around the country, need not have a telephone and are often unavailable during working hours. For groups of volunteers to meet may involve a considerable amount of time and expense.

- Managers in the voluntary sector have to take their staff as they find them. Whilst few volunteers will be perfect, their contribution is likely to be better than nothing, which is generally the alternative. Even if they are more of a hindrance than a help, they cannot normally be fired because this would get around and make it very difficult to recruit anyone else. The most challenging part of managing in the voluntary sector is working out how to get the best from less-than-perfect, or even incompetent, volunteers.

It is in these circumstances that devolution and empowerment yields dividends. Giving people responsibility and allowing them to make the decisions makes them feel important and gives them job satisfaction. Not only will they be less likely to leave, but their enthusiasm will spill over and encourage others to join. If we accept that our systems of communications can never be that good, then it makes sense to adopt a method of working that does not depend on perfect communications all the time and it is always best to have a system which cannot be harmed too much by failures.

24.7. How volunteers can achieve their objectives

It is now proposed to consider the ways in which the modern management culture of devolution and empowerment can be applied to help voluntary rights of way workers to achieve their objectives. Note that the starting point is taken to be a number of people with a shared objective, for example to protect and improve the network of rights of way. To achieve this some form of organisation is likely to be needed, but this should be seen as a means to the end. It is wrong to see existing organisations as an end in themselves. Situations change and systems that produced good results in the past may be capable of improvement, or even have outlived their usefulness.

For many years the rights of way voluntary sector has been dominated by relatively large organisations covering the whole of Britain. Their structure tends to be hierarchical with a central organisation and local organisations dealing with successively smaller areas. For example, the British Horse Society operates at both a regional and county level whilst the Ramblers Association has a similar approach with areas and local groups. And this is merely the structure of management committees; there are inevitably further layers of the volunteers who actually carry out the work. Generally speaking the management of such organisations tends to follow the centralised model described above, with detailed orders being produced at the centre and passed down the tree.

There must be increasing doubt as to whether this model will best achieve the objectives. As was pointed out in Chapter 6, the best way of influencing local authorities is through the actions of local people rather than through national organisations. Similarly, it will have become clear that the objective of getting more rights of way on the definitive map can only be achieved through a great deal of very detailed local work. In other words, the achievement of the objectives depends much more on the work of the local volunteers than that carried out at the centre.

If we follow the principles of devolution and empowerment, it will be seen that the centre should be setting the objectives and let the local organisations work out the best way of achieving them. It should not be necessary for the centre to be constantly sending out instructions nor checking whether they have been carried out. Given that the objectives themselves are widely accepted, there is little need for even these to be passed down. Arguably, the only task that really leads itself to the handing down of objectives is that of handling the various public path orders that are sent to the central organisations as required by law. It is essential that it is known which local organisation will deal with the orders in a precisely defined area, and it will be necessary for the centre to ensure that they are properly considered. For the great bulk of the work, including checking the paths, pressing for the removal of obstructions, researching missing paths and pressing for the creation of new routes, there is no need for the centre to give any instructions at all.

The implication is that the traditional hierarchical structures in rights of way work may well not be necessary. Instead a form of flat pyramid is indicated with a central organisation carrying out the essential national tasks and a whole variety of local organisations empowered to carry out the local work. Moreover, there is no reason why the local organisations should be an integral part of the national organisation; so long as all the groups share the same objectives there may well be advantages in them retaining their autonomy. This gives the greatest opportunity for innovation and minimises any harm done if a group should not be as efficient as it might be.

It might be felt that this approach would severely limit the role of the central organisation. This is not so; it is simply that it has a different role. Within an organisation with a culture of devolution and empowerment, management retains a vital role of facilitating the work of the staff. Within a structure of voluntary organisations, a similar role is even more important because volunteers may well lack the knowledge, experience or self-confidence to carry out the work. So training and support should be the contribution of those at the centre, rather than any attempt to pretend that they are in control of the whole process. This approach has been the motivation behind this book which has been written to facilitate the work of all volunteers who share the same sorts of objectives as the British Horse Society.

Another important role of a central organisation is in facilitating good communications. Now one of the main arguments for a devolved system is that the need for communications upwards and downwards is reduced and that failures of communication do not matter as much. This does not mean that there is no need for any communications; on the contrary there are great advantages in having good sideways links between the grass-roots organisations so that information and experience can rapidly be passed around. After all, a system which is intended to encourage innovation is not being used to the full unless successful new ideas can rapidly be disseminated.

Traditionally, this sort of role has been filled mainly by newsletters and the organisation of occasional conferences and seminars. In the near future there may well be an increasing role for new methods such as use of the internet. Whatever the method used, there seems to be an important role for central rights of way bodies in organising rather than controlling the networking between the various groups taking action at the local level.

24.8. *Organisation within a local rights of way group*

In the light of the principles just discussed, it is hardly the role of the author to lay down hard and fast rules as to how local rights of way organisations should conduct their affairs. However, on the basis of experience of successes and failures in local organisations, it is proposed to at least give some ideas.

It will be assumed that the organisation is a democratic one and that the overall control rests in the hands of the individual members. It will, of course, be impossible for the detailed management to be carried out by the members at large. It will be difficult enough to persuade them to attend an annual meeting to elect a management committee.

It will be equally impossible for the management committee to carry out the day to day work that is required. This will need to be done by voluntary officers who have been appointed by the members. This is usually done at the annual meeting, but it is equally possible for them to be appointed by the management committee. What needs extremely careful consideration is the split of duties between the committee and the individual officers.

On the principle of empowerment, the committee should restrict itself to considering the overall objectives and should give freedom to the officers to work out how to achieve them. The committee will also need to set out any constraints such as the finances available and any matters that must be referred to the committee for consideration. For example, it might be decided that all decisions relating to public path orders should be taken by committee. This has the advantage that the committee as a whole become the target for anyone who feels aggrieved rather than an individual officer bearing the brunt.

This example demonstrates clearly the need for a careful balance in devolving responsibility. In general, letting people make their own decisions gives them more satisfaction. However, too much empowerment may mean people feeling exposed and stressed. It is also important to note that many people take up voluntary work for the companionship, and this will be lacking if they are constantly working on their own. The golden rule is to be flexible and to adopt a system that individual officers feel comfortable with.

The same rule needs to be adopted in respect of the tasks that individual volunteers undertake. Only a few tasks of a rights of way group are absolutely essential, for example monitoring any orders and making the appropriate objections. Most of the work, although desirable in the long term, can be carried out at whatever pace turns out to be feasible. So rather than assuming priorities to start with, it is better to see what the volunteers want to do and help them to achieve it. Remember that not only is the best work obtained from those who are enjoying themselves but also that enthusiasm is infectious. People who are clearly enjoying themselves are the best possible advertisement to encourage others to join the gang!

To those brought up in a tradition of a hierarchical system where all the volunteers work to a plan carefully devised by the centre, the ideas put forward in this chapter may seem a recipe for anarchy. It is important to remember that the objective of the exercise is the protection and improvement of rights of way, rather than the maintenance of some archaic power base.

25
WORKING WITH THE MEDIA

25.1. Introduction

This chapter looks at how rights of way workers can use the news media to their advantage. In order to do this it is necessary to understand something of the way in which the media operate and to appreciate that the best way forward is to work with journalists rather than against them. That way both sides benefit; the journalists get an interesting story and the rights of way cause gets useful publicity. Thus this chapter looks at the way in which the media works and suggests techniques for generating stories that are to the benefit of both parties.

25.2. Who are the media?

The media is a collective term for the various methods by which news is disseminated to the public. Generally the term is taken to mean the press, radio and television. In this section we will look in more detail at the various parts of the news business, starting with the most important area for our purposes, that of the press.

It is important to appreciate the different types of newspapers. At one extreme are the dailies which are the morning papers. These divide into two types, the regional dailies like the Western Mail, Liverpool Post or Northern Echo and the national dailies such as the Telegraph or the Sun. The national dailies do not have an even coverage of news but tend to give greater prominence to events in London and the South-East. This gives rise to the curious fact that the most populous region does not have a regional daily paper.

There are also a large number of daily evening papers. These are usually based on a single large town or city. They cover any major stories that have broken since the morning paper, but their real stock in trade is the more local stories that do not reach the national or regional dailies. Their catchment is the town or city and its surrounding area, although having an urban base their coverage is often more slanted to the urban area.

The opposite applies to the weekly papers. These are generally based in towns too small to boast a daily evening paper. They have little chance of competing with daily papers for the very latest news and so concentrate on the very local stories which do not reach the daily papers. They are often helped in this by the limited coverage of rural areas by the evening papers. It is not uncommon for the catchment of a weekly paper to include a town with its own evening paper in which case there is often very limited coverage of town stories. This is because the townspeople are unlikely to buy a weekly paper if they can get the town news on a daily basis; thus trying to cover town stories does not help to sell the weekly paper.

Finally, it is important not to ignore the "free sheets". These are weekly papers which are now common in both urban and rural areas. They are mainly advertising and are distributed free to all houses; increasingly, however, they contain some news items to reduce the chance of householders throwing them away unread. As the news side is produced on a shoe-string with normally only one or two reporters, it is particularly easy to get stories into the free sheets.

Radio works in a way which is comparable to newspapers. There are national channels, mainly those of the BBC but now including some national commercial channels such as Classic FM. The equivalent of the regional dailies are the regional channels of the BBC (Radio 5) and recently some regional commercial stations. However, unlike newspapers the radio channels are mainly for entertainment with limited news coverage. This means that little time is available for more local issues.

Then there are local radio stations. These are the equivalent of the local evening papers, and normally cover similar catchment areas of a large town and its surrounding area. There is an important distinction here between BBC local radio and the commercial stations. The latter mainly broadcast records and advertisements; their news coverage is limited. The BBC stations, by contrast, have taken a policy decision that they will concentrate on a separate market by dealing mainly with news and current affairs. It follows there is a good potential for getting rights of way stories onto local radio.

Television has been left until last because, although it is potentially the most influential medium, it is the hardest to get coverage on. This is because TV stations are national or regional; there is no equivalent of the local paper or local radio. It follows that developing a strategy for getting rights of way stories onto the media must mainly concentrate on the press and radio. That is not to say that TV should be ignored, but it should be regarded as a bonus that may fall to us from time to time.

25.3. *Why we need the media*

Most rights of way workers never give a thought to the media, and assume either that their work is not newsworthy or that they would in any case gain no benefit from media publicity. This is an error; rights of way workers can gain great benefits from media coverage in two important ways.

Firstly, it is a commonplace among rights of way workers that there is far too much work for the limited number of people carrying it out. If this is to be remedied, there is a vital need to recruit many more enthusiastic people. It must be obvious that nobody is going to volunteer for a job that they do not even know exists, yet this is precisely the current position; a surprising number of path users of all types who do not even know that there are volunteers hard at work protecting the routes that they use. If we are to recruit the people we need, then it is vital that we publicise the fact that we exist. Media coverage of issues gives us that publicity.

Secondly, it is important to appreciate the influence that media coverage has on the way in which decisions are made. We are frequently in the position of trying to persuade central or local government to take decisions in matters that affect rights of way. In many cases they have full discretion and there is no appeal mechanism if they do not go along with us. Even where there is an appeal mechanism, this is likely to cause delay and a great deal of extra work. Clearly, it is vital to influence the government body to take the right decision in the first place.

In a democracy it is only right that the ultimate test is the ballot box. At first sight it might be thought that most rights of way issues are so local and so few people are directly involved that even a local council could take any decision it liked without significantly affecting voting patterns. However, this is true of almost all issues; in practice voters are influenced not by the individual issues themselves but by an overall impression of how reasonable and competent the council or government is in dealing with all issues. The public can only gain this impression from things that they know about, which in practice mainly means those that have had media coverage. So where a path issue has no publicity, then the decision taken will indeed have little or no effect on voting patterns. An issue that has wide media coverage is quite another matter. The public are never inhibited from coming to an opinion on a matter by the fact that they have no personal interest in that matter. If central or local government are seen to act unreasonably or incompetently on any issue then the bad publicity will potentially affect the public perception of the controlling party and hence voting patterns at the next election. Politicians are understandably nervous about media coverage, even on issues that appear to directly affect very few people.

The implication is that obtaining media publicity can be a powerful weapon in ensuring that rights of way problems are at least dealt with fairly and efficiently. Of course, this will only be the case if rights of way workers are skilled in presenting their case to the public via the media in the best possible way; the purpose of this chapter is to show how this can be done.

25.4. Why the media need us

Having looked at why we need to cultivate the media, let us look at the other side of the coin: why do the media need us? The matter is quite simple. News media only exist because there is news to be reported. Not only has there to be news, but the media have to find out about it and make it into a story. There are a limited number of journalists, and timescales are extremely short. So it should be clear that they will be grateful to anybody who helps them, through telling them about a potential story and even more by helping to present the matter in a way that is likely to interest the public.

It is important not to fall into the trap of thinking that the media are against us. Whilst newspapers may well have an editorial bias to a particular political party (local radio has to be neutral) they are unlikely to have a pre-conceived idea about rights of way. It is necessary to appreciate that the media can only succeed if the public are interested in the stories. It is the journalist's job to make them interesting. So, if your story seems simply boring to the outsider then it is not going to make it to the public. Even if a good story, it might get pushed out if a bigger story breaks. That is not the media's fault; it is just bad luck, or even your own fault if you could have presented the story to the media in a more interesting way.

On the other hand, a journalist might well see the potential in a story even though it has been presented in a boring way. The best stories have "human interest" and this is often achieved by exaggerating the extent of any dispute. Do not be surprised if a radio interviewer adopts a devil's advocate style of questioning, or asks you to confront on the air a representative from the other side of any dispute. The journalist is not against you; he is simply doing his job to make his story as interesting as possible.

25.5. How the media works

Have you ever wondered how it is that there is always enough news to fill a newspaper or radio news slot? What would happen if some day there was no news at all and the paper had to come out blank? This never happens because of the way in which news editors operate. They do not just wait for the news to come in; instead they plan ahead to ensure that each edition is filled.

Relatively few stories are completely unexpected events, and when they are the coverage is often patchy. A news editor with his finger on the local pulse will know many of the stories that are likely to come up during the next few days. For example, it is known in advance when criminal cases are listed to be heard in the courts and the editor will know which are likely to interest the public. Or if there is a political row brewing, the editor will know that it is likely to surface at the local council meeting. With a reasonable idea of what stories are likely in the next few days, the editor can ensure that reporters are assigned to cover them. Those involved in the production of a daily newspaper or radio news programme will have a good idea of the contents of tomorrow's edition and at least some idea of what will be in the following day's.

Whilst this system ensures that there should always be something to put in the paper or news programme, it does not follow that there will always be news of equal significance. If there are a number of important stories, lesser news will not be covered. On days when news is short, editors have to seek out less important stories. Cycles can often be discerned. For example, local evening papers often have difficulty in finding good stories for the Monday edition. This is because with a mid-morning deadline the paper will rely for most of its bread and butter news on community events of the previous day; little such news arises on a Sunday. This sort of cycle can be used to advantage. If it is suspected that a particular story will have difficulty in getting in the paper then it is best to try and arrange for it to be available to the news editor at a period when there might be difficulty in finding enough news to fill the paper.

It is important to bear in mind the planning stage when trying to get a story in the media. The media like to give the impression of immediacy and thus try to report events as they happen. There has to be some kind of event, even if one is effectively manufactured for the purposes of the story. But to get coverage it is vital that the news editor has the information sufficiently far in advance so that the potential story can be allowed for in planning the paper or news programme.

It is also worth bearing in mind the extent to which the media borrow each other's news. A survey was once carried out to establish where newspapers got their stories from. The result included the surprising fact that by far the greatest source of information was stories in other papers! The implication for us is that getting an item in one paper or on the radio may well be the key to obtaining a good deal more exposure in other places.

25.6. Making friends with the media

A story might start in one of two ways. There may be some issue on which we want to get media coverage and where we will need to start the process. On the other hand, stories often commence with some other event which prompt the media to seek a response from us. As an example, a local councillor may say in some public forum that bridleways ought to be closed because horses make them muddy. The media might spot a confrontation story and would look for conflicting views from walkers and riders.

Either way, it is very useful to know and be known by individual reporters. If we are initiating the story we need to bring it to the attention of the media. It is possible to do this by sending a news release to the paper or radio station in question. If the story is thought to be worthwhile then they will arrange a reporter to follow it up. However, reporters are supposed to be on the lookout for stories, and are often given a quota of how many stories a week they should file. If a reporter is tipped off on a personal basis he may take this as a kindness and be more prepared to write sympathetically.

Knowing the individual reporters is of particular advantage when a story breaks that has not been initiated by us. A reporter will have very little time to prepare his story and if he is to get a comment from an expert, then he will need to get it quickly. It follows that he will have to know who to contact. An efficient journalist will have a list of contacts on every subject; someone who is on that list as rights of way expert is thus able to get media coverage on any rights of way issues that arise. Bringing to the attention of the journalist an interesting rights of way story may well secure your place on his list of experts.

Some environmental bodies use a combination of national stories and local contacts to good effect. For example, they may secure the assistance of a sympathetic MP to make a speech deploring some evil which he alleges is nationwide. This may well not be important enough to reach the national media and will not be of interest to local media without a local angle. But if the national pressure group provides the media with a list of local contacts, and they can come up with local examples of the problem, then a great deal of media coverage can be secured.

25.7. Telephone approaches

Being on a journalist's list of experts means that an approach may be made without warning. A journalists is always in a rush and will normally telephone. He may be simply seeking information, but it is more likely that he will want a quote. People generally find a "human interest" story more interesting which means that journalists are trained to look for the person behind the news. So anyone who has any position within a bridleways organisation is likely to be expected to act as spokesperson.

Ideally, a journalist will want the information or comment straight away so that he can get on with the story. If you can provide this, then do so. Avoid being too carried away with the urgency. As explained earlier, news programmes are planned in advance and the journalist should have allowed at least some time to make the contact. If he claims that a delay of even half an hour would be too much, then he is either lying or not a very good organiser.

It is often best to avoid making comments immediately but first to try and establish what the story is. Find out what information is required and if a comment, what the question is. It may well be that you do not have the answer and need to contact someone else to establish it. Even if you know it is often better to pretend not to and claim that it is necessary to check something. This little ruse gives time to make sure information is accurate and to give a little thought on how to present a comment in the best possible way.

However, this ruse should not be overdone. Reporters do have deadlines to keep and will need an answer promptly. The golden rule is to carry out any promises. If you say that you will find the answer and ring back within an hour, then you must do so. Otherwise you are likely to be regarded as unreliable and crossed off the list of experts.

25.8. News releases - the story and its timing

Although some stories do result from approaches by journalists, it is far better to take the initiative and thus be better able to control the situation. A key part of this is the preparation of news releases, that is to say short notes addressed to news editors tipping them off about some item of news. As indicated above, in some cases where a good relationship has been established with an individual journalist it might be better to send the release there rather than the news editor but the principle is the same.

The first stage is to establish what the story is. Remember that the media are interested in news; something has got to have happened. The actual event may be quite mundane, but it should be possible to put a date and time on it. For example, a dispute over an alleged right of way may have been simmering for years and is not news. However, a decision by a council on an application, a public inquiry or a decision by an inspector are all actual events that can form the basis of a story.

Events of this sort are outside our control but might well not be picked up by news editors without assistance. It is also possible to generate events that create a kind of synthetic news. A careful study of local newspapers will reveal that such things are quite common. If people in a neighbourhood feel that a new pedestrian crossing is needed, then that is not much of a story. If they demonstrate outside the Town Hall demanding a crossing, then something has happened. You may be sure of one thing: no protester today would think of organising a demonstration without informing the press in advance! Or ask yourself why the opening of a supermarket always seems to be graced by some star of sport or television. It is, of course, to make the event into a story and thus obtain press coverage and hence free advertising.

There is no reason why rights of way workers cannot generate their own synthetic news. For example, where a new path is created than a simple opening ceremony could be arranged with the press invited. Or suppose a local paths group is frustrated with lack of action by a local council. The simple fact would not be news but a speech by the president of the group at the AGM would be. Even if only a handful attend, and the press know this, there is still an event on which a story can be hung.

This brings us to the question of timing. Where we control the timing of an event then we can arrange it so that the news comes at a time when other news is scarce and hence more coverage is likely. Even when the actual event is outside our control, the timing of the news release is important. The key point is that information about the event must be available to the news editor sufficiently far ahead for him to include it in his plans. He might want to send a reporter to cover the actual event, or he may take the facts from the release. Either way he will want to present the news immediately it happens and will want to include it in his planning.

On the other hand, a news editor receives many news releases and may well lose or forget one that deals with events too far ahead. The ideal is for the release to reach the editor about the time he begins to start planning the edition in which the story is intended to be in. This depends on the type of media; three or four days notice is probably best for dailies and local radio, whilst around ten days would probably be better for a weekly paper.

344

Sending out retrospective releases is not usually so successful as by the time they reach the paper the news is too stale. However, where the advance notice fails it might be worth having another go afterwards. Consider the example above where the chairman of the paths group slates the local council at his AGM. A press release could be sent out a few days before giving details of what he is going to say. If this gets no coverage then it is always worth sending another immediately afterwards saying what he did say. The free sheets in particular are always short of news and may well fall for a ready-made story of this type.

Finally, the use of embargoes should be noted. This is a common tactic of politicians who want coverage of a speech but do not want information to leak out before it is made. They will often issue a news release which says that the news is "embargoed" until a particular time, that is to say it is not to be printed before that time. For our sort of news it is difficult to see much value in this sort of device, although some amenity groups do seem to use the technique to give an impression that the news is more immediate than it really is.

25.9. Writing a news release

Writing a news release is a skill that needs to be practiced to give the greatest chance of the story being selected by the news editor. The first thing to appreciate is that news editors are always in a rush and do not want to read long documents. News releases are normally typed double-spaced and ideally should fit on a single sheet of A4; in any event it is recommended that the maximum should be two sheets. This means that around 500 words should be aimed for and the story has to be condensed into that space.

A release is more likely to be used if it is in a journalistic style. This is both because the style is deliberately intended for easy reading and thus more likely to catch the editor's eye, but also because a journalist in a rush can more easily incorporate much of the release without alteration. The styles used by newspapers should be studied. In general, they use short sentences and avoid the use of excessively long or jargon words. News releases should be written similarly.

Another journalistic trick worth cultivating is that of utilising the first sentence to summarise the whole release. The idea is to catch the interest of the reader straight away so that the whole release is read. An extension of the same concept is the use of footnotes. The idea is to avoid confusing the main body of the release with too many details. If the reader is still interested, then the footnotes at the end give more details. For example, a news release concerning a bridleways association might have a footnote saying when the association was formed and how many members it has. However, this technique should be used with care. Carried to excess, it can give a very cluttered release which defeats the whole object.

It has already been pointed out that journalists like "human interest" stories. This means that news releases are more likely to be used where they have an individual touch. Ideally, try and find someone who is personally affected by the matter in hand and get a quote from them. Failing this, include a quotation from some activist, even if it is yourself!

It is necessary to be aware of the conventions of news releases. It has already been mentioned that they should be typed double-spaced. It is also conventional to put ENDS at the bottom of the last sheet and MORE at the bottom of any other sheets to avoid bits getting lost. The last thing on the release should be a contact name and telephone number of someone who can give additional information.

Traditionally, releases were posted to the appropriate news editor. Today, faxes are increasingly used and are to be recommended. They seem to strike a chord with journalists who like to feel that they are getting information precisely as it happens. With a fax machine even the assistant hack on a free sheet can imagine himself in Fleet Street. Thus faxes seem to have a better success rate than posted releases and also have the advantage that they allow a more accurate timing of precisely when the news editor will receive them.

25.10. Radio interviews

News releases sent to local radio stations will often result in a request for a spokesperson to give an interview. This is another area where a little planning can pay dividends.

There are various types of radio interviews. You may be asked to meet a radio reporter at some location. The reporter carries a tape recorder and carries out the interview on the spot. Or you may be asked to visit the radio studio to give an interview. There are also telephone interviews where a technician rings up a few minutes before, checks the line and then asks you to hang on to give the interview. A surprising amount of local radio coverage is live so do not be surprised to hear that your telephone is connected straight through to the local radio transmitter. Live interviews have the advantage that it is not possible for the interview to be cut in ways that give a different impression from the original interview.

Whatever type of interview is used, remember that it will be short. It is an unfortunate aspect of the media today that proper debate on an issue is rare. Instead the business is one of *soundbites*: glib statements that are intended to sound impressive but on analysis mean little. Listen to any politician speaking on TV or radio and you will get the idea. But unsatisfactory as this is, we have to adopt the same style to get our arguments over. Any lengthy explanation of our position is likely to be cut off by the interviewer so it is vital to try and work out a way of explaining things in a very few sentences.

In the interview itself, it is essential to keep calm. A clearly stated reasonable argument will impress the listener. On the contrary, anyone getting angry will make a very poor impression. However, radio interviewers have the job of making interesting listening and will have their own idea of how the story should go. So be careful of leading questions which may try and lead you to say things that you will later regret. Do not be afraid to disagree with the interviewer where necessary, only do it politely and in a conversational type of voice. Having said that, do not get too worried about the approach that a radio interviewer may take; local radio staff deal mainly with ordinary people and are a far cry from the aggressive interviewers reserved for pursuing national politicians.

25.11. Television

The opportunities for TV coverage are limited, which is probably just as well because it is a tricky medium for the inexperienced to handle. The main difficulty is that there is very little live coverage and a great deal of material that has been filmed is never used. This gives a great opportunity for cutting of the material which may give a different impression to the original interview. In addition, the public tend to believe what they see on television to a greater degree than what they read in the papers; after all they are convinced that they actually saw the interview take place.

However, there is not much that can be done about this. Essentially, the techniques for dealing with television interviews are the same as for radio and you just have to hope that the result will not be too distorted!

NOTES

NOTES

NOTES

NOTES